THE DRAVIDIAN PATHWAY

THE DRAVIDIAN PATHWAY

How the DMK Redefined Power and Identity in South India

VIGNESH RAJAHMANI

context

cntxt

First published in the United Kingdom by C. Hurst & Co. (Publishers) Ltd in 2025

Published in India by Context, an imprint of Westland Books, a division of Nasadiya Technologies Private Limited, in 2025

No. 269/2B, First Floor, 'Irai Arul', Vimalraj Street, Nethaji Nagar, Alapakkam Main Road, Maduravoyal, Chennai 600095

Westland, the Westland logo, Context and the Context logo are the trademarks of Nasadiya Technologies Private Limited, or its affiliates.

ISBN: 9789371979252

10 9 8 7 6 5 4 3 2 1

Typeset by Jojy Philip
Printed at Manipal Technologies Limited, Manipal

CONTENTS

Abstract vii
Note on Terminology ix
Acknowledgments xi
List of Tables xvii
List of Figures xix

Introduction 1
1. Periyar and the DMK: Forging a Horizontal Dravidian-Tamil Solidarity 27
2. Disseminating the Dravidian-Tamil Ethos through Reading Rooms 65
3. The DMK's Manoeuvres in Madras State: Political Opportunism Revisited through the Prism of the Dravidian-Tamil Repertoire 99
4. A Meticulous Underdog and a Seemingly Lax Stalwart: The Tale of the 1967 Madras State Assembly Election in Virudhunagar Constitutency 147

Conclusion 185
Epilogue: The Dravidian-Tamil Ethos Today 191
Appendices 217

Notes 221
Bibliography 251
Index 263

ABSTRACT

Most research on social movements and electoral politics tends to focus on the outcomes, rather than exploring how these two forces—movements and politics—actually interact. In this book, I take a different approach and trace the transformation of a socio-cultural movement into a political party that could compete successfully in elections. It tells the story of how the Dravida Munnetra Kazhagam (DMK) transformed the Dravidian Movement into a political force in what was once Madras State, now Tamil Nadu.

The book uses Christophe Jaffrelot's 'integrated theory of ethnic nationalism' to frame its argument. The theory lays out a few steps: first, creating an identity based on ideology that unites different groups to challenge a dominant power; next, spreading that ideology and bringing marginalised cultures into the mainstream; and finally, growing the movement and turning it into a mass-based political party. The theory is applied to explain the Dravidian movement's journey from the early 1900s through to 1967, when the DMK rose to power in what was then the State of Madras.

I build on this theory by marshalling evidence that shows how different versions of the original ideology and political platform kept the movement alive, adaptable, and relevant over the years. This book also looks at how ethnic groups can be shaped in ways that gradually address the needs of marginalised communities when it comes to recognition, redistribution, and representation.

I argue that Periyar E.V. Ramasamy played a key role as a 'chief aggregator', bringing together anti-caste and egalitarian political ideas from the Saivites, reformers like Iyothee Thass and B.R. Ambedkar, and other social reform movements that came before him. The DMK's creation of a Dravidian-Tamil identity as a political platform was shaped by Periyar's influence, with C.N. Annadurai and M. Karunanidhi also playing a strategic role in making it broad, inclusive, and democratic.

To understand how the political message spread and how the people of Madras State got politically engaged, I look into the previously unexplored network of reading rooms and other public spaces set up and run by DMK members and sympathisers. These spaces became places where ordinary people could get involved in activities that made them politically aware. I use Sandria Freitag's framework on public arenas and Narendra Subramanian's framework on organisational and social pluralism to analyse political engagement in Madras State.

In less than two decades, from 1949 to 1967, the DMK went from being a secessionist party to a major electoral force. I chronicle how its responses to key political developments in Madras State during this period helped it to advance its agenda. To explain this shift, I use Subramanian's framework of leadership flexibility. I have also gathered data on the party's social profile in the State Legislative Assembly to show how the movement developed and how its ideology played a key role in that process.

I also take an ethnographic look at how a student leader from the DMK managed to defeat the Congress party's most popular leader, K. Kamaraj, in the 1967 elections. I argue that the DMK's ability to adapt and adjust its long-term goals to changing circumstances helped it connect with people, transforming it into a political force that could represent their shared aspirations. This flexibility and openness created a society where different communities could coexist peacefully and work together towards their goals and aspirations.

I argue that the movement, led by marginalised groups, was characterised by opportunism—something that challenged the hegemonic idea of purity. In the end, the book reflects on the political history of Madras State, placing it within the larger context of post-independence India.

NOTE ON TERMINOLOGY

Throughout the book I use multiple categories to denote social groups on the lines of caste, class, and religion. Broadly, they can be classified into ritual, socio-economic, and administrative classifications. Almost all castes in Madras State except the Tamil Brahmins are deemed Shudras and, therefore, if ritual classification were to be exactly translated into socio-economic and administrative classification, all caste groups would be regarded as lower castes.

To bring in the important element of regional nuance and the communities' socio-economic position, the categories used in the book mean the following: Upper castes include Tamil Brahmins, non-Tamil Brahmin communities, and a few non-Brahmin groups, like some Chettiyar and Vellalar, Mudaliar, and Reddy/Reddiar communities. Intermediate castes are those with a higher standing compared to the Shudra communities but lower than that of the upper castes in the regions within the scope of this book. This category includes Pillais, Rajus, Udayars, and Naidus. Depressed Castes, Scheduled Castes, Adi Dravidars, and Dalits are used interchangeably to denote the formerly untouchable castes.

Lower castes and backward classes are used to denote the castes that occupy a lower position in the socio-economic and ritual hierarchies, but not Scheduled Castes. The word marginalised has been used to denote a larger and polysemous collective of the poor, the Scheduled Castes, the backward classes, gender and religious minorities and, at times, the intermediate and a few upper-caste groups mentioned above as well. For instance, in the context of representation in government posts in the late 1800s and early 1900s, non-Brahmin upper castes such as the Vellalars and Mudaliars had a minuscule representation, thereby making them a marginalised group.

ACKNOWLEDGMENTS

At this important moment in my academic career, I am deeply grateful to many people, and this section is my way of thanking them all, even those I may not have mentioned below.

This book is the result of my parents' unwavering faith in me. My father, Rajahmani, taught me the importance of dreaming big, while my mother, Vairam, showed me how to stay focused on making those dreams a reality. My younger brother Ramakrishnan has been my rock—consistently providing unconditional support, but especially since 2016, when this book was nothing more than an idea in my mind.

My intellectual growth and ongoing support have come from my mentors. Professor Christophe Jaffrelot has shaped my thinking since the first class I took with him at King's College London in 2012, during my master's programme. He supervised my master's dissertation, opened up numerous academic opportunities for me, and continues to guide me in many ways. Dr Kriti Kapila has spent countless hours over the past decade—starting when I was a prospective master's student in 2012—helping me refine my ideas and teaching me how to pursue them academically. Most importantly, she continues to support my academic and career growth.

I am truly grateful to the King's India Institute for giving me the freedom to pursue my research. I also want to thank the libraries that supported me along the way, including the SOAS Library, the British Library, the Nehru Memorial Museum & Library, the Tamil

Nadu State Archives, the Roja Muthiah Research Library, and the library at Anna Arivalayam.

The central idea of this book was inspired by two key works: *India's Silent Revolution: The Rise of the Lower Castes in North India* by Professor Christophe Jaffrelot and *Brahmin and Non-Brahmin: Genealogies of the Tamil Political Present* by the late Professor M.S.S. Pandian. I am also deeply grateful to Dr J. Jeyaranjan, Professor M. Vijayabaskar, Dr Karthick Ram Manoharan, Professor S. Anandhi, and Dr Andrew Wyatt. Their thoughtful discussions and close engagement with my project from its early stages have greatly enriched this book.

Dr Manoharan played a key role in providing important opportunities for me to present my work. First, at the 'Anti-Caste Thought: Theory, Politics and Culture' conference at the University of Wolverhampton in 2021, part of his EU Horizon 2020 project *Freedom from Caste: The Political Thought of Periyar E.V. Ramasamy in a Global Context* (supervised by Professor Meena Dhanda), which led to a special issue in *CASTE: A Global Journal on Social Exclusion* published in May 2022. Second, at a panel he co-organised with Professor Dhanda at the Political Studies Association Conference 2021, which has now been included in the *Cambridge Companion to Periyar* that Dr Manoharan is co-editing with Professor A.R. Venkatachalapathy.

I would like to sincerely thank Professor Louise Tillin, whose feedback was vital in helping me clearly define the scope of this work. I'm also deeply grateful to my thesis examiners, Dr Indrajit Roy and Dr Kalaiyarasan Arumugam, for their critical insights and constructive feedback, which significantly improved the quality of my research. Additionally, I am thankful for the invaluable advice from Professor Pradeep Chhibber, Professor Srinath Raghavan, Professor A.R. Venkatachalapathy, Dr Nilanjan Sarkar, Dr Sunil Mitra Kumar, and Dr Subir Sinha throughout this project.

My collaboration with Dr Srilata Sircar in the form of *Confronting Caste*, a seminar and podcast series from the King's India Institute that discusses caste as a system of power, has helped me revisit my fieldwork notes and present my findings more effectively. Along with Dr Sircar, Dr Sudhir Selvaraj, Dr Niranjana Ramesh,

Dr Shyam Krishna, and Tusharika Deka have been generous with their help and motivation.

A major source of steadfast support is Ajay Chandra Vasagam, who has helped me pursue this journey in more ways than one; without his support, the timely completion of this project would have been impossible. I am especially indebted to Saumya Gupta for her encouragement, engagement, and feedback since 2019. Raghunath Nageswaran has been supportive throughout the process, closely engaged with my work, and provided useful inputs over the years. Conversations with Vishal Vasanthakumar were always marked by valuable insights.

I am also very thankful to M.K. Venu, Pragya Singh, Rammanohar Reddy, Roman, Samas, Seema Chishti, Siddharth Varadarajan, and Srinivasan Ramani for giving me the opportunity to share my work on semi-academic and popular platforms. This book benefited from the intellectual camaraderie of Professor Arun Swamy, Dr Kamini Gupta, Dr Parag D. Parobo, Professor M.V. Rajeev Gowda, Professor Mukulika Banerjee, Ajaz Ashraf, A.S. Panneerselvan, Dr Nirali Joshi, Dr Pradyumna Jairam, Dr Rahul Ranjan, Dr Shounak Set, Jeyannathann Karunanithi, Johanna Deeksha, Sharik Laliwala, Shireen Azam, Dr Priyam Sinha, Manuraj Shanmugasundaram, Yazhini P.M., and Barath Pandian. I wish to acknowledge V.M. Subagunarajan's vital support in constructing the dataset pertaining to the social profiles of the members of Madras State legislative assemblies between 1952 and 1967. In the same vein, I wish to thank Gilles Verniers for the opportunity to work on building the dataset pertaining to Tamil Nadu as a part of the Social Profile of India's National and Provincial Elected Representatives project (LIA SPINPER) at the Trivedi Centre for Political Data, Ashoka University. I owe my sister, Kasturi Ramanathan, greatly for her infectious affection and continuous support over a decade.

My journey was a people-backed endeavour both in terms of resources and networks. I am deeply grateful to C.R. Kesavan, S. Senthilkumar, M. Gunasekaran, Chandrasekar, Anand Srinivasan, Meesam Ali, Laxman Pararasasingam, Yash Sripuram, Dr Uday Chandra, Subramanian Saravana, and Deepika Padmanabhan for the help they extended in the form of mobilising resources and their own timely support.

My earnest gratitude to Thangam Thennarasu for helping me secure access to reading rooms, DMK office bearers, and interviewees in Virudhunagar. My heartfelt gratitude to Kanimozhi Karunanidhi for taking time out to discuss my work on multiple occasions and giving me thoughtful feedback. Sincere thanks to Palanivel Thiaga Rajan, Tiruchi Siva, and N.R. Elango for making time to interact with me and engage with my work.

I also thank Thamizhachi Thangapandian, Suba Veerapandian, Pollachi Umapathy, Viduthalai Virumbi, Viduthalai Rajendran, K. Thirunavakkarasu, A. Gopanna, A. Sivasubramanian, Fathima Muzaffer, Gandhi Balasubramanian, S.R.S. Dhanabalan, and Yogesh Kanna for intriguing conversations and their help in facilitating my fieldwork.

I would like to acknowledge the generous support and freedom extended by Prashant Kishor and Esha Singh Alagh in my engagement with M.K. Stalin and the senior leadership of the DMK. I am also deeply thankful to the cheerful octogenarian and nonagenarian interviewees for their time and effort in having long conversations with me, sometimes taking a day or two to recall and share their memories.

I am indebted to Arunkumar S. (Cheyyaru), Poo Ko Saravanan, Suriya Krishnamoorthy, and Gowtham Raj for their help and support in accessing archival material. I owe my friends Joanny Bert Gomez, Vinay Gupta, Ashraf Ali, Rashan Sultan, Sai Prathish, Avantika Dureha, Anushree Rai, and Gayathri G.L.—thank you, for your warmth and constant motivation, and my apologies for my intermittent presence in your lives. Life in London would not have been smooth, enjoyable, and eventful if not for Sanam Arora, Aishwarya Mishra, Jyoti Mangal, and Vijaya Priyadarshini. As a small team managing a pan-UK students' union, we were each other's company and endured the COVID-19 pandemic together.

The long and tough process of turning my thesis into a book manuscript was made much smoother thanks to the careful and intuitive work of my editor, Mimi Choudhury, who worked closely with me in the rewriting. Many thanks to Pragya Singh for her invaluable last-minute support in bringing this book to the finish line. My heartfelt thanks to Michael Dwyer, a compassionate person and a dedicated publisher, whose support ensured the book's speedy publication and wide distribution.

I am grateful to Ajay, Jeyannathann, and Premkumar Natarajan for their generous assistance with the book's cover. My sincere thanks to the two anonymous reviewers for their thoughtful and encouraging feedback.

Last but certainly not least, I want to express my special gratitude to my partner, Sukanya. Since we first met in 2020 during the height of the COVID-19 pandemic, throughout our courtship leading up to our wedding in late 2021, and our move to London in 2022, she has been incredibly patient and supportive, even though she is used to being around people who have well-organised routines—unlike mine! I'm truly grateful for how she has brought so much joy and energy into my life, especially in London.

My sincere apologies and heartfelt gratitude to anybody I may have missed.

LIST OF TABLES

1. Literacy Rate in Madras State 77
2. Caste Composition of MLAs – 1952 State Assembly Elections 109
3. Partywise Caste Breakdown of MLAs – 1952 State Assembly Elections 110
4. Caste Composition of MLAs – 1957 State Assembly Elections 122
5. Partywise Caste Breakdown of MLAs – 1957 State Assembly Elections 122
6. Caste Composition of MLAs – 1962 State Assembly Elections 129
7. Partywise Caste Breakdown of MLAs – 1962 State Assembly Elections 129
8. Caste Composition of MLAs – 1967 State Assembly Elections 170
9. Partywise Caste Breakdown of MLAs – 1967 State Assembly Elections 171
10. Election-wise Breakdown of Caste Composition of DMK MLAs 174
11. Caste Composition of Madras State Cabinets (Fieldwork Findings) 176

12. Education Profile of MLAs (TN Assembly Archive) 177
13. Tracking Caste References/Titles in Names of MLAs – 1952 179
14. Tracking Caste References/Titles in Names of MLAs Supported by DMK – 1952 179
15. Tracking Caste References/Titles in Names of MLAs – 1957 180
16. Tracking Caste References/Titles in Names of MLAs – 1962 180
17. Tracking Caste References/Titles in Names of MLAs – 1967 180
18. Women Candidates and Women MLAs between 1957 and 1967 182

LIST OF FIGURES

1. Membership of Dravidar Kazhagam between 1944 and 1949 73
2. Decadal Variation in Madras State's Population between 1931 and 1961 74
3. Comparison of the Density of Reading Rooms in 1957 and 1967 79
4. Correlation between the Electoral Participation of DMK in 1957 (L) and 1962 (R) Assembly Elections and the Density of Reading Rooms in 1957 (M) 84
5. L–M: Correlation between the Electoral Success of the DMK Alliance and the Spread of Reading Rooms in 1967 M–R: Positive correlation between the density of reading rooms and district-wise literacy rates in Tamil Nadu 85

INTRODUCTION

Back in the 1950s, a decade full of socio-cultural and socio-political changes, few could have predicted that the word 'Tamil' and the politics surrounding it would go on to dominate the electoral scene in Madras[1] State for more than fifty years. This book investigates how the Dravidian movement—rooted in anti-caste struggles, the socio-economic uplift of marginalised communities, and the Tamil language[2]—transformed into a powerful electoral force.

The Dravida Munnetra Kazhagam (DMK),[3] which means the Dravidian Progressive Federation, was founded in 1949 as the political arm of the Dravidian movement.[4] This book examines the role the DMK played in spreading the principles of the Dravidian socio-cultural movement, leading to the party's first decisive electoral victory in 1967. It explores how the DMK developed a broad political identity around Dravidian-Tamil to shift the Dravidian Movement from a socio-cultural movement to a political and electoral force. Along the way, the book tackles two key questions: why does a socio-cultural movement shift into party politics? And who made up the social engine behind this transition in terms of castes (*jatis*)?

The book argues that the Dravidian movement grew out of the social conflicts in Madras Presidency, Madras Province, and then Madras State, focusing more on the socio-economic mobility of lower castes than on promoting the Tamil language in a nativist sense. It also takes a closer look at the sociology of the DMK to understand how it shifted from a socio-cultural movement into a political party that could actually compete in elections.

The Dravidian-Tamil identity was a political idea that started to take shape in the early 1900s. It was built around addressing the specific grievances of marginalised communities, making sure resources and opportunities were fairly distributed, and giving these communities a voice in power. It was not a fixed idea—it could shift, adapt, and evolve through changing contexts. Its constitution was marked by simultaneous bottom-up and top-down approaches.

Building on M.S.S. Pandian's work (2007: 130), I argue that this transitivity—evolving nature—of the Dravidian movement has, over time, allowed it to spark challenges against dominant systems of power, like the Brahminical value system. This value system shows up in discriminatory social relations, the unequal Centre-State relations mandated by the Constitution though they hurt regional aspirations, and the cultural privilege given to the Sanskrit language, among other things.

The term 'Dravidian' refers to both a historical region and a people connected to egalitarian values, while 'Tamil' refers to the oldest language in the Dravidian family. In the political realm, the term Dravidian emerged in the early twentieth century thanks to the anti-caste activist Iyothee Thass. Meanwhile, 'Tamil' made its political shift following the 1937 anti-Hindi agitations.

However, the expression Dravidian-Tamil is more than the sum of its parts. It represents a pluralist mindset focused on empowering marginalised communities that act as interest groups. The identity is capacious, inclusive—there's no room for exclusion based on gender, caste, class, religion, or language—and it can be subscribed to. As a result, the phrase retains its core meaning while gradually taking on new layers as more communities and their aspirations are included.

This book argues that the formation of the DMK in 1949 marked the start of the Dravidian movement's shift from a socio-cultural movement to party politics in post-independence India. The creation of the Dravidian-Tamil identity, mainly by Periyar[5] E.V. Ramasamy and C.N. Annadurai[6] in the 1930s and 1940s, and its spread in the 1950s and 1960s through reading rooms run by the DMK and its supporters, led to the rise of a Dravidian-Tamil community and the gradual politicisation of ordinary people in Madras State. The DMK's strategic balance between ideological commitment and political opportunism helped the Dravidian movement successfully transition into the electoral arena, defeating the Congress party and tasting the first of its many successes in the 1967 elections. The loss of Congress leader Kumaraswami Kamaraj to a DMK student leader is seen as a turning point in the transition. After that election, no national party could form the government in Madras State (now Tamil Nadu).

The book builds its arguments using two primary sources. First, it looks at previously unexplored materials, like Periyar's speeches in caste associations and publications circulated in the reading rooms run by the DMK and its supporters. Second, it draws on fieldwork conducted in 2019, 2020, and 2021, all in line with pandemic regulations.

Illuminations and Inquiries: A Systematic Exploration of Scholarly Works

The existing literature is grouped based on its relevance to the central argument of the book—the role of a political party in the transition of a socio-cultural movement to party politics. I have sorted these works by their focus on different aspects of the Madras region's polity and the Dravidian-Tamil identity. Along with pointing out the key overlaps in the works discussed, I also highlight the gap in the literature and explain how my book fills it.

Problematising Identity: From Non-Brahmin to Tamil

This study draws on three key frameworks to understand identity-building and the formation of the Dravidian-Tamil identity in Madras since the 1860s: the scholars of the Cambridge school, the Ethno-Populist school, and the Subaltern Cultural Studies school. Eugene Irschick, Christopher Baker, and David Washbrook are part of the first framework, which sees socio-economic competition as the main force behind the creation of a non-Brahmin identity and the politics surrounding it.

The second framework, put forward by Arun Swamy and Narendra Subramanian, focuses on the transactional nature of the relationship between the political class and the general public. The third framework, developed by M.S.S. Pandian and based on Nambi Arooran's (1980) work, describes the non-Brahmin identity as a socio-cultural construct that stands in contrast to the Brahmin identity.

Irschick (1969) explores in detail the early years of the organised challenge to Brahmin dominance in the Madras presidency. His book looks at the period from 1916 to 1929, when two main streams of thought emerged: one led by Annie Besant, and the other by leaders of the Justice Party like T.M. Nair and P.T. Chetty. The Justice Party's rise to power in the 1920s brought a series of reforms, which came about through negotiations with the British.

This book focuses on the conflict between Brahmins and non-Brahmins, which revolves around challenging the inherited social hierarchy and working to build a new order, mainly by opening up opportunities for non-Brahmins to share in power. The problem, however, is how Irschick views the rise of the Justice Party as happening at the expense of nationalist movements. This argument treats the Dravidian movement as a tool of the imperial government, which downplays its role in promoting socio-economic empowerment for the backward sections and helping them gain political power.

Washbrook (1976) and Baker (1976) argue that the Dravidian movement was shaped by economic conditions that helped the elite within the non-Brahmin communities improve their material well-being. These elites were seen by the British as an alternative to the 'Mylapore Brahmins',[7] whom they wanted to replace. The Mylapore group's entry into the Indian National Congress, under the banner of nationalism, was supported by Annie Besant, who defended the *varna* system. In response, the Justice Party equated Congress nationalism with Brahminism which allowed the social injustices perpetuated by Brahmins to continue.

The Cambridge scholars' focus on economic factors and power dynamics overlooks the extensive social dominance of Brahmins, while downplaying the Justice Party's push for social justice and equitable access. In this way, the social realities of the caste system weren't considered as a reason—though not necessarily as the only reason—for the formation of the Justice Party. Additionally, these works overlook the crucial role early Dravidian leaders played in reviving the Tamil language and challenging Sanskrit influences. While the Justice Party was made up of elites from non-Brahmin communities, its decline and the rise of the Self-Respect Movement—which questioned the prejudices of those elites—point to a strengthening of the equality ideal preached by early Dravidian Saivite leaders like Maraimalai Adigal.

Arun Swamy (1996) and Narendra Subramanian (1999) have traced political and social outcomes in Tamil Nadu from the 1930s to the 1990s to explain broader questions about conflict, development policies, and the political class's motivations for focusing on specific societal issues. Both scholars use the term 'populism', which has many different and often conflicting definitions, to explain these political processes. In the context of Dravidian-Tamil identity, populism served as an ideology that helped lower castes fight for a fair share of power and resources, which had been controlled by a small section of upper-caste elites.

Swamy defines populism as "a doctrine that holds that ordinary people have been robbed of their due owing to no fault of their own" (Swamy, 1996: 72). On the other hand, Subramanian says populism is used to describe "movements, parties, and regimes which articulate notions of a 'people' defined by special norms rooted in its history" (Subramanian, 1999: 8).

Based on these definitions, they identify two kinds of populism—what Subramanian also defines as subcultures—in Madras State (now Tamil Nadu). Their works complement each other, but there's a difference in emphasis that makes them work well together: while Subramanian focuses on the *style of political action*, Swamy stresses on the *alliances of classes* that backed these parties (Harriss, 2001: 12).

To explain why and how alliances are formed, Swamy outlines two variants of populism—*empowerment populism* and *protection populism*. Empowerment populism sees the problem as stemming from a privileged elite (whether alienated or seen that way), with the solution lying in the hands of aspirational groups who attack the sources of privilege. On the other hand, protection populism views the issue as coming from the misconduct of aspirational or middle groups, with the solution being the elite's 'duty' to protect the poor.

The success of 'protection populism' depends on the effectiveness of 'sandwich tactics', which involve bypassing the interests of middle-level groups through an alliance between groups at the top and the bottom.

Swamy points to the DMK's success in forging an identity that spoke to the concerns of multiple groups within a discursive realm—where debates on meaning and identity take place—as a prime example of empowerment populism. He also sees the rise of M.G. Ramachandran (M.G.R.), the founder of the All-India Anna Dravida Munnetra Kazhagam (AIADMK), and his protection populism as a strong contender to the DMK's empowerment populism.

Subramanian's starting point is ethnic conflicts in plural societies. He uses Tamil Nadu as an example of how distinctiveness can shape political processes, arguing that South Indian states used political action to curtail violent ethnic conflicts (Subramanian, 1999: 30). His main point is that Dravidian parties successfully united middle- and lower-level groups under one political umbrella. He discusses two other variants of populism—*assertive* and *paternalist*. Assertive populism involves political actions that challenge discrimination and defend entitlements from the elite 'other'. Paternalist populism, on the other hand, is when a poor community looks up to a leader, party, or state for support and protection from oppression.

Subramanian also brings in the idea of *organisational pluralism*—comprising leadership flexibility, cadre autonomy, and supporter autonomy (ibid., 39). He argues that these elements, along with *social pluralism*—multiple independent organisations, separate from the state and one another (ibid., 3)—support his larger framework, in which language and caste are essential elements of the political processes in Tamil Nadu.

Swamy examines Tamil Nadu within the broader context of India in a comprehensive, comparative manner, while Subramanian focuses on non-Tamil examples only to highlight the distinctiveness of Tamil Nadu. Swamy's approach, therefore, contextualises developments in Tamil Nadu within the broader national framework of the time. By looking at Swamy's work alongside Subramanian's, I offer a fresh perspective on Subramanian's analysis. A case in point is the re-organisation of states based on language in 1956 —a momentous episode that Subramanian discusses only briefly.

Despite extensive fieldwork, Subramanian's book *Ethnicity and Populist Mobilization: Political Parties, Citizens and Democracy in South India* does not provide detailed explanations or reasons for his inferences and observations. For example, he touches on social and organisational pluralism but doesn't fully explain how such distinct groups could unite. While he identifies the anti-Brahmin stance as the rallying point for their unity, this is limiting as a sole explanation. Also, his broad six-decade scope means he misses some of the earlier, more formative years of the DMK, particularly the crucial details about how it eventually came to power. As a result, both these works cover the breadth of the Dravidian movement more than its depth. My book attempts to bridge this gap, exploring how a large and inconvenient 'other' was forged into a strong political identity that sticks together to this day.

M.S.S. Pandian's book, *Brahmin & Non-Brahmin: Genealogies of the Tamil Political Present,* challenges the usual way of looking at the Brahmin-non-Brahmin antagonism as just a straightforward caste struggle in Tamil Nadu. As a subaltern scholar, he took a step back from both Indian nationalist and Marxist approaches. Instead, he traces the development of Brahmin and non-Brahmin identities against the backdrop of colonialism.

He suggests that the colonial experience hybridised Brahmin identity in a way that made Brahmins appear both modern and the true guardians of culture, thus helping them claim authority. At the same time, this transformation both supported and restricted non-Brahmins. Dalit Buddhist leaders like Iyothee Thass offered a cultural critique of the true Brahmin, while the Justice Party highlighted how Brahmins dominated jobs, education, and wealth. Pandian argues that this hybridisation of Brahmin identity—in which discrimination based on caste, for instance, was reframed as a matter of hygiene—shaped non-Brahmin identity too (Pandian, 2007: 30). In other words, the non-Brahmin identity reconfigured itself on the basis of the Brahmin identity where the Brahmin stood for everything that was oppressive and hegemonic, and the non-Brahmin was comprehensively inferiorised by the Brahmin.

Pandian's work offers a valuable challenge to the perspectives I discussed earlier, but it also opens the door for a deeper understanding of how identities are built in the political arena—something my book aims to explore. Building on Subramanian's critique of Pandian, that it looks at identity mainly through the perspective of top leaders and overlooks how ordinary people respond (Subramanian, 2002: 127), my book fills that gap by incorporating the views from the grassroots level, drawn from my own fieldwork. By interviewing party workers from that time as well as leaders from both the DMK and Congress, my book offers a fresh perspective on how the movement functioned on the ground. This is something Pandian's work does not address.

Through my work with archival material, including writings from leaders and their ideas, I aim to show how the DMK could reconcile social conflicts across different castes. I argue that its promotion of the Dravidian-Tamil ethos continues to shape the politics of Tamil Nadu to this day.

To sum up, scholars from the Cambridge School focus on the economic mobility of a few non-Brahmin castes as they fought against the Brahmins, often portraying the Justice Party leaders as proxies for the imperial government. In contrast, M.S.S. Pandian traces the roots of Dravidian-Tamil identity back to the relationship between Brahmin and non-Brahmin identities. Meanwhile, Arun Swamy and Narendra Subramanian examine the political developments of the time only through the lens of the political style practised by the DMK and AIADMK.

Identity and Tamil Language

Sumathi Ramaswamy (1997) explores issues of caste and nationalism by examining them through the lens of the Tamil language. She highlights the tensions between groups like the neo-Saivites, Dravidianists, the classicists like Swaminatha Iyer and Robert Caldwell, and Indianists such as Rajagopalachari, who disagreed on the meaning of Tamil and what it stood against. Ramaswamy starts by challenging the idea of 'one language, one nation' and questioning the centrality of language in imagining a national identity. She traces the politics of language and the development of Tamil identity through the language from the 1890s to the 1970s.

Using the concepts of *Tamilparru* (devotion to the Tamil language) and *Tamiltay* (Mother Tamil), Ramaswamy traces the rise of Tamil identity, positioning *Tamilakam* (home of the Tamils) against a Hindi-dominated India that embodies the North Indian Aryan Brahminical ethos. On the question of the Tamil language serving as a unifying force for various, sometimes hostile groups, she presents the case of Periyar, who, despite not supporting *Tamilparru,* endorsed Tamil identity in response to the anti-Hindi agitations.

Despite its anti-Brahmanical stance, the image of *Tamiltay* resembled a Hindu deity, suggesting a paradox. While discussing the non-Brahmin supporters of the Tamil identity, Ramaswamy does not directly engage with the Dravidian movement. Here, too, my book intervenes by bringing the Dravidian movement into the picture, helping to explain Periyar's change of stance and engaging with the post-Independence tensions to explore the political aspects of Tamil identity formation.

Marguerite Ross Barnett's 1976 work on the Dravidian movement details the prolonged struggles of the movement's popular leaders to shape a political identity and establish themselves as a dominant political and electoral force. She presents a wealth of data on the status and class of the people involved in the movement, highlighting a broad coalition that transcended caste, religion, and class, all united under the Tamil identity.

Additionally, she includes data on elections, as well as excerpts from speeches and writings. She challenges the view that the movement was anti-modern or 'primordial', as suggested by the 'Primordial sentiments-Civil politics' dichotomy put forward by Geertz (1961). Her arguments on cultural nationalism advocate for understanding the Tamil identity as a key component of the idea of India, rather than a challenge to it—provided that the concept of India fosters cultural pluralism.

I have explored Ross Barnett's suggestion about the movement's accommodation of multiple social groups. The goal of engaging with her work is to better understand the motivations behind the unification of various, often conflicting, groups under the broad Dravidian-Tamil identity.

Paul Brass (1981) noted that Barnett's perspective aligns with the 'instrumentalist' school of ethnic and nationality studies. This school views the groups involved in such movements as "cultural categories transformed into self-conscious communities by leaders, elite groups or the state, and seeking to provide social, economic and political advantages for the group in question" (1981: 451). However, Barnett's claim that the DMK's altering of Dravidian ideology i.e., shifting its focus to language instead of secession, is problematic. She argues that for the DMK, winning elections became an end in itself, rather than aiming for secession, which she believes should be the goal of a party promoting cultural nationalism. (Barnett, 1976: 106). She writes, "Thus, while the outlines of the radical Dravidian ideology were maintained, the meaning of basic symbols and overall emphasis were changed…" (ibid., 318).

I contend that the DMK was—and continues to be—an insurgent force against hegemonic nationalism, with elections not being an end in themselves, but rather a powerful tool to achieve its objectives. During my fieldwork, I discovered archival material that supports my argument. This book will, therefore, examine the Dravidian ideology promoted by the DMK, drawing on previously unexplored archival material and supporting it with interviews to assess the arguments presented by Barnett.

Bernard Bate's book *Tamil Oratory and the Dravidian Aesthetic: Democratic Practice in South India,* part of the 'Cultures of History' series, is an important work that explores the different types of

Tamil and communication styles of Dravidian movement leaders. Bate describes the use of *Centamil* (literary Tamil), which carries a feminine overtone (2009: 170) and symbolises antiquity and authenticity, in political communication during public gatherings from the 1950s (ibid., 52).

Bate notes that the variant of Tamil spoken by politicians and used to convey their messages in public meetings was viewed as ancient, distinctively original, and deliberately separate from Sanskritised Tamil. This distinction set apart a Brahminical Congress leader from a non-Brahmin Dravidian leader, with the latter portraying the former as the 'other'.

Bate also observes that Dravidian-Tamil politicians aligned themselves with a rich lineage of Tamil kings and gods in their connection with the public and voters. Their supporters, in turn, elevated them to godly status through praises and poems. His central argument revolves around how leaders employed traditional language styles to convey modern and democratic ideas. He argues that these traditions were invented and crafted as 'a primary modality of modernity' (ibid., xvii). Bate's account helps this book discuss the Dravidian-Tamil identity as a modern construct that wields tradition to assert its authenticity in the cultural realm.

A Comparative Perspective: Caste Emancipation and Linguistic Assertion and Statehood in Andhra Pradesh, Uttar Pradesh, and Tamil Nadu

The creation of Andhra State in 1953, followed by Andhra Pradesh in 1956, and the later Jai Telangana Movement in 1969 and the Jai Andhra Movement of 1972, as well as the bifurcation of Andhra Pradesh in 2014 show that the Telugu identity—rooted in the Telugu language—struggled to unify the Telugu-speaking population across regions. One key reason for this is the caste and sub-regional conflicts that have been simmering among the Telugu-speaking population for decades.

Ramakrishna V. (1990: 570) points out that the modern Telugu language movement, which was all about pushing for social reform, really took off in 1919 with the efforts of Gidugu Ramamurthy. This breakthrough followed over a century of contestation with traditional Brahminical pandits, going all the way back to Charles Philip Brown, a British civil servant, who made the first attempts to modernise the language. After Ramamurthy passed away in 1940, the modern Telugu movement shifted its focus. What had once worked to steer clear of Sanskrit influence started to incorporate ideas from Western literary movements and Marxist principles (ibid., 570).

From 1900 to 1930, the non-Brahmin movement was at its peak in the Telugu-speaking regions of the Madras Presidency. K.C. Suri (2000: 3) connects this rise of lower-caste Congress leaders, the early development of the communist movement before Independence, and the founding of the Telugu Desam Party in 1980 to the non-Brahmin movement. This movement was largely led by a section of landowning Telugu non-Brahmins, both in the Tamil- and Telugu-speaking regions of the Madras Presidency.

Uma Ramaswamy (1949: 300) points out that the tensions between the upwardly mobile non-Brahmin castes—like the Kammas, Reddis, and Velamas—led to the decline of the non-Brahmin movement after 1930. Worse still, it sparked competition among these groups for superior status. The tussle among the Kammas, Reddis, and Velamas ultimately alienated the Other Backward Classes and Scheduled Castes. The unresolved caste conflicts among the non-Brahmin castes held back the development of an inclusive Telugu identity. Though there was debate about creating an inclusive identity, it largely ended up reflecting the caste pride of the Kammas, Reddis, and Velamas.

On the other hand, K.V. Narayana Rao (2007: 155–56) argues that the "Dravidanadu of E.V. Ramasamy was not a province like the Andhra province but a separate autonomous unit based on self-determination". In other words, the linguistic reorganisation movement of the 1950s took on a different form in the Tamil-speaking regions of the Madras State.

In Uttar Pradesh, the most populous state of India, a movement similar to the one in Andhra Pradesh emerged, where the State's geographical territory was viewed as the 'heartland' (Kudaisya,

2006: 391–92 in Tillin, 2012). Louise Tillin argues that the defenders of Uttar Pradesh used the idea of "an organic Hindu social order", rooted in the *varna* system, which is central to Hindu nationalist thought, to paradoxically stress the unity of the State. (Tillin, 2012). It is also suggested that both the suppression of opposing views from the Jats of western Uttar Pradesh in the 1950s and the State's bifurcation in 2000 were results of caste-based political mobilisation.

The failure of political leaders to create a common identity that could bring together horizontal groups—those with similar socio-political standing—in Uttar Pradesh is also considered an important reason for its bifurcation. By comparing with Uttar Pradesh and Andhra Pradesh we can bring our discussion on the Dravidian movement to life, highlighting the potential for its replication, as well as the challenges and limitations it faces in other parts of the country and across the broader Global South context.

Caste Associations as a Means to Politicise Caste

Caste was integral to mobilising people in Tamil Nadu, with most of the early popular associations being caste-based. Periyar himself participated in and spoke at numerous caste association meetings. While some scholars might view caste as 'pre-modern', any analysis that ignores caste would struggle to explain why people participate enthusiastically in elections, or why the fight for education and economic empowerment became central to improving their social position.

Rudolph and Rudolph talk about how the role of caste associations changed over time. They trace their origin to British rule (1960: 7) and explain that as the idea of democracy spread, the focus of these associations shifted. In a democracy, simply having a certain rank no longer guaranteed power. Unlike caste, which you're born into, caste associations were formed voluntarily—you had to choose to join, even if you were born into that caste. They also operated in a more organised way. As a result, the meaning of caste itself started to change (ibid., 9). To illustrate this, Rudolph and Rudolph cite the Shanan (Nadar) protest of 1858, through which they demanded the right of women to wear the upper cloth, showing how caste associations played a key role in securing people's rights through democratic means.

The central argument is illustrated through the case of the Vanniyars, a numerically dominant caste in Northern Tamil Nadu that includes agricultural labourers, cultivating landowners, and petty landlords. Initially, they wanted to improve their social status and made representations to the census commissioner. Later, they lobbied for reservation in the civil services and in 1952, they sought representation in elected bodies. When these demands were ignored, they formed political parties and began participating in elections. Village caste organisations were then used to encourage people to vote for these parties and to address the community's social and economic backwardness.

"Caste has been able to play this curious political role as bearer of both India's *ancien régime* and its democratic political revolution by reconstituting itself into the sabha, with characteristics of both the natural and the voluntary association, of caste defined in terms of both dharma and democracy" (ibid., 22). This process of coming together as a negotiating force can be applied to most caste groups in Tamil Nadu. Jaffrelot (2003: 172) calls this process across castes a "bureaucratic creation aimed at empowerment", which helped flatten the hierarchy and bring them together. In my work, I would like to explore how this political identity came into being and became an electorally potent force.

I have studied the scholarly literature about the Nadars for two reasons. First, Kamaraj, who features prominently in this book, belonged to the Nadar community. Kamaraj Nadar, the name he went by till the late 1960s, clearly exhibited his caste identity. Second, the area where my study is focused, the Virudhunagar Assembly constituency, has a large population of Nadars. Historically, the Nadars were considered a lower caste, even viewed as 'half-polluting'. They were seen as occupying a middle ground in the caste hierarchy—between the lower Shudras and the outcaste untouchables.

In the early nineteenth century, the women of a section of the community were not permitted to wear upper-body garments, and the men were forced to pay multiple taxes,[8] but by the early twentieth century, they had transformed into a prominent and successful mercantile community in Tamil Nadu. Studying the Nadars and their rise is also important because of the impact of missionaries and influential community leaders such as W.P.A. Soundarapandian and social reformers like Periyar (Jaffrelot, 2003: 167).

To truly understand the dynamics of the Nadar community, it's crucial to look at their history, mobility, and political engagement. The works by P. Rajadurai (1983) and Robert L. Hardgrave (1969) are particularly insightful in this regard. They give us a detailed look at the community, including the birth of local institutions and intra-community efforts to improve the lives of its members. The Mahajana Sangam was at the helm, and *uravinmurai*, a group of merchants who joined forces to claim certain powers, was affiliated to it. *Uravinmurai* levied *mahimai*, a tax on goods purchased and sold, and owned *pettai*, a place for the merchants to rest and store their goods during transit.

There existed local *uravinmurai* associations that helped resolve disputes among Nadars. This system was not tied to religion, so it did not matter whether someone was Hindu or Christian. The main focus of Hardgrave's book is on how the Nadars interacted within their families and with others in the community, striving to protect themselves from potential threats from other communities in the domains of trade and social dealings (Hardgrave, 1969: 70). These structures later became crucial in helping the community and driving change when leaders of the Dravidian movement reached out to work with caste organisations.

Hardgrave's work spotlights prominent community figures like W.P.A. Soundarapandian and V.V. Ramasamy Nadar, showcasing their contributions. While Rajadurai's work (1991) focuses extensively on Soundarapandian's role, Ramasamy Nadar was elected to the legislative assembly in the first State Assembly elections in 1952 as an independent candidate from Virudhunagar—the constituency where I carried out my fieldwork.

Rajadurai's work, *WPA Soundara Pandian's Tenure in Tamil Nadu Legislative Assembly* (1991), explores his role as the most revered leader in the community's development. He was influenced by Periyar's principles and was known as the uncrowned king of the Nadar community (Hardgrave, 1969: 319).

Finally, Rajadurai's thesis (1992) provides an insightful look into the Self-Respect Movement's impact on the Nadar community. By engaging with these texts, I've gained a fresh perspective on the regional developments, particularly from Ramasamy Nadar's tenure between 1952 and 1957, to Periyar's disagreements with the DMK and his support for Kamaraj. Kamaraj then went on to contest three more elections in 1957, 1962, and 1967, losing in the third. My book argues that the Dravidian movement's shift into party politics was partly driven by the politicisation of caste, which must be seen as one of the key outcomes of the democratisation of political life in Madras State.

This book fills a critical gap in the literature by offering a detailed exploration of how a socio-cultural movement evolved into full-blown party politics, reaching its apex with the seismic electoral shift in 1967. While the scholars from the Cambridge School mostly overlook this period, both Swamy and Subramanian focus on the political styles embraced by the DMK and AIADMK. However, Subramanian's treatment is rather cursory, leaving the deeper significance of events I engage with unexplored.

Barnett's preoccupation with the Dravidian Movement as an example of cultural nationalism leads her to overlook a crucial aspect: how the movement evolved into a party. Instead, her analysis suggests that the movement's programmatic collective ideals were watered down, transforming into a more pragmatic, brokerage-style, or umbrella party. Ramaswamy's engagement with various factions pushing Tamil interests misses the opportunity to directly address the Dravidian movement. While Pandian traces the genealogies of Brahmins and non-Brahmins—terms that are still rich with meaning in the Dravidian-Tamil public sphere—he does not address how the movement transformed into a political party either.

My book will scrutinise the emergence of Periyar and the Self-Respect Movement in the Tamil speaking regions of the Madras Presidency. I will examine the role of his speeches in caste associations in the 1920s in forging horizontal solidarity among the non-Brahmin lower castes and forging the inclusive Dravidian-Tamil identity. Annadurai's strategic articulation of the Dravidian-Tamil identity, which the DMK effectively propagated both at a personal level and on a larger scale during the 1950s and 1960s, will also be examined.

This book contends that the Tamil language served to bind its speakers, who believed in the socio-economic mobility of lower castes, irrespective of their mother tongue. For instance, it is worth noting that Periyar did not prominently take part in the contestations over the State's borders during the creation of linguistic states. I seek to explain why and how the DMK's distinctive brand of regionalism is rooted more in the politics of solidarity among marginalised castes. The socio-economic advancement of these caste groups, rather than just the linguistic assertion of dominant communities, shaped the DMK's political agenda.

Methodology

The book employs a mixed-methods approach, combining archival research with interviews. Given the historical scope of the study, the primary reliance is on archival materials, which include writings and recorded speeches by key figures such as Periyar, Annadurai, Karunanidhi,[9] and the newspapers they ran. The selection of archival content is based on the relevance to the chapters.

Elections have long been a critical marker in the intersection of social, economic, and political forces. In Tamil Nadu, where rival regional parties with a shared political identity have dominated since the 1970s, pre-1970s elections provide crucial insights into examine the development of this identity.

Jaffrelot (2018) argues that a combination of methods and interdisciplinarity is essential to understanding identity and the politics surrounding it in India. He emphasises that robust research requires not only quantitative data to explain ground realities but also extensive interviews to provide a more nuanced understanding. In this context, I examine the critical 1967 election in the Virudhunagar constituency of Madras State and a series of elections leading up to the year from 1951, considering the role of the dense network of reading rooms to explore the depth and scope of the transformation of the Dravidian-Tamil identity.

Interviews

The book rests firmly on qualitative, unstructured interviews with key figures from major political parties of the time, including the DMK, Congress, Swatantra Party, and the Communist Party of India. It also draws from interviews with family members aware of the developments or associated with party activities. Additionally, the research includes insights from activists and journalists with memories of the 1950s and 1960s, and regional historians and scholars who have studied and written about the movement in Tamil.

I have constructed a purposive sample of interviewees that can be broadly classified into three categories. First, persons belonging to the political class, that is, party workers, office bearers and leaders, and the close family members of the above-mentioned political parties. Second, octogenarian and nonagenarian reading room visitors and reading room managers in Virudhunagar. Third, sub-regional historians and senior journalists, who were active in the 1950s and 1960s and/or have produced material about the said time period.

I have constructed this sample of interviewees, drawn using the snowball-sampling method. These interviews helped my research in two ways: first, by way of providing an oral account of the past—at times, firsthand—thereby richly informing the book about events, their background, and how they shaped the Dravidian-Tamil identity. These interviews are key to chapters 2, 3, and 4. Second, the interviews provide direction while referring to the extensive archival material.

Quantitative data

I rely on election data provided by the Election Commission of India on the assembly polls held between 1951 and 1967. The base dataset was compiled by retaining the candidates in the top two positions of the elections in each constituency and, in select cases, the third position if they belonged to the DMK or its alliance.

To this dataset, three new classifications were the added to build a sociological profile of the candidates—caste (at the *jati* level) of the winners, the social status of these castes in the Tamil Nadu context, and a yes/no category tracking the caste reference in the candidate's name. The resultant dataset allowed me to track the representation of candidates from various caste groups across the social hierarchy and provide evidence of the outcome of DMK's efforts to facilitate the entry and socio-political mobility of lower castes.

The Scaffold and the Story: Theoretical Groundwork and Chapter Outlines

One possible reason the transition of the Dravidian movement into party politics hasn't been fully explored is the limitations inherent in the theoretical frameworks used by scholars. The Cambridge School argued that the competition among social groups for economic resources and political power in colonial South India shaped the movement in the late nineteenth and early twentieth centuries. Swamy (1996) and Subramanian (1999) looked at the region's political developments through an ethno-populist lens, covering over six decades of political change, from the 1930s to the 1990s. However, this broad scope restricted their ability to give more detailed attention to the decades of the 1950s and 1960s.

On the other hand, a more recent study by Krishnan, Sriramachandran, and Subagunarajan (2022) examines how the DMK created a counter-hegemonic force in the 1950s and 1960s. However, their analysis is marked by some internal inconsistencies, partly in how they treat the term 'Tamil' within the Dravidian-Tamil phrase. They seem to consider it an empty signifier within the context of left-populism,[10] which weakens their intervention. Similarly, Pandian and Aaroran's interpretations of the movement through the subaltern studies and cultural studies framework, respectively, fall short of fully explaining the transition of the movement into a successful mass party.

Barnett's use of the instrumentalist framework helps shift the focus from socio-economic tensions to cultural nationalism. However, it misses an important part of the picture—the process of shaping an ideology, which is then tied to the cultural symbols and tropes used by cultural nationalists. To address these gaps, I turn to Jaffrelot's (2005: 47–48) integrated theory of ethnic nationalism, which looks at both simultaneous and sequential processes.

As a result, the book has two parts, three chronological phases, and four chapters in a chrono-thematic format.

The first part of this book looks at how the Dravidian-Tamil identity was formed and disseminated while it became politicised. This process of identity formation took place through the first half of the twentieth century and underwent various stages. The second part shifts focus to how this identity spread through electoral politics between 1951 and 1967, examining both the smaller, local level and the larger, overarching trends. At a micro level, the Virudhunagar assembly constituency is examined from the early 1960s leading up to the 1967 elections, which saw the surprising defeat of Kamaraj, a towering figure in both Tamil Nadu and India.

On a macro level, this section looks at the sociological profiles of the winning candidates in each constituency for the State Assembly elections between 1951 and 1967. This helps track how the profiles of representatives changed over time and offers insights into the success—or failure—of the Dravidian movement's transition into electoral politics.

The first phase, which focuses on the 1920s, explores the rise of Periyar during a time when the (neo)Saivite movement, Iyothee Thass, and the Justice Party were challenging the prevalent Brahminical hegemony. This phase looks at how a political identity was formed around an ideology centered in anti-caste discourse, the socio-economic uplift of marginalised communities, and the Tamil language. It also examines how Periyar—and later Annadurai in the 1940s and 1950s—created the concept of 'the people' and 'the other'.

The second phase begins with the formation of the DMK as a political party in 1949, marking the movement's shift into party politics. During this phase, the party works to spread its ideology and solidify the Dravidian-Tamil identity throughout the 1950s and 1960s. The third phase represents the full realisation of this transition, culminating in the 1967 State Assembly elections. In this landmark election, the DMK-led alliance secures a decisive victory, and from this point on, no non-Dravidian party could come to power in the State.

The movement is marked by a constant struggle between different communities across social, economic, and political spheres. The icons of the movement work to devise an ideology that effectively targets the dominant group, aiming for a broad-based emancipation rather than just change in one area.[11] The new social order is often envisioned as a 'Golden Age' (Fallers, 1961: 677–78) that is more often than not carefully constructed.[12] Later, Jaffrelot introduces conflict-based theories, similar to Gellner's ideas, to explain how the movement shifted into politics.

Gellner suggests that social structures like race or religion can play a powerful role in bringing a marginalised culture into the mainstream, especially in the context of socio-economic conflicts.[13] He also points out that education is vital force to recasting a section of the subalterns (proletariat) as the intelligentsia to lead the movement. Essentially, Gellner's focus on the processes that spark socio-economic conflicts (1964: 165–70), combined with the strategic ideological approach mentioned earlier, helps explain how the movement gained political power. Chapters 1 and 2 provide evidence of how these two processes came together, contributing to the success of the DMK on the political turf.

Finally, Jaffrelot blends the instrumentalist theory with ideas from nation-building schools to track how the movement gained mass support and ultimately transitioned into politics. Brass (1979: 69) argues that the movement's leaders offer their own interpretations of the issues facing society, cleverly embedding these with cultural symbols of the movement.

Deutsch (1969: 97), from the cybernetic approach to nation-building, which foregrounds the role of technological advancement, emphasises that the cohesion of a nation and its growth depend on an effective communication strategy that can connect a diverse population. He also notes that factors like newspaper readership, student enrolment, urbanisation, and the strength of the postal network are useful indicators to assess the movement's strength.

Chapter 2 examines the surge of journalistic activity in Tamil, driven by members of both dominant and non-dominant communities, a tool of politicisation too significant to be overlooked. In the 1950s and 1960s, around three hundred to four hundred newspapers and magazines were active, and the writings of movement leaders helped foster a shared sentiment around key issues across the Madras State. The impact of this vibrant journalistic activity can be best understood through the lens of print capitalism, as proposed by Benedict Anderson.

In his book *Imagined Communities*, Anderson writes, "The very conception of the newspaper implies the refraction of even 'world events' into a specific imagined world of vernacular readers; and also, how important to that imagined community is an idea of steady, solid simultaneity through time" (Anderson, 1983: 63).

Jaffrelot (2005: 11) also notes that theories of ethnicity align closely with theories of nationalism. When it comes to ethnicities, he cautions against an overemphasis on continuities and stresses the possibility of qualitative change (ibid., 38). Criticising the essentialist views of primordialists and the material focus of instrumentalists as the central reasons for the construction of ethnic groups, Jaffrelot gravitates towards the interactionist approach put forward by Frederik Barth.

Barth argues that ethnic groups are characterised by continuous change (1969: 21). He believes that multiple communities, even if they have cultural differences, can function as an ethnic group as long as the underlying basis for their belonging remain intact (ibid., 18). Thomas Eriksen builds on this idea, defining ethnicity as a relationship between groups rather than within groups, which frames it as something collectively created. He explains that cultural differences within an ethnic group are continually communicated and maintained, without disrupting the group's social relations. Ethnicity, he argues, is both relational and situational, meaning that while communities within an ethnic group can stay distinct, they can also be mobilised to assert as a unit when faced with external pressure or pressure from the 'other' (Eriksen, 2002: 58).

In the modern context, Glazer and Moynihan (1975: 7–8) propose that ethnic groups can act as interest groups. While modernisation may reduce some cultural differences, the historical inequalities and varying social and economic positions still make ethnic groups strong forces for mobilising people and pushing for their collective aspirations.

This book explores how Periyar and Annadurai forged the Dravidian-Tamil identity as an ethno-nationalist platform that aimed to serve the interests of a variety of communities united under the Dravidian-Tamil banner. It also looks at how the boundaries of this ethnic group shifted in response to political changes in South Asia and, more specifically, Madras State. Lastly, the book argues that the DMK's goals include addressing the specific grievances of marginalised communities, redistributing resources, and securing representation in power—all by framing the Dravidian-Tamil ethnic group as an interest group of numerous marginalised communities.

The first chapter examines how the Dravidian-Tamil identity was formed, arguing that it emerged from the development of non-Brahmin and Dravidian movements, with a particular focus on how it became political in the late 1940s. To understand how this identity was created, the chapter looks at Periyar's ideas about the caste system and how his views challenged its hierarchical structure, along with the conflicts that arose from this.

By exploring Periyar's take on caste, the chapter also highlights how the Dravidian-Tamil identity developed in opposition to Brahmins, leading to the formation of what is called 'horizontal solidarities' (Jaffrelot, 2000: 107) among the lower castes. The impact of this process on Dravidian-Tamil identity gives a glimpse into how a political identity is formed. The chapter starts by looking at the existing research on caste to provide some context for the system's hierarchical structure. It then contrasts this with Periyar's unique approach, that aimed to flatten the hierarchy in ways that Dumont didn't envision and Ambedkar didn't operationalise. I explore Periyar's views on caste by drawing on archival material, including his writings in his newspapers like *Kudi Arasu* (Republic) and *Revolt,* as well as his public speeches, especially those made in caste association meetings.

The second chapter looks at how *padippakams* (reading rooms/ libraries) helped spread the Dravidian-Tamil identity among ordinary people. Most of these reading rooms were either informally inclined towards the DMK or were actually run by party members. My research highlights Kamaraj's loss in the 1967 Assembly elections in Virudhunagar as a key moment when the socio-cultural movement shifted into party politics. With a focus on the Virudhunagar constituency, the chapter traces how *padippakams* emerged and developed there.

The chapter starts by looking at the journalistic work of DMK leaders, especially in relation to the material that was shared in the reading rooms. It then argues that these reading rooms became a powerful way to spread the writings and speeches of DMK leaders on a daily basis, helping to create a shared sense of identity among people across Madras State. The chapter mainly draws on interviews with politicians from the DMK, Indian National Congress, and Communist Party of India, along with senior journalists, regular reading room visitors, those who ran the reading rooms, and local Tamil historians. These conversations provide insights into how the reading rooms functioned and what topics were commonly discussed there.

The third chapter takes a closer look at how the DMK responded to critical political events: the Constitution (First Amendment) Act, 1951 that secured the existing system of affirmative action; the Modified Scheme of Elementary Education in 1953; the passage of the States Reorganisation Act in 1956; the Sino-Indian War of 1962; the Constitution (Sixteenth Amendment) Act, 1963 a.k.a. Anti-secession Act; the anti-Hindi protests of 1965, and the rising prices of essential commodities, primarily rice, in 1965 across the Madras State. I argue that DMK's responses to these events catalysed the spread and reach of Dravidian-Tamil identity, turning it into a force with electoral possibilities. It also looks at how Annadurai's writings and speeches, widely read and discussed through the network of reading rooms across Madras State, played a big role in shaping public opinion. These are buttressed with notes from interviews to understand how people's perceptions of the Dravidian-Tamil identity and the DMK changed over time.

Chapter four focuses on the 1967 election in the Virudhunagar Assembly constituency, where student leader Seenivasan defeated Kamaraj. After winning, Seenivasan went down to meet Annadurai to ask for a position in the council of ministers. However, Annadurai turned him down, saying that he was just a 'bullet' (Thangapandian, Personal Communication, 25 November 2019).[14] Annadurai's response to the election results suggests that there is more to the Virudhunagar election than just an underdog's victory. It is an apt micro-level case study to evaluate how successfully the Dravidian movement transitioned into electoral politics.

Periyar had supported Kamaraj since 1954. To understand Kamaraj's success in the elections during the period covered by this book, I relied on records kept in Tamil by local caste organisations in Virudhunagar to compare the profiles of Kamaraj and Seenivasan. The comparison shows that Kamaraj had an edge in earlier elections leading up to 1967. It's too simple to attribute Kamaraj's defeat solely to mismanagement by the Indian National Congress in the Madras State before 1967, as some senior Congress leaders and media reports suggest. After all, he did win the 1969 Lok Sabha by-election from a constituency in the neighbouring Nagercoil district. Moreover, he was an astute politician who understood caste and communal factors (Gnanadason, 1969: 1337).

It is thus cogent to locate Kamaraj's defeat beyond misgovernance and caste and communal factors. To unpack his defeat, I relied on interviews with people who were involved in Seenivasan's campaign, as well as other senior leaders who were active at that time. In other words, Kamaraj's defeat offers a great opportunity to explore how Dravidian movement made the shift into party politics.

Chapters 3 and 4 also look at the sociological profiles of the winners in all the constituencies of Madras State for the Legislative Assembly elections held between 1951 and 1967. This includes details about the caste (*jati*) of winners and where those castes stood in the social hierarchy. I gathered this data through fieldwork and networks within the DMK. The data is presented to show the caste composition of the elected representatives, which allows us to discuss how successfully (or not) the Dravidian movement transitioned to electoral politics.

The sociological profiles show how people from backward sections began moving into positions of power. Along with the rise of lower castes, the data also looks at whether or not caste references appeared in the names of candidates in terms of elected representatives and candidates across the elections in Madras State between 1951 and 1967. This analysis helps us understand how the Dravidian movement created 'horizontal solidarities' among different caste groups at a personal level, especially in public life. The idea here is that by avoiding caste titles in their names, people were taking a step towards breaking down caste divisions. It's also worth noting that today, most people in Tamil Nadu do not have a caste reference in their names, which is seen as a major success of the Dravidian movement.[15]

The Conclusion takes a closer look at the lasting impact of the Dravidian-Tamil identity and how things have changed in Madras State, which later became Tamil Nadu. In doing so, it revisits the two key questions of the book: how did a party transform a sociocultural movement into party politics? And how relevant are the motivations behind that process in shaping the State's present and future?

The Epilogue reflects on what followed the DMK's transformative shift into party politics. It explores the trajectory of the Dravidian-Tamil identity after its institutionalisation, questioning how its core ideals have endured, adapted, or been contested in Tamil Nadu's evolving political landscape.

1

PERIYAR AND THE DMK

FORGING A HORIZONTAL DRAVIDIAN-TAMIL SOLIDARITY

The campaign song[1] of the Dravida Munnetra Kazhagam (DMK) for the 2021 Legislative Assembly elections became the most-watched political campaign song in India. It goes like this: "Those who try to impose [the Hindi] language, and those who seek to politicise religion, dare not step foot in Tamil Nadu. We have someone [M.K. Stalin] to stand against such forces. We carry the fire ignited by Periyar within us." While the song is about preserving the pride of the Dravidian-Tamil identity, it also emphasises two key elements of social justice: equal opportunity and self-respect.

Throughout my fieldwork, I noticed a powerful, broader sense of identity that went beyond just caste identity, and a thriving discourse around caste-based social justice—especially when it comes to empowerment and representation. Over a hundred years after the 1916 non-Brahmin manifesto put forward by the South Indian Liberal Federation (better known as the Justice Party), which pushed for better representation for non-Brahmin groups, the Tamil Nadu Legislative Assembly remains one of the most diverse in terms of caste representation.[2]

The diversity seen in the assembly is often linked to the inclusive Dravidian-Tamil identity, which has shaped the politics of Dravidian parties since they first came to power in 1967. This identity, linked with an ethos, has created strong connections across various non-Brahmin lower-caste groups that, despite their traditional caste-based divisions,[3] have come together in 'horizontal solidarities'. These bonds are rooted in shared social and economic goals and cultural aspirations of these caste groups. The ongoing strength of these solidarities can be traced back to Periyar's radical yet gradual and ever-evolving anti-caste ideas and activism.

In my work, I've explored Periyar's ideas and how they can be found in the writings of other thinkers—both within and beyond the academic world, not just in the subcontinent but globally. His anti-caste ideas and brand of activism are not just about demanding adequate representation for the numerically dominant non-Brahmins or from an antagonism towards Brahmins. It's about embracing pluralism in identity politics, challenging the outdated views on caste, and providing it a modern and practical context. At the heart of his philosophy is the idea of self-respect, which has been central to the struggle against oppression and social degradation—an idea that has shaped the Dravidian parties' politics for over fifty years.

A quick overview of the literature on Periyar is important in the context of this chapter. Sumathi Ramaswamy (1997), V. Geetha and S.V. Rajadurai (1998), Narendra Subramanian (1999), and M.S.S. Pandian (2007) have critically examined prominent activists and social reformers from the late nineteenth and the early twentieth centuries in the Madras region. They later focused on how the Dravidian parties altered social relations among communities in a caste-based society, particularly through the contributions of activists like Periyar. These studies also discussed the strengths and limitations of these movements in fighting inequality in caste and class systems.

Although their views on the movement differ, Pandian, Ramaswamy, and Subramanian all agreed on the vital role Periyar played in broadening the scope of the Dravidian-Tamil identity. Subramanian noted that even though lower and depressed caste groups faced uneven political and developmental outcomes, ethnic conflicts were kept under control, helping foster growth and development. Pandian, in addition to discussing Periyar, also highlighted the contributions of non-Brahmin Saivite leaders and depressed-caste intellectuals like Iyothee Thass when conceptualising the non-Brahmin identity. He expressed concerns about the stability of this identity due to tensions between lower-caste groups and Dalits.

Despite some notable omissions, such as the absence of Iyothee Thass in her work, Ramaswamy classifies activists based on their contribution to the Tamil language and its political significance. She positions Periyar as a political opportunist rather than a passionate advocate of the Tamil language and its storied past. Geetha and Rajadurai's work on social reformers of the nineteenth and twentieth centuries places Periyar and his writings at the heart of debates around the complexities of non-Brahmin politics.

G. Aloysius (2019 and 2022) explores Periyar's ideas in specific contexts—modernity and category-wise rights, for instance. In his book *Periyar and Modernity*, Aloysius argues that Periyar's idea of self-respect was his rational response to Brahminism pretending to be nationalism. This approach was critical of the past, rooted in modernity, and focused on addressing current issues. In his 2022 work on category-wise rights, he highlights how Periyar pushed for communities, big or small, to take political action and assert their agency for the nation's development. This was in contrast to the idea of blending one's identity into a larger nationalist framework, which, in his view, would not be as representative when it comes to who holds power.

While these authors engage with specific aspects of Periyar's work, others like Anita Diehl (1978), E. Sa. Visswanathan (1983), and Karthick Ram Manoharan (2022) have written full-length books about Periyar's life and his interventions in the social and political spheres in South India. Diehl looks at Periyar's views on religion, caste, women's empowerment, and how he used rationalism to fight gender and caste discrimination against women and the lower castes. She concludes that Periyar wasn't a philosopher in the traditional sense, but more of a practical preacher, whose messages were at times repetitive and a bit superficial. Hjejle (1979: 75–76) argued that this view ignores the varying educational levels of the audiences that Periyar was reaching out to. The next chapter presents a picture of the reading rooms across Madras State that were key spaces for spreading the DMK's ideas, and how they communicated with the less educated.

Visswanathan's biography of Periyar, focusing on the years between 1920 and 1949, explores Periyar's rise in the political scene of Madras Presidency until the DMK's split away from his movement, the Dravidar Kazhagam (Association of Dravidians, or DK). Visswanathan (1983: 344) acknowledges Periyar's ability to mobilise crowds and organise agitations, noting that he wished to build a *monolithic non-Brahmin community*. However, the later sections of the following chapter mobilise evidence to show Periyar's nuanced approach to lower-caste and depressed-caste groups, thereby refuting Visswanathan's claim. Citing Periyar's engagement with Rajaji, Visswanathan also argued that Periyar chose to give up his core ideals for political ends, which Visswanathan saw as unethical and dishonorable (ibid.).

Karthick Ram Manoharan (2022) offered a detailed response to these claims. Earlier, in 2017, Manoharan had explored Periyar's views on anti-caste activism, framing them around the universal grievances and specific aspirations of marginalised communities within the caste system as a power structure. In his more recent work, Manoharan places Periyar in the anarchist tradition, portraying him as an 'anti-philosopher' who unsettles traditional ideas of philosophy to create something entirely new. He sees Periyar's political atheism as an effort to question all forms of established power—whether it's Brahminism, patriarchy, or religious majoritarianism—that keep marginalised communities oppressed.

In my view, Periyar's contributions are better understood when we don't see him just as the leader of the Dravidian movement, but rather as a pragmatic and insightful aggregator-in-chief—someone who brought together the ideas of earlier reformers. These ideas were then carried forward and adapted into the political realm by leaders like C.N. Annadurai, M. Karunanidhi, and political parties like the DMK.

A Chronicle of the Isotopes of the Dravidian-Tamil Identity

By the late 1920s, Periyar and his ideas were gaining popularity, and he became a central figure in shaping the Dravidian-Tamil identity. This identity revolved around three main ideas: socio-economic mobility, cultural uniqueness, and the Tamil language, in that order. While Periyar wasn't the first to address the question of Dravidian-Tamil identity, earlier efforts often relied heavily on just one or two of these aspects, which limited their impact—a point we'll discuss later in the chapter.

It was perhaps Periyar's gumption that he could blend these three vectors into a single, powerful vision of the Dravidian-Tamil identity. This vision still features in the politics of Tamil Nadu, pushing for social change that is democratic, rational, moral, and just, all of which helped humanise the economy, society, and culture. As M.S.S. Pandian wrote, "E.V. Ramasamy's (Periyar's) concept of politics freed history from any notion of Saivite utopia, invoked a number of inferiorised identities and as a result expanded the realm of politics to include a range of oppressed groups, and, above all, invested them with active political agency. More importantly, it had the quality of being perennially contestatory: the telos of history and rationality were interminable and hence there could be no certitude about the finality of any political resolution. Struggle had to go on..." (Pandian, 1994: 100).

Periyar's intimate alloy of the three vectors was not always an obvious or natural fit for a Dravidian-Tamil identity—it took a series of versions and refinements. But through it all, the ideological core remained the same: challenging social hierarchies and working towards flattening them out.

Caste System in the Dravidian Region

According to the 2011 Census of India and NSSO Report No. 563,[4] upper castes made up 2.79% of Tamil Nadu's population,

Scheduled Castes were 20.01%, Scheduled Tribes 1.1%, and Other Backward Castes 76.1%. The religion-wise breakdown was: Hindus 87.58%, Christians 6%, Muslims 5.86%, others 0.56%. To make sense of these proportions, the caste system in the region must be clearly understood.

At least two frameworks of social classification exist, both of which overlap with and differentiate from the Hindu *varna* order. The earliest classification, i.e., of the Sangam era, was based on topographic distinctions that were somewhat similar to ideas of environmental determinism. The region was divided into five sub-regions: *Kurinchi* (mountains), *Mullai* (forests), *Marutham* (agricultural plains and valleys), *Neythal* (coastal belt), and *Palai* (desert and wastelands). Each of these areas had its own inhabitants, called Kuravar, Ayar, Ulavar, Parathavar, and Maravar. K.K. Pillay (1977: 16) suggests that in the Sangam age, a person's occupation determined their social identity, leading to a mix of both horizontal and vertical groupings. He also points out that sub-castes began to take shape within the occupational framework, without conflicts over inter-dining (ibid., 17).

The Satavahana period—around the second century BCE in the Telugu region and first century BCE in Tamil region—is when the varnashrama system began to emerge, as mentioned in *Tholkappiyam*[5] (ibid., 14–15). Under the Pallavas, the Brahmin community gained influence, and the *varnashrama* system became more established (ibid., 17–18). This system continued to evolve and expand during the Chola and Pandya periods between the tenth and fifteenth centuries.

Brahmins started taking on roles beyond priesthood, becoming ministers, commanders, and administrators. New (lower) social categories were created for children born from inter-caste marriages, discouraging such unions. While the Brahmins' position was consolidated, Kshatriya communities didn't feature prominently.[6] The relationship between the Vaisya and Shudra communities was largely determined by their social status and economic power within the sub-regions (ibid., 21–22).

Another complex social framework developed around the Idangai (left-hand) and Valangai (right-hand) castes, which existed in the regions that are now Karnataka, Andhra Pradesh, and Tamil Nadu. There are several theories about how this classification came to be, which lasted from the eleventh to the eighteenth centuries (ibid., 46). One version suggests that the soldiers recruited by the Cholas from the armies of defeated kingdoms, like the Pandyas, were regarded as 'left-hand' castes. For example, the Pallans or Pallars, now called Devendra Kula Vellalars, fit this category (ibid., 42).

In some cases, the classification was gendered, with men and women from the same caste group being classified differently. For instance, in the Sakkiliyar (now called Arunthathiyar) and Palli (now called Vanniyar) communities, women were part of the right-hand group, while men belonged to the left-hand group. Broadly speaking, according to Niels Brimnes (2019: 27), the right-hand castes were mostly agriculturists and landed communities, whereas the left-hand castes constituted the artisanal communities. Brahmins and Vellalars were considered outside or above these categories, with the right-hand castes claiming to be ritually superior. However, these categories were not strictly defined and were full of exceptions and shifting interests, indicating that society was in constant flux.

Aloysius (1998: 25–27) offers a classification of the Tamil region's history based on the availability of water for irrigation and divides it into three periods: the Pallava-Chola period (ninth to twelfth century), the Vijayanagara-Nayaka period (twelfth to early eighteenth century), and the British colonial period (late eighteenth to twentieth century). He argues that during the first period, the irrigated regions were controlled by Brahmins (Brahmadeyas) or Vellalars (Periyanadus), and discrimination in land ownership and access to resources was the norm.

The forests and arid regions, however, were fluid spaces, with landholding being more democratic and limited surpluses, which made it harder for a rigid social structure to take root. The culture in these regions was different from and not influenced by the Aryan or Brahminical system.

As people from these regions moved to the river valleys, a more complex social order began to form. In the second period, Aloysius argues, lower-caste groups involved in warrior or merchant occupations began challenging and unsettling the Brahminical hierarchy. *Amarams*—grants to soldiers—which were taxed heavily, emerged in the place of Bramhadeyas and Periyanadus in this time (ibid., 29). The mobility of lower-caste groups like the Marakkairs or Mukkuvars along the southern coast, combined with the royal dependence on artisanal communities rather than just agriculturalists. It meant that the social order was in constant flux. Many lower castes asserted their cultural presence by embracing non-Brahmin religious practices, with priests from non-Brahmin and depressed castes (ibid., 32) leading these ceremonies.

By the end of the second time period, social relations were marked by a kind of liminality among most communities, except in relation to the Brahmins. This created an opening for these communities to come together and rally for change.

Attempts at Redefining Identity and Social Relations around and after the eighteenth Century

The efforts to flatten social hierarchies can partly be traced to the prevalence of the ryotwari system, where the average size of land holdings was relatively small. As kingdoms weakened and the land was redistributed, the elite who had once controlled social hierarchies in villages lost their power (Bayly, 1988: 73). There was a gradual regulation of economic capital through land redistribution. However, this shift alone wasn't enough reason to challenge the discriminatory caste relations.

At the same time, in the late eighteenth century, the prosperous *dubashee*[7] entrepreneurs and smaller kingdoms lost ground to the British. A section of the *dubashee* entrepreneurs turned their surplus into assets, becoming a rent-seeking community that owned land, lent money, and relied on rents and offices for income. Consequently, Madras Presidency saw the rise of a fairly strong non-Brahmin public. By the turn of the nineteenth century, there was an influx of *dubashees* and people from rural ruling and landowning communities into Madras city. This was alongside Tamil and Telugu[8] speaking literates also arriving, who belonged to the Brahmin *jatis* like Iyer and Iyengar.

C.A. Bayly (1988: 73) observes that there ensued a churning among the urban communities, with new settlers in Madras city starting to define and, at times, reshape social hierarchies. While some people tried to hold on to the traditional social structure, creating a "more rigid form of modern Hinduism", others used this as an opportunity to reimagine the status of different *jatis*.

By the latter half of the nineteenth century, language and social hierarchy became central to the conversations in the Presidency, with print culture playing a major role in regional politics. A flood of publications, made possible by the printing press, came from social activists and reformers who sought to unsettle the traditional hierarchy that was based on Sanskrit and Brahmin dominance. These texts can be seen as early attempts to define the Dravidian-Tamil identity and its core values.

Robert Caldwell's *A Comparative Grammar of the Dravidian or South Indian Family of Languages,* published in 1856, played an important role in engendering the opposition to Sanskrit-Brahmin supremacy (Thapar, 1971: 408). Caldwell argued that the Dravidian languages, of which Tamil was the oldest, were fundamentally different from Sanskrit, and didn't derive from it. This opened up an opportunity to reimagine social hierarchies and helped establish a clear difference between the lives and beliefs of the Sanskrit-supporting Brahmin *jatis* and non-Brahmin *jatis* who rejected Sanskrit dominance.

The challenges to Sanskrit-Brahmin supremacy were at odds with Dipankar Gupta's argument (2000: 21) that only measurable or quantifiable concepts should be included in constructing a hierarchy, with everything qualitative being viewed as a difference. Gupta's view didn't quite capture the complexities of society. While he argued that language cannot determine hierarchy, in practice, various forms of the Dravidian-Tamil identity recognised differences within communities, though always in a way that aimed to challenge hegemonic identities and cultures—like Sanskrit supremacy—which legitimised Brahminical practices.

The idea of branding the caste system as something foreign can be traced back to differences in language. In the Madras Presidency, primarily two kinds of publications surfaced that challenged the supremacy of Sanskrit and the Brahmin *jatis*. The first focused on radically rethinking caste histories, with the goal of building new identities that would elevate their status (Rudolph & Rudolph, 1967: 50). But many of these redefined identities still mimicked Brahminical practices (Jaffrelot, 2003: 183–84).

For instance, Ayyakannu Nayakar's *Vanniakula Vilakkam* (A Treatise on the Vanniyar Caste), published in 1891 and *Varuna Darpanam* (Mirror of Castes), published in 1907, argued that the Vanniyars were descendants of the Pallava dynasty, and petitioned the British to recognise them as Kshatriyas (Rudolph & Rudolph, 1960: 14). Similarly, the Nadars[9] attempted to gain Kshatriya status by claiming to be descendants of the Pandya rulers, who were overthrown by the Nayakas in the sixteenth century (Damodaran, 2008: 179).

The works of Iyothee Thass (1845–1914), a medical practitioner and social activist who advanced an early Dravidian construct based on a Buddhist re-reading of Tamil classics like *Periya Puranam* and *Harichandra Puranam* continued the trend of revisionist publications, albeit on a contrasting tangent.[10] According to Thass, the Buddhist essence was the original culture of the land and the untouchables were its native inhabitants. In 1891, Thass founded the Dravida Mahajana Sabhai and fought for the rights of the untouchables, who, he argued, were not Hindus. Thass prescribed identifying as 'Dravidian' rather than by their caste, advising the untouchables to register as casteless Dravidians in the 1901 Census.

While Thass drew on the ancient texts and traditions, there was an inherent struggle within these efforts to define Dravidian-Tamil identity—a struggle centered on the rights of the oppressed.

In addition to his books, Thass ran two magazines, *Dravida Pandian* (1885), which he co-founded with Rev. John Rathinam, and *Thamizhan* (1907), staying actively involved in the publishing culture of his time. While he sought support from Henry Olcott, co-founder of the Theosophical Society, to spread Buddhism, Thass's criticism of both the caste system and the freedom movement later put him at odds with the Theosophical Society under the leadership of Annie Besant.[11]

Despite his strong critique of Brahmins and caste hierarchy, Thass claimed that the native followers of Buddhism, the Dalits (Paraiyar), were the Yatharththa Brahmana or True Brahmins and the Aryan invaders were Vesha Brahmana or Pseudo Brahmins. According to him, before the Aryans arrived in the Dravidian land,[12] the native residents followed Buddhist principles where the social divisions of Brahmana, Vaishya, Kshatriya, and Sudra were based on the division of labour. Thus, changes to birth-based caste divisions were due to the Aryans.[13] This view somewhat contradicted his vision of a casteless or hierarchy-free Dravidian identity. Nevertheless, Thass's work in fostering an insurgent culture—one that challenged caste-based oppression—remains relevant (Leonard, 2021: 357). Notably, half a century later, Ambedkar, too, would turn to Buddhism to fight the oppression and inequality inherent to the caste system.

In the realm of revisionist publications, another approach to constructing an identity counter to the Brahminical order was presented by non-Brahmin Tamil Saivites, which is also called Vellalar[14]-inspired Dravidian identity. I engage with the ideas of Maraimalai Adigal (1876–1950), whose writings offer a contemporary understanding of the Saivite approach. Vaitheespara (2015) points out that the non-Brahmin Saivites drew from colonial missionary critiques of the Vedas and Puranas to forge an identity in opposition to the Aryan-Sanskritik-Brahminic framework. This identity revolved around Saivism and non-Brahmin Tamil nationalism. In it, Tamil language was celebrated as superior to Sanskrit, which was regarded as a dead language (Adigal, 1975: 11).

Adigal promoted medieval Tamil literature and scriptures[15] through the Thani Tamil Iyakkam (Tamil Purist Movement),[16] which helped early Dravidianists argue that the caste system based on birth was an alien concept, not native to Tamil land. In this framework, the agriculturist or Vellalar was placed at the top of a hierarchy based on occupation, and the Vellalar was portrayed as a compassionate figure, unlike the Brahmin, who was viewed as both non-native and an oppressor. It was the Vellalar's duty to uplift those engaged in other occupations and help them become Vellalars—agriculturalists who refrained from 'lowly' activities.

However, as summarised by M.S.S. Pandian (1994: 94–95) and A.R. Venkatachalapathy (1995: 767), this early Vellalar-Saivite identity aimed to unsettle the Brahmin but ultimately replaced the Brahmin with a Saivite-Vellalar personification of compassion. Unfortunately, this construction did not grant political agency to non-Vellalar communities. In other words, while the Saivites contended that the caste system was foreign to the Tamil way of life, a new hierarchy still existed in the Saivite construction of Tamil society.

Ultimately, between the two approaches to constructing the Dravidian-Tamil identity, the Saivite approach endured longer, mainly due to the influence of Adigal and the lack of a successor after Thass. The approaches of Thass and the Vellalars were similar in two key ways: both argued that Brahmins and the Sanskrit language were foreign elements, and both imagined a common Dravidian identity as a counter. However, these revisionist attempts to reshape caste hierarchies by creating newer ones, revisiting older texts within the boundaries of tradition, and relying heavily on a glorified view of Tamil language and culture, continued to uphold inequality and prejudice. They failed to create a horizontal solidarity across communities.

As a result, while Periyar's newspaper *Kudi Arasu* (Republic) initially supported the Saivite-Vellalar criticism of Brahmins, Periyar eventually developed a strong critique of the Saivite construct. He denounced the tendency to look at the past for solutions to contemporary issues. Drawing on the Western enlightenment framework, like the early Dravidianists (Madras Secular Society et al.), Periyar began to question, in works such as *Periya Puranam* and *Thiruvilayadal Puranam,* the contradictions within the Saivite-Vellalar version of Dravidian-Tamil identity. He pointed out the contradictions between their promotion of caste inequality and conflicts and their inability to foster horizontal solidarities across communities despite their claims of fostering an equal society (Meikandar,[17] 1928, in Pandian, 1994). Rational thought and reason were at the heart of Periyar's critique of these ancient texts.

On the other hand, some publications brought out by a section of non-Brahmin landlords (and others) directly challenged caste hierarchy and drew on enlightenment, Buddhism, and a blend of multiple traditions. The Hindu Free Thought Union (MFTU), formed in 1860 and later renamed the Madras Secular Society (MSS) in 1886, was one of the earliest associations to re-read and stridently critique the Hindu Puranas. Appathoaray Chettiyar, Masilamany Mudaliar, Munesawmy Naicker, and Attippakkam Venkatacala Nayakar were the most notable figures associated with the MSS. The MFTU/MSS published two magazines, *Tattuva Vecini* and *The Thinker*, which opposed the *varna* system, promoted atheism, supported widow remarriage, advocated for women's education, and featured writings on figures like Voltaire, Benedict Spinoza, and Charles Darwin.

Kaali (2018. np) identifies several strategies used by the MSS to challenge the Puranas. These included the use of logical reasoning and modern empiricism, structural deconstruction of myths in a comparative manner, and offering counter-narratives to existing lores. For example, they reinterpreted *Asuras* as the native inhabitants of India, defeated by the invading Aryans through deceitful means.

At the same time, other individuals and groups who shared MSS's opposition to Brahmins and Sanskrit, but who were not aligned with MSS's rational thought and atheism, also contributed to the discourse. The Vallalar[18] sect, popular in the northern regions of the Madras Presidency, opposed casteism and promoted charity. Many caste associations also worked for the rights and welfare of specific lower-caste groups, such as the Nadars and Vanniyars (Rudolph & Rudolph, 1960: 13–18).

While MSS's work did not glorify Tamil texts or the past, it ultimately faced a similar fate to that of the Vellalar-Saivites' or Thaas' work on Dravidian-Tamil identity. It could not evolve into a mass movement. The limitation was likely due to the fact that the key figures in MSS were mostly landed elites, who were able to develop intellectual and structural anti-caste principles but failed to address the grievances and socio-economic aspirations of the numerous non-elite communities.

At the end of the nineteenth century, the expansion of British occupation of India provided many communities a means to express their socio-cultural conflict through socio-economic means. After the 1890s, communities in Madras city and the Presidency as a whole could compete over places in administrative and official positions. This sparked, between the 1890s and 1910s, a cultural conflict between Brahmin and non-Brahmin *jatis* over the Brahmins' disproportionate representation in government positions.

With social hierarchies in flux, economic mobility and formal power or authority became a route to claim superiority. Irschick (1969: 14–19) demonstrated the rising competition between literate Brahmins and the non-Brahmin communities—namely, the *dubashee* entrepreneurs-turned-rent-seekers, the non-Brahmin landlords, and other upwardly mobile *jatis*. The competition in both entrance-test-oriented and support- or endorsement-based appointments grew fierce. A considerable non-Brahmin section lacked formal education, English proficiency, and were also divided along language and *jati* lines, while the Brahmins were seemingly united, well-educated, and proficient in English.

The struggle for socio-economic mobility was no different from socio-cultural conflicts elsewhere and represented the interests of numerous communities. As a result, it became the backbone of the Dravidian-Tamil identity, which often transcended the boundaries of caste, though with only limited success at the time.

However, the competition between Brahmins and non-Brahmins was not confined to socio-economic spheres, it also permeated the political space. Tamil-speaking non-Brahmins actively advanced their cause, emphasising the distinctiveness of their Dravidian identity vis-à-vis the Brahmins (Pandian, 1994: 85). Following sustained conflicts with the Theosophical Society and Annie Besant, who defended the caste system and founded the Home Rule League, a group of prominent non-Brahmin leaders launched the Non-Brahmin Manifesto and established the South Indian Liberal Federation, popularly known as the Justice Party, in 1916–1917. The Justice Party won the provincial elections in 1920 and stayed in power for thirteen years between 1920 and 1937.

During its time in office, the Justice Party implemented several defining policies, including proportional representation for various communities through a quota system, the reversal of the prohibition on women becoming legislators, gender-neutral voter qualifications, the renaming of Dalit *jatis* as Adi-Dravidars (native Dravidians), and the introduction of compulsory elementary education for children. Notably, the Justice Party created a strikingly composite identity for the non-Brahmin identity.

In a 1920 debate on 'Indianising' the administration in the Madras Presidency Legislature, when the allocation of posts in the police service was discussed, C.V. Venkataramana Iyengar proposed a motion to allocate a few posts to Indians, in addition to Europeans. In response, one of the Justice Party's founding fathers, Dr Natesa Mudaliar, called for a revision to the motion to add a new category: 'Non-Brahmin Indians'. This category included non-Brahmin Hindus, Mohammedans, Indian Christians, Jains, Parsis, and Anglo-Indians (Anwar S., 2018). Essentially, this identity transcended the boundaries of religion and culture, bringing together diverse communities in opposition to the hegemonic Brahmins.

While there was a momentary sense of relief among non-Brahmins due to their socio-economic gains, the dominance of Telugu-speaking communities[19] within the Justice Party's governments/leadership remained conspicuous. This dominance began to shift, but gradually, with the short-lived Justice Party government under Sir K.V. Naidu (April–July 1937). The 1920s and 1930s also were periods of consolidation of communities within the broad non-Brahmin umbrella, despite divisions along linguistic and caste lines in Tamil-speaking regions of the Madras Presidency.

While the Justice Party was busy fighting Congress in the provincial elections, pushing for a fairer system with proportional representation for all communities, Periyar was taking up a similar cause within Congress itself. In 1925, at the Kanchipuram Provincial Congress Session, which was focused on choosing delegates and resolutions for the All-India Congress Committee at Patna in preparation for the 1926 elections, the big issue was whether or not to contest in the elections to enter the councils. Periyar proposed a resolution for proportional representation for all communities, but for the second time, it was rejected on technicalities. He walked out of the General Session, organised a separate meeting for non-Brahmins, and put forward a new resolution: that all communities should be given their due representation in all offices and institutions, but again, it was rejected.

This repeated disregard for proportional representation made Periyar seriously question the Congress's motives. On top of that, in his discussions with Gandhi, he noticed that Gandhi was more focused on preserving the exclusive claims to knowledge of the Brahmins and was hesitant to challenge the foundations of Hinduism, calling it too complex and vague to change.[20] This drove Periyar away from Congress, concluding that the noise it made about socio-political reforms and its claims to radicalism were merely smokescreens, masking a power transfer from the British to the very same privileged elites, especially the Brahmins, under the guise of freedom (Aloysius, 2022: 126).

Periyar's Tryst with Self-Respect: Radical yet Steady

In the mid-1930s, Periyar sensed an opportunity to get Depressed Castes politically mobilised and be more assertive. On 15 March 1936, he wrote about the changing political situation. He noted that, unlike before, when the colonial government had given special treatment to Brahmins, they were now trying to win over both Brahmins and non-Brahmins because of the animosity between these groups. Periyar argued that the Brahmins, therefore, used nationalistic propaganda against the government,[21] while everyone—the Brahmins, the government, and the non-Brahmins—was now seeking the support of the Depressed Castes to secure or retain power.

Periyar saw this as an opportune moment for the Depressed Castes to rise in the political landscape, thanks to the rifts between Brahmins and non-Brahmins, as well as between Brahmins and the government. However, he pointed out that each group was reaching out to the Depressed Castes not because they wanted to genuinely address their problems but simply for their own narrow political gain. Periyar cautioned the Depressed Castes to be careful of the Brahmins' tactics and advised them to negotiate with the government for social benefits even though they might have differences with it.[22] He urged them not to rebel.

Building on Karthick Ram Manoharan's (2022: 62–63) interpretation of Periyar within the anarchist tradition, we can say that Periyar had a clear, methodical approach to challenging existing societal norms. He consistently relied on rational thinking when tackling cultural or secular issues. I see Periyar's politics through Nancy Fraser's (2004: 375–81) famous triad of recognition (acknowledging particularistic grievances), redistribution (fair distribution of resources), and representation (in power), with self-respect as the key to achieving these goals. In response to political disempowerment of lower castes, Periyar advocated for *suyamariyathai* or self-respect as central to his vision of Dravidian-Tamil identity.

Self-respect, an intimate yet broad principle, allowed Periyar to challenge the caste system in a comprehensive way. He expanded his critique to include gender inequality and the struggles of lower caste groups and untouchables, moving beyond the narrow framework of Brahmins versus non-Brahmin Vellalars. Through the Self-Respect Movement, Periyar also took aim at leaders of the Justice Party, criticising them for their elitist approach and their disconnect from the masses.

The idea of self-respect was central to Periyar's approach to the caste question and building a horizontal Dravidian-Tamil solidarity. He rigorously critiqued the numeric majority, that is, the Shudras, and punctured their idealised sense of history and self-worth. Periyar believed that without this critical examination, these communities would continue to play the role of foot soldiers within the larger, oppressive framework of Hinduism.

By positioning Hinduism and Brahmins as the outsiders and promoting a politics based on empirical socio-economic and political realities, he successfully flattened a hierarchical Dravidian-Tamil society, making it inclusive of marginalised communities, embracing those from other religions as well. For Periyar, this was about attacking the very core of caste-based oppression—the denial of dignity and self-worth. His solution, *suyamariyathai*, was not just a temporary fix, but a lasting and fundamental answer to the problem.

Periyar's ideas about caste, dignity, self-respect, and oppression stand in contrast to how scholars like Dumont, M.N. Srinivas, and others theorised the caste system in India. Dumont, for example, explained caste system and Indian society using ideas of hierarchy and purity and pollution. He believed that caste wasn't just about wealth or power but about maintaining this deep, rigid, social order based on hierarchy. (Dumont, 1972: 20). According to him, even if a Brahmin was poor, they would still be at the top of the hierarchy, higher than someone like a wealthy, landed Vaishya or Shudra (ibid., 65).

But M.N. Srinivas disagreed with Dumont. He argued that the caste system wasn't totally fixed. Instead, there was room for movement, especially in the middle sections of the hierarchy. He introduced the idea of Sanskritisation, the central argument of his book, *Religion and Society Among the Coorgs of South India* (1952: 32). His idea of the caste system was that it had an element of fluidity and movement. Following Vedic practices, or Sanskritisation, was a route towards mobility, although, ritually, it is not permitted to mimic the life of a twice-born. He argued for Sanskritisation instead of Brahminisation, for Vedic practices were followed by the non-Brahmin twice-born castes too.

Drawing conclusions on the basis of his fieldwork, he concluded that the caste system had two parts: the 'ritual structure', which had to do with purity, food, and religious practices, and the 'secular structure,' which involved access to power, wealth, and education. While he argued that the ritual structure was weakening, the secular structure was becoming more dominant.

In other words, he believed Dumont's model differed from empirical realities, as 'hierarchy' was achievable and not set in stone as Dumont argued. But contrary to Srinivas, even the one source of hierarchy he acknowledged—the ritual structure—has remained resilient and powerful. A very recent example of it is the president of the Bahujan Samaj Party of India, which claims to be the voice of the untouchables, using a religious slogan, "*Hathi*

Nahi, Ganesh Hai"[23] (It's not an elephant—it's Lord Ganesha) while describing the elephant that is her party's symbol.

The idea of a single, unchanging hierarchy, as Dumont proposed, or even Srinivas's focus on the growing importance of secular power structures, overlooks that caste is capable of not only reproducing older connections, but evolving through newer inequalities, differences, and associations. Two prime examples of this are the dominant castes'[24] demands for reservations since 2015 and, conversely, how during the 2020–2021 farmer protests, historically rival communities, like dominant castes and Dalits, came together in a shared moment.

Periyar's engagement with dignity as a concept gave him the flexibility to think about mobility in ways that didn't just focus on demands for gaining access to higher positions, but also on building solidarity across different groups. He didn't follow Dumont's template of sticking to a rigid caste hierarchy, nor did he ignore the role of religion and rituals in these struggles like Srinivas did. For example, while Periyar saw Buddhism as a philosophy of reason and an antithesis to Brahminical Hinduism (Periyar, 2005: 12), he also viewed Islam as a way for lower castes, including Dalits, to escape discrimination and untouchability (Periyar, 2004: 13–19). He believed Islam could help unite backward castes into a more equal solidarity. However, his support for Islam was based on its core principle of equality, and he remained wary of practices that hindered the liberties of women (Manoharan, 2022: 98).

Also, in Tamil Nadu, Muslims were not viewed with the same suspicion as in other parts of India during the immediate pre-Independence period, which was marked by riots. P. Daud Shah, the editor of *Darul Islam*, an influential Tamil magazine published until 1957, argued for the use of Tamil to both understand Islam and as the medium of instruction. He also cautioned the Muslim community against adopting Brahminical stances on 'national' issues. A slogan that became popular in those times is: "*Islam engal vazhi, inba Tamil engal mozhi*" (Islam is our path, sweet Tamil is our language) (Fakhri, SMAK, 2008: 72).

Periyar's approach to challenging the rigid social structure was to focus not just on the material aspects of power, but also on how these positions had metaphysical significance in society. This view contrasted with the traditional Marxist ideas, which argue that caste in itself does not influence people's material conditions. To put it simply, Marxists saw caste as the effect and not necessarily the cause of inequality. Therefore, ending the caste system would require addressing its historical and material roots. In the Marxist framework of 'Base–Superstructure', the caste system was seen as a part of the superstructure, which masks the class inequalities in society while giving a few groups legitimacy to exploit others. Dipankar Gupta summed it up by saying, "Marxists consider the caste system to be a myth, but only that the caste system justifies exploitation by the superior classes on the basis of the myth of 'natural superiority'" (Gupta, 1981: 2093).

In a speech in 1964, Periyar argued that if the hegemony of caste groups were to be unsettled, positions of authority and power must be made representative and democratised. "The feeling of caste superiority and assumption of this superiority as a 'right', stems from Brahmin and Mudaliar holding the position of village accountant and Pillais and Gounders holding the position of Maniyakarar. So, a plan should be made to reserve these positions for the Paraiyars, Devendra Kula Vellalars, and Arunthathiyars. Similarly, the positions of Constable, Head Constable, Sub-Inspector be given to them as well. Once given, the arrogance associated with caste position would dissipate. Without implementing these structural changes, the rallying cry for annihilation of caste, rings empty" (Periyar in Subagunarajan V.M., 2018 ed: 361).

One thing that stood out was how both Periyar and the Justice Party used the language of assertion and caste identity in shaping the Dravidian-Tamil identity. Caste associations played a crucial role in helping Periyar tackle the massive challenge of galvanising a mass movement out of socio-economic and political aspirations, transforming *suyamariyathai* (self-respect) into widely accepted, conventional wisdom. Periyar actively participated in various caste conferences from mid 1920s until the late 1940s, and in about half of these, the focus was on the Depressed Castes. Influenced by Periyar's ideas, these caste associations worked to improve the socio-economic and educational standing for lower- and depressed-caste communities.

After the Self-Respect Movement[25] was formed in 1925, Periyar's speeches at caste organisations became central to spreading awareness and empowering lower-caste groups in the Madras State. He would begin almost every speech by saying nobody is above, nor anyone below, the people he was addressing. One would argue that Periyar was an ardent pragmatist who internalised and endorsed Ambedkar's conception of the caste system. Ambedkar observed, "There is no such thing as caste. There are only castes" (Ambedkar, 1916 in Moon, 1979: 20).

In other words, the caste system thrives in relational terms, where the underlying point of differentiation was ritual purity. Ambedkar argued that every caste internalised ritual hierarchy, thereby making it a resilient system, defended not just by the upper castes but also by those in the middle, seeking to secure their position in society. He regarded this as the reason for the naturalisation of violence in the name of caste (Ambedkar, n.d.).

While Ambedkar's thinking certainly aligns with structuralist ideas, he emphasised the need for political action to address the material manifestations like deprivation, thereby making this a good first step towards revisiting how we understand the caste system. However, Ambedkar's political action engaged with the extreme ends of the caste system, that is, the Brahmins and the Dalits, while Periyar worked a lot more in the more restive and warring intersection of the lower castes and depressed castes.

Periyar's constant emphasis on equality among lower caste groups in his speeches was central to both deepening the antagonism against the Brahmins and working to flatten the hierarchy among the lower caste communities themselves. This approach sought to correct a critical flaw in the early Dravidian identity movements, which sometimes overlooked the complexities and divisions within non-elite castes. He was categorical that the empowerment of the depressed castes was possible only through their own will and actions, and not through the assistance of any other caste community, given the entrenched graded inequality of caste.

In his speech to the Adi Dravidar[26] youth in Erode in 1932, Periyar encouraged them to prepare for a bold revolution. He challenged them to ask themselves why they were in a 'depressed' position, and if they thought that it was due to God, they should break the idols; if it was due to religious belief, they should dismember the religion; if it was monarchy, then to destroy it, and if it was through trickery and selfishness of individuals, then to assertively declare that this could not go on.

Periyar specifically addressed the grievances of Adi Dravidars, without seeking to moderate the intensity of their concerns, nor attempted to smother clear differences[27] between them and other non-Brahmins by clubbing them together. With time and concerted efforts, he could position himself and other like-minded individuals not as voices or representatives of the cause of Adi Dravidars but as comrades who got together to forge an equitable society (Manoharan, 2020: 8). This conscious acknowledgment of the variance of grievances allowed for a more stable allyship, where no interest group had to surrender to the numerical or social might of the other.

Periyar also critiqued the conventional use of names like Devendra Kulathar and Arunthathiyar, which, despite being high-sounding, still failed to address the real, lived issues of these communities. He argued that the names should clearly identify the oppressor, suggesting that they add the prefix 'non-' to it. He said that this would remind them of the oppressor and the nature of the oppression, and ignite thought and action to overcome it. He suggested that instead of the term 'Depressed Classes' or *Odukkappattor*, they adopt the term 'Non-oppressor' or *Odikkanavar Alladhor* (Periyar in Subagunarajan, 2018 ed.: 37).

He criticised the practice of segregating social infrastructure, such as wells, temples, and schools, exclusively for the Adi Dravidars. Periyar abhorred government measures that perpetuated exclusion and social segregation, such as separate colonies, separate wells, and separate schools that were tailored to not disturb the caste status quo. Instead, he called for the government to settle Scheduled Caste families within the traditional spatial boundaries of the village, as in *agraharams* (exclusive sections of villages reserved for Brahmins), and on streets from which Scheduled Caste families were excluded, so that they did not end up being called 'New Paraiyar Street', referring to a Depressed Caste group (Periyar in Subagunarajan, 2018 ed.: 355–56).

Periyar thus demanded the radical integration of Adi Dravidars into the mainstream rather than creating even more segregated spaces that failed to address the roadblocks preventing integration. By doing so, he attacked the sources of pride from which the lower-caste groups derived their social distinctiveness. For Periyar, questioning caste, mindfully acknowledging differences between communities, and advocating self-respect were not ends in themselves but ways to carefully craft a layered Dravidian-Tamil identity that could claim socio-economic mobility and socio-political representation for the marginalised communities.

Despite Periyar's disinclination towards electoral politics, socio-political representation continued to be one of the commanding ideas in his struggle against Brahminism. He had an unusual relationship with electoral politics, wherein he sought distance from it, but appreciated its role in cementing and developing the ideas of self-respect and social justice in the public sphere.[28] Politics, for Periyar, was a means for subalterns to unsettle discriminatory social relations and incrementally forge and deepen collective social consciousness among communities (Manoharan, 2022: 62).

Periyar also believed that electoral politics, by its very nature, was characterised by compromises made in the pursuit of power. He argued that this kind of tactic was something a rationalist, anti-caste movement could not afford in a society ridden with graded inequality. For this reason, he chose to lead a social reform movement rather than a political party, as the latter would inevitably have to grapple with the machinations of electoral politics.

Despite his disinclination to party politics, Periyar's stance was never one of indifference towards electoral politics. In fact, his approach helped forge one of the most significant alliances in Tamil politics—the one between him and Annadurai, who would become his most trusted lieutenant in the years to come.[29] In Annadurai's preference for electoral path and Periyar's emphasis on social action and mobilisation, we can see the unbounded plurality and fluidity of the Dravidian-Tamil ethos. This unique ability to adapt, where politics reflects the changing realities of caste relations and struggles, allowed the Dravidian movement to derive meaning and legitimacy through both socio-cultural movements and institutional politics. And one key moment where both the institutional and electoral paths converged was during the protests against the imposition of Hindi as the sole official language of India.

The Justice Party suffered a humiliating defeat in the 1937 provincial elections,[30] which brought the Indian National Congress, a party that was seen as dominated by Brahmins, to power. C. Rajagopalachari (Rajaji) became the Premier of Madras Province, and his introduction of Hindi as a compulsory subject in schools across the Madras Presidency sparked widespread outrage. The policy was met with fierce opposition from the Justice Party, Periyar's Self-Respect Movement, and many other Tamil organisations, who organised protests throughout the Province. These protests continued until the policy was revoked in 1940. Two years earlier, Periyar took over the Justice Party, elected to the position through the support of its leadership, due to his popularity as well as the party's need to appeal to the poor.

From then on, Periyar, who had been addressing the socio-economic and cultural mobility of the lower sections of society, began to explicitly engage with the question of language, while still framing it within his principles of self-respect and equality. Tamil language became a key tool for Periyar and later Dravidianists, helping to unite diverse interest groups under a shared Dravidian-Tamil ethos (Ramaswamy, 1999: 6). As a result, the Justice Party under Periyar evolved from a political entity representing a few to a social reform organisation that drew in many people. This transformation culminated in 1944, when the party rebranded itself the Dravidar Kazhagam (DK)—one of the rare instances globally where a political party transformed itself into a social organisation.

An 'Anti-Nationalist's' Rendition of a Nation Building Project: Periyar's Tryst with Communities and Particularistic Grievances

Congress's push for making Hindi compulsory, coupled with its indifferent stance on dismantling caste hierarchies and reconciling diverse interest groups, only deepened Periyar's scepticism towards its vision of nationhood and nationalism, a stance he maintained until his death. In fact, in a 1973 speech, Periyar raised a series of questions that struck at the caste core of the Congress's idea of nationhood. He asked, "You say [that] India is a nation. You say, we are all children of the same mother. But do you treat us with love? I ask you, what is the relationship between you and me? Who are you and who am I? You say that you were born from the forehead of Brahma and I was born from Brahma's feet. Given this crude irony, you compel me to be as one with you" (Periyar in Subagunarajan, 2018 ed.: 405; Own Translation Lit.).

He viewed the nationhood of India as an embodiment of the hegemony of Brahmins over subalterns and, until his last breath, he questioned Brahminical hegemony. At the risk of being termed an anti-national, he questioned the nation-building project.

Congress's idea of nationalism, especially when it came to caste, was already facing sharp criticism back in 1916 when the Justice Party released its Non-Brahmin Manifesto. "In these days of organised effort, they (non-Brahmins) maintain no proper organisations for protecting and promoting their common interests and for preventing professional and other politicians, with hardly any corresponding stake in the country, from posing as their accredited spokesmen, nor have they a press of their own to speak the truth on their behalf. Their political interests, therefore (as compared with those of the Brahmins who number only about a million and a half), have materially suffered."[31]

Unsurprisingly, the nationalists of the time were agitated. They quickly dismissed the views of the non-Brahmin leaders of the South Indian People Association (SIPA), arguing that they were rooted in rivalry and pride. They claimed that it would hurt the efforts to create a unified national identity. Caste associations were seen as hurdles, too, often criticised for lacking legitimacy, not even claiming the support of the very castes they claimed to represent.

Periyar had a very clear stance when it came to caste associations. He believed they were legitimate, as long as they were focused on empowering and helping people move up in society, especially in the face of Brahminical oppression and subjugation. He urged non-Brahmins to think more rationally about nationalism. Instead of buying into a hollow sense of unity, he emphasised that real equality was what mattered most (Periyar in Subagunarajan, 2018 ed.: 33).

One could say that when Periyar questioned Congress's stance on nationhood, he wasn't trying to obstruct the anti-colonial struggle. Instead, he was pointing out how the Brahminical order of Hinduism was reinventing itself through the Congress's ideas of nationalism. For Congress, nationalism was about creating an imagined sense of unity, where communities were supposed to forget their differences rather than actually addressing them. While they were fighting for freedom from British rule, they were unwilling to confront caste inequalities or the cruelty that it came with. Plus, the Congress wanted a continuity in government once the British left, keeping Brahminical power and supremacy intact in the affairs of the country.

For Periyar, Congress's nationalism was akin to a self-fulfilling prophecy—if people adopted it to gain self-rule and freedom, it would just give Congress an unquestioned, idealistic legitimacy to take over the country. He feared that the Brahmins, through their close ties with the British, would end up shaping a newly independent India into a country still firmly structured around caste and Hinduism. On the other hand, Periyar's version of nationalism was fiercely anti-Brahminical. However, first, we must look at how Periyar viewed the colonial government when it came to caste and the Brahminical social order.

Aloysius (2022: 143) suggests that Periyar was very clear in pointing out how the Brahminical classes evolved under British rule. They went from being "an indolent, parasitical and a merely consumer group" to "meritorious" and "forward-thinking" in every aspect of life. This transformation made them partners in the colonial project. Periyar argued that in doing so, the British identified the large working-class population as lower castes and rendered them unworthy of higher positions and aspirations.

Now, it might appear that Periyar, like Nicholas Dirks, saw the colonial administration as responsible for the caste system. However, while Dirks blamed the replacement of local kingships in the post-1857 period for shaping the caste system as we know it (Guha, 2003: 459), he didn't really blame the pre-British era for the state of caste. He pointed to M.A. Sherring's *Hindu Tribes and Castes* (1872) as the moment when things shifted, claiming, "Gone is the ubiquitous reliance on Manu; orientalism has become empiricist rather than textual… It also eclipsed earlier enthusiasms for things Indian, even if, as in the case of most early orientalists, these enthusiasms were exclusively for ancient Indian civilization…" (Dirks, 1992: 66–67). In other words, Dirks argued that the system of caste became more Westernised and stabilised during British rule.

But Periyar didn't let the Brahminical order off the hook for its role in creating depravation, exclusion, and discrimination before the British arrived. He was more focused on criticising the British for becoming complicit in it. Interestingly, today, Hindu nationalists cite Dirks's work on India to demonise the colonial administration, and if you follow that line of thinking, it paints a picture of a 'glorious past' where, among other things, the caste system was fluid.

Since Periyar's views on nationalism were the complete opposite of Congress party's stance, it also meant that the caste hierarchies that the Congress model supported would inevitably be carried over into their idea (and the era) of self-rule. And for Periyar, that had to be challenged. The key to opposing this elite caste-dominated version of nationalism was the idea of category-wise rights. Periyar's vision of nationalism came out of a movement for category-wise rights, which was, in essence, an extension of his anti-caste struggle for social justice, grounded in lived experience and empirical realities (Aloysius, 2022: 127–28).

A Horizontal Identity vis-à-vis Differences and Aspirations

Periyar's idea of category rights saw the differences between communities not as something to divide them, but a part of their unique contribution to nation-building. While Congress's Brahminical elite wanted to create a unified identity by dissolving differences without any real change in the lived experiences and material realities of a large section of the people, Periyar favoured a society where differences could exist and co-exist through open contestation and political action.

Chantal Mouffe (2000) and Shruti Kapila (2021) have emphasised that conflict is an inherent part of democratic politics in plural societies. Kapila argues that conflict and contestation are actually essential for a vibrant democracy; Mouffe highlights that politics must be seen as a struggle among diverse groups with deeply held, sometimes irreconcilable, differences. Both of them reject the notion that democracy should always strive for consensus, calling it a form of democratic deficit (Mouffe, 2000: 13–17). Striving for consensus can undermine pluralism, which is foundational to democracy.

Kapila (2021: 192), drawing from Ambedkar, emphasises that democratic representation should not just reflect the will of the majority but also protect minority rights and perspectives (Kapila, 2021: 277). Periyar, a staunch supporter of Ambedkar, similarly sought to build an identity based on solidarity across conflicting groups. This solidarity allowed each subaltern community to have the agency to assert its rights and strive towards socio-economic and political mobility. In other words, the Dravidian-Tamil identity was consensus-driven when outlining broad contours. However, everything else concerning fulfilling each community's aspirations was done through encouraging contestations and supporting coexistence. For Periyar, a nation's unity was stable only when empowered communities came together[32] on equal terms.

For Periyar, if any community that was politicised felt left out or oppressed, its assertion for dignity and mobility had to be recognised. Each subaltern group had its distinctive place in the nation, and so, the nation was really a sum of these categories. Unity—any cross-community solidarity—was not something Periyar assumed or took for granted in his conception of nationhood. It was something that had to be worked for, and required active political action towards supporting the cause of equal rights for all these different categories[33] (Aloysius, 2022: 130).

To fully understand the larger ambitions behind Periyar's politics and his motivations to create a horizontal Dravidian-Tamil solidarity, it helps to look at William Connolly's ideas. Connolly (1996: 255–56) talks about the 'politics of becoming'—when a community that has been subjugated in a given society decides to transform itself by rethinking its identity in relation to the differences around it. Such revisions are not openly acknowledged or accepted because they challenge the existing power structures. In the case of India, that structure is the deeply ingrained social hierarchy. Connolly suggests that this kind of struggle pushes communities to engage in persistent, experimental, and sometimes militant political movements to make their voices heard and their grievances part of the mainstream. In the epilogue to this edition, I present a couple of examples of such mainstreaming on the lines of caste (Dalits) and gender (with non-binary genders).

To sum it up, Periyar's struggle wasn't just against colonialism or Brahminical oppression, nor was it simply about fighting one specific social group. His fight reflected his broader vision of Dravidian-Tamil identity. The idea of self-respect, his push for category-based rights, his alternative vision of nationalism, and his commitment to substantive equality were all key parts of what made up Periyar's isotope of Dravidian-Tamil identity.

His approach created a space where multiple communities could assert themselves and work towards socio-economic and political mobility. Over time, it opened up opportunities for more groups on the margins to do the same. This capaciousness to accommodate also gave his vision resilience, allowing it to pass the test of time, adapting and evolving to stay relevant to contemporary realities.

Annadurai and the DMK as Praxis: Between Periyar and Pragmatism

The Dravidian-Tamil identity serves as a template for incrementally acquiring new meaning, significance—and new social groups. Annadurai's vision of this identity was not too different from Periyar's or anyone else's before him, but it was able to reinvent itself and revive in response to contemporary experiences of the Tamil socio-political landscape. What makes this identity so adaptable is how it has shifted and changed in relation to various important factors. We can see this by looking at how it interacted with traditions and identity, its relationship with Brahminism and Brahmins, how it connected to the struggles and events around Indian Independence, and how the people who identified with it were named or referred to over time.

Annadurai, who was Periyar's trusted lieutenant, played a crucial role in the decisive electoral success of the Dravidian movement. He took Periyar's idea of the Dravidian-Tamil identity and spread it far and wide in various ways. But while Periyar's vision was deeply sceptical of the past—especially the idea of glorifying traditions—Annadurai had a somewhat different approach. He relied on history and 'invented tradition' (Hobsbawm, 1983: 14) to create meaning. This made Annadurai's approach clash a little with Periyar's, which was all about moving beyond historicised identities and averse to relying on past glory to find solutions for contemporary problems.

To spread the Dravidian-Tamil ethos, Annadurai returned to the Sangam era[34] (sixth century BCE to third century CE). By revisiting the Dravidian-Tamil conceptions of the early Dravidianists, Annadurai learned to avoid the mistakes they committed. In his celebrated work *Ariya Mayai* (The Aryan Illusion), Annadurai crafted a political identity framework that drew inspiration from the Sangam era but was placed firmly in the present. Like the early Dravidianists, he maintained that the caste system was foreign to the Dravidian lands. But instead of focusing on the Bhakti period like his predecessors, Annadurai emphasised a hierarchy-free society akin to Periyar's vision, steering away from the idea of occupational hierarchy that the early Dravidianists clung to.

Barnett (1976: 73–74) observed that Annadurai's approach in *Ariya Mayai* pivoted around four key ideas: nature of oppression, its causes, an alternative idea, and a call to action. The nature of oppression stemmed from the caste system, rooted in Hindu traditions, and the cause of it, according to Annadurai, was the widespread false belief in Aryan supremacy. His alternative? A rational, egalitarian, Dravidian society—one that could only be achieved through anti-caste propaganda rooted in reason.

Annadurai leaned on the Sangam era, using it as a foundation to weave a distinct cultural identity, one that felt grounded in a historical past but was also marked by equality and was relevant to the present. His engagement with the past was not completely divorced from rationality. Instead, it came from the extremely pragmatic understanding that people often find identity, legitimacy, and meaning in their history.

While Periyar advanced rational thought, Annadurai espoused rationality at a personal level. He sought to contain the excesses of believers through aggressively promoting powerful slogans: "*Onre Kulam Oruvaney Devan*" (One community, one God) and "*Makkal Sevai Magesan Sevai*" (Service to people is service to God). By looking back to the Sangam era to claim a 'Golden Age', Annadurai tried to help people move past the 2,000 intervening years, which were popularly understood as the era marked by casteism and conflict. Through his writings and speeches, he found a way to revisit Periyar's ideals, preserve them, and then repackage them in a way that would be more politically engaging and relatable.

Seldom did Periyar distinguish Brahmins from Brahminism. Consequently, his relationship with Brahmins was never above a degree of suspicion. His relationship with Rajaji is a case in point: while he considered Rajaji a good and selfless man, he could never completely trust him with Tamil politics or governance. The impact of this lack of complete trust reduced the scope of their engagement. However, in the later part of his public life, Annadurai tried to moderate the hate against Brahmins by clearly distinguishing between Brahmins and Brahminism.

A DMK leader defined Brahminism as something that represents "the particular system and practice of life preached by the Brahmins...based on irrational beliefs and superstitions. It is not peculiar to Brahmins as these practices have permeated over the centuries to all castes" (Ryerson, 1988: 118). In his famed epistle to his brethren *Aariyam Irukkum Idam* (The site of Aryanism, meaning Brahminism) published in the Tamil weekly *Dravida Nadu*, Annadurai said: "Brother, Aryanism does not lie with Aryan alone, it has been propagated among Dravidians too, and the Dravidians that do not look like Aryans are defending and conserving [it]... To rid the society of Aryanism we should not set fire in an *Agraharam* (Brahmins' enclaves) but ignite the minds of people by propagation of knowledge (rational thought)... It is Aryanism when an Iyer (Brahmin) says, 'Get lost you Shudra...' It is Aryanism when a Mudialiar (non-Brahmin elite caste) says, 'Do not come near me you slum dweller.' Saying, 'So much wage hike for a Padayatchi?' (a lower middle caste) is also Aryanism. 'Walk respectfully in front of a Maravar...' 'Thevar is coming, stand up...' 'Nadar is calling, run and come...' 'Chettiyar is asking, give carefully...' are multiple ways in which Aryanism blatantly manifests itself, brother... multiple ways"[35] (Original Translation Lit).

The epistle effectively took Ambedkar's concept of graded inequality and applied it to Tamil society in a way that people could easily relate to. It's safe to say that both Periyar[36] and Annadurai[37] wanted to dismantle the irrationalities and brutalities of Brahminism, but Annadurai was more agile when it came to adapting the process to the changing realities of Tamil society. His efforts to bring Tamil Brahmins into the fold of Dravidian politics earned the DMK support from Rajaji in the run-up to the 1967 elections. This support weakened the Congress's organisational structure and provided the DMK with a much-needed fillip, allowing it to sustain its social justice and welfare politics in Tamil Nadu for more than half a century.

By offering an olive branch to Tamil Brahmins, Annadurai may have strengthened the horizontal solidarity that Periyar had emphasised. Conceptually, this approach helped shape the Dravidian-Tamil identity in a way that it became something people could choose to embrace—consciously subscribe to—rather than be born into it—an ascribed identity. In other words, the identity is forged based on changing boundaries: both in terms of how the subaltern communities wish to come together, as well as regarding the relationship between these communities and the elite. Notably, many of the stalwarts of the Dravidian movement who died during the anti-Hindi agitations, and those who stood by the Sri Lankan Tamils, were actually native Telugu speakers and their attackers were chauvinistic Tamil nativists.

The differences between Annadurai's faction and Periyar's faction spilt out in the open at the time of India's independence. While Periyar saw independence as a transfer of power from the British to Brahmins and observed Independence Day as a day of sorrow, Annadurai saw it as a moment of respecting the Dravidian lives lost in the struggle for freedom (Saraswathi, 1974: 110). He did concur with Periyar on Brahmin or Aryan domination, and he opposed British rule too, which gave his political agenda wider appeal while staying rooted on Periyar's turf. In effect, Annadurai forged the Dravidian-Tamil political identity as a collective insurgence against Aryanism, Brahminism, Sanskritic traditions, and so on by infusing it with an element of transitivity. In his view, all these words—Aryanism, Brahminism, Sanskritic traditions—meant domination and decimation, which the Dravidian-Tamil ethos must resist.

Annadurai also drew a conceptual boundary between 15 August—the day the Brahminical government took power—and the struggles before it to overthrow the colonial government. For him, it was all part of an ongoing struggle—the British colonists were out, and now was the time to challenge the new power structure on its own issues.

As Tamils joined the Self-Respect Movement in large numbers, they also became part of the Dravidian-Tamil community, while Annadurai found new ways to strengthen the sense of horizontal solidarities that Periyar had started. One key way in which he did this was his use of the word *udanpirappu*, which is a gender-neutral term for 'brethren'. Periyar insisted on using *thozhar* (comrade), to encourage a non-familial, egalitarian sense of identity. But Annadurai referred to partymen and the public as *udanpirappu*, which emphasised a sense of fraternity across caste groups and had a more 'familial' ring. While *thozhar* was a radical call to disparate individuals to forsake their caste identities and unite as Dravidian-Tamils, *udanpirappu* helped build relationships between communities, from which flowed an identity that transcended local limits.

Annadurai's conception of the Dravidian-Tamil identity made it flexible and accommodating, helping to create a historical bloc that remains a powerful voting force today. Seemingly warring factions or communities unite in Tamil Nadu under the supra-local Dravidian-Tamil identity—where they choose to act as interest groups. The policies of Dravidian governments have actively addressed the specific grievances of various social groups, focusing on fair redistribution of resources and ensuring access to political representation.

That said, these polices have benefited different caste groups in varying ways. First, the benefits were programmatically delivered to each community based on their needs. Second, the identity relied on history and cultural idioms. As a result, despite its inherent focus on egalitarianism, communities weren't motivated to transform their social relations in ways that would increase interdependency. They tended to focus inward, achieving their own aspirations instead of actively working to nurture networks of dependence between caste groups.

Periyar gave the depressed and marginalised sections socio-political ideas that empowered them to reject the Brahminical order and stand up for themselves. However, it was Annadurai's political vision that gave them the capacity to aspire.[38] Annadurai's wit, humour, and use of rhymes made him much more popular and relatable than Periyar, allowing him to influence public discourse through accessible forms like cinema. The reading rooms he established across Madras State helped spread the message of Dravidian-Tamil ethos widely, and those who frequented them supported the DMK's protests between 1949 and 1967, when they finally voted it to power.

The Dravidian-Tamil political identity has remained strong, in part because of its cross-religious inclusivity, with the Tamil language being its central feature. It was seen and developed as a language of subaltern resistance. Muslims, who predominantly belonged to subaltern castes, were integral to both the inclusivity and resistance aspects of Tamil. For instance, even today, one of the most popular contemporary Tamil poets is *Kaviko* (King of Poets) Abdul Rahman. Another influential figure was Manavai Mustafa, also a Muslim, who published Tamil glossaries on topics like computers, medicine, and science and technology, and campaigned for Tamil to be recognised as a classical language.

But Annadurai struggled with the gender question in Tamil politics, even after he shaped the Dravidian-Tamil identity into a dynamic and largely egalitarian vision that pivoted on socio-economic mobility, dignity, social justice, and the Tamil language. Periyar tried to build distance from traditional gender roles, especially by pushing for education and equal inheritance rights for women. Many Dravidian scholars produced a serious body of work on self-respect marriages in which both genders are equalised within a deeply unequal institution. Yet, despite these efforts, gender could not be adequately dealt with in the Dravidian fold (Karthik & Baskar, 2021).

It's possible that Dravidian political leaders struggled to imagine womanhood beyond traditional roles, as seen in their heavy reliance on the cult goddess of chastity, Kannagi, as a symbol. The way they contrasted the chastity of Kannagi with "the sexual obscenity" of the Sanskritic tradition (Pandian, 1998: 549) in their fight against Brahminical supremacy was deeply ignorant of women's autonomy and agency, in all realms including sexuality. I've argued elsewhere that attempts to empower women have failed to increase their representation in the political sphere. The current, alarmingly low levels of female representation make the welfarist, progressive, inclusive electoral viability of Dravidian politics less sustainable in the long term (Karthik & Baskar, 2021).

The ideological foundations laid by Periyar, the DK, and the DMK paved the way for some of the boldest and most effective affirmative action reforms, which are still debated today. The makers of the Indian Constitution generally agreed that graded and ascriptive inequality needed substantial redress, but they often disagreed on how to achieve it. Ajantha Subramanian (2019:

208) highlights that one key point of debate was the appropriate constitutional language for social differentiation—specifically, whether caste should be legally recognised. She points out that Dravidian governments challenged the liberal norm of formal equality in two ways: first, by prioritising the caste collective over the individual citizen, and second, by opposing the inclusion of class criteria alongside caste.

That said, the Dravidian governments' sustained resistance to formal equality also shifted the balance between merit and affirmative action. Formal equality didn't seem as important as addressing historical social injustices and achieving substantive equality.[39] The mobilisation through an identity that is supra-local—beyond local limits—allowed communities to assert themselves and unite politically, which has helped prevent restiveness from escalating into conflict, something often seen in other parts of the country. However, the shift in social relations towards harmonious cross-community interdependence is an unfinished project and needs further development.

Conclusion

This chapter has demonstrated Periyar's understanding of caste as a system of power and how this informed the DMK's approach as it worked to transform the Dravidian movement into electorally viable party politics. I have provided a brief overview of the South Indian region and how the caste system evolved, and the social reform efforts that preceded Periyar's influence.

The constant social upheaval—especially regarding control over resources, social relations, and migration-related factors—made definitive categories, analogous to Kshatriya or Vaishya, absent. This, in turn, helped form a Dravidian-Tamil political identity that was both accommodative and accessible, thanks to Periyar and Annadurai's interventions.

I have presented them not as the fountainheads but as social and political icons who skillfully framed the Dravidian-Tamil identity to address the specific grievances of individual caste groups while fostering horizontal solidarity. The focus was on self-respect, dignity, and socio-economic empowerment of the marginalised along with primacy to the Tamil language, creating a universalist insurgency against the existing discriminatory social relations and concentration of power and opportunities in the hands of a few.

While the DMK's representational matrix did not prominently feature women, they were emergent in Periyar's movement. More crucially, this approach to caste did not radically unsettle the private lives of caste communities but encouraged them to come together in secular and political spaces. One could argue that the popularity of self-respect marriages had a ripple effect on private lives in some cases. The Dravidian-Tamil identity remains accommodative and resilient politically and electorally, continually evolving while staying true to its core principles and adapting to new political realities.

In the next chapter, I discuss how the DMK, under Annadurai's leadership, worked in the 1950s and 1960s to politicise Tamils and build the Dravidian-Tamil public sphere.

2

DISSEMINATING THE DRAVIDIAN-TAMIL ETHOS THROUGH READING ROOMS

The previous chapter traced the development of the Dravidian-Tamil identity, focusing on the non-Brahmin and Dravidian movements from the 1890s to the 1940s, led by prominent political figures and activists. This chapter tackles two main questions: First, how did the DMK, a political party founded by Annadurai after splitting from the DK in 1949, communicate its political message and build mass appeal? Second, how did the DMK go beyond messaging to actively politicise the public, turning passive audiences into engaged political participants? While the questions aren't new, this chapter takes a different approach to the existing discourse.

Previous research (such as Hardgrave, 1973; Pandian, 1986, 1989, 1991, 1992, 1996; and Krishnan, 2009), has largely found answers in the use of popular media such as theatre, street plays, and films that promoted ideas of rationalism, egalitarianism, and dimensions of caste injustice. While these forms were certainly critical, most literature, with the exception of two key works, doesn't fully recognise other forms of mediation.

Subramanian (1999) offered a broad account of the Dravidian movement and the electoral rise of both the DMK and AIADMK, while Bate (2009) explored the influence of public speakers in the Madras State on spreading these ideas within a democratic framework. However, the reasons behind the popularity of plays, films, and Tamil oratory culture deserve further exploration. This chapter focuses on the emergence of a network of reading rooms, using Virudhunagar—a district in southern Tamil Nadu—as a case study, to show how these spaces helped create a vibrant counterpublic sphere.

The chapter argues that the formation, spread, and use of reading rooms in the Tamil region in the 1950s and 1960s was critical for forging the Dravidian public sphere. It shows that *paddipakams* and *mandrams*[1] (loosely translated as reading rooms and associations) that housed tens of newspapers, magazines, and periodicals, and were frequented by ordinary people, were pivotal to creating social awareness. The reading rooms also mediated between the subaltern[2] public and the ideas of the Dravidian movement. The reading room culture resembles *adda* (Chakrabarty, 1999: 110) in Bengal to the extent that they were sites of deliberation, debate, and dissemination of ideas among people. However, while the *adda* was marked by exclusion or domination (ibid., 145), the reading rooms were run by subalterns and relatively more inclusive.

Andrew Wyatt (2014: 158) concurred with the subaltern nature of the reading rooms, though he critiqued how effective they were in inducing radical social change. Citing the 1980s and 1990s when a series of political activities valorised caste identities and led to a spate of clashes between lower castes and Scheduled Castes, he questions how inclusive the Dravidian counterpublic sphere was in accommodating members of Dalit castes.

The scope of this chapter is restricted to the 1950s and 1960s when Dalits ran reading rooms and participated in their activities, but also responds to pertinent concerns raised beyond these decades. The fieldwork is a significant addition to the work of Francis Cody on the Arivoli Iyakkam (Light of Knowledge or Enlightenment Movement)—a mass literacy movement in Tamil Nadu between the 1990s and 2009. The Arivoli Iyakkam promoted access to knowledge including the sciences, helping improve the political participation of the rural population, especially women.

Cody notes significant similarities between the Arivoli Iyakkam reading rooms and those run by Periyar and the Self-Respect

Movement between 1926 and 1949. He refers to the cultural appeal of Arivoli being far higher than Dravidian mobilisation (Cody, 2013: 53). This chapter does not discuss Periyar's reading rooms in detail, but it shows that the DMK's reading room network, supported by allied groups in the 1950s and 1960s, successfully mobilised the masses to significantly and decisively alter the course of elections and politics in Tamil Nadu. I follow the works of Sandria Freitag (1989) and Christopher Alan Bayly (2002) to demonstrate how the DMK forged the Dravidian public sphere.

In *Collective Action and Community: Public Arenas and the Emergence of Communalism in North India,* Freitag uses what she calls a 'processual analysis' of activities of groups in Varanasi in the late eighteenth and early nineteenth centuries in public arenas. In these, "the community has been expressed and redefined through collective activities in public spaces" (1989: 6). The activities of the communities include religious ceremonies, festivals, and later, riots and protests. Discussing the formation of a broad-based identity around seemingly religious activities and symbols, she notes that such events were also political, allowing different groups to negotiate their rights while colonial occupation changed social relations. The overtones of religious symbols over time are seen as a reason for the emergence of a communalism that is at once political and religious.

Bayly describes the presence of knowledge networks in the early modern decades in northern India. Departing from the Habermasian public sphere, he terms the indigenous public sphere as the 'Indian ecumene', where print media and oral communication were complementary. He notes that dialogue and debate took place through public congregations, personal and institutional letter-writing, and placarding (Bayly, 2002: 179). He also uses Garcin de Tassy's argument about how Western distinctions in politics, literature, and history were inapplicable in India, and how a strong political undercurrent exists in art and fiction (ibid.).

In this context, the chapter draws from Freitag's concept of the making of a politicised community by engaging in group activities in and around reading rooms meant to disseminate knowledge of the Dravidian-Tamil ethos. Given the DMK's approach of engaging through multiple media—theatre, drama, film, poetry, public talks, letters, newspapers, magazines, and reading rooms—the chapter also engages with Bayly's concept of ecumene, specifically within the Tamil reading rooms.

I present findings from my own fieldwork in and around Virudhunagar district, which serves as an apt site to study the role of reading rooms in the 1950s and early 1960s. The DMK benefited from the presence of a group of committed Justice Party leaders in Virudhunagar who supplemented its efforts to establish reading rooms and, at times, provided financial support. In the 1967 elections, K. Kamaraj and the Indian National Congress lost in Virudhunagar and the Madras State, respectively. This outcome was suitable to evaluate the efforts of the DMK and allied groups in enabling the Dravidian-Tamil identity to spread through the reading rooms.

The chapter employs the concepts of 'social pluralism' and 'organisational pluralism' put forth by Narendra Subramanian (2002) to analyse and understand the role the reading rooms played. By social pluralism, Subramanian refers to "the existence of many active associations significantly autonomous of the state and of one another" (Subramanian, 2002: 126). Using the concept, the chapter enumerates the different groups that established and ran the reading rooms in Virudhunagar. They were run by or with the support of Nadar associations, some affluent Justice Party members, and a few private individuals.

A good number of reading rooms that emerged before independence were run by affluent Nadars who belonged to the Nadar Sangam and/or the Justice Party, and many more sprang up after the DMK was established. These reading rooms ran alongside the ones that were DMK-run. The second concept, 'organisational pluralism', refers to the "extent of autonomy and flexibility characterising both relations within an organisation and transactions between the organisation and society" (ibid.). According to Subramanian, organisational pluralism has three components—cadre autonomy, supporter autonomy, and leadership flexibility, the first two of which are useful in the context of this chapter. Cadre autonomy denotes "the autonomy of local party units, party factions and party-affiliated associations from party leaders" (ibid.). Using this concept, the chapter also discusses what inspired the groups that engaged in creating and running the reading rooms.

The success and longevity of the reading rooms were a direct result of the strength of the DMK's organisational structure. As Annadurai had envisioned, Karunanidhi built a well-knit, multi-level framework that was more formal and agile than the loose structure of the DK. The core unit of the DMK's organisation was the Branch Office (*kilai*), which existed in both rural and urban areas, and consisted of at least twenty-five members, including office-bearers. At the next level, the Taluk Committees brought together the secretaries from each branch office.

The most powerful unit in the DMK's structure was the District Committee, made up of five elected members from each Taluk Committee, along with respective secretaries. The District Secretary had significant power within the party. Above the District Committee was the General Council, the party's highest decision-making body. To be eligible for the General Council, members needed at least three years of party membership. District secretaries were ex-officio members of the General Council, alongside ten elected members from each District Committee.

The General Council also elected members to key positions, including the party's Parliamentary Board, Trust Board, Appeals Committee, Audit Committee, Treasurer, General Secretary, and Chairperson. The General Secretary then formed a working committee with fifteen members and five secretaries, each in charge of a specific area—headquarters, organisation, propaganda, trade union activities, and party publications (Sampath, 1960 in Hardgrave, 1965: 33–34).

A Wedding in Tamil Nadu and the 'Present'

To set the context for my experience of interviewing people who had frequented or been involved in running the reading rooms, I'll share an incident that highlighted the ongoing influence of reading material in common gatherings in Tamil civil society. During my time in Virudhunagar, I had an opportunity to attend a wedding in Madurai, about 35 miles away, where I saw how social events like weddings can be used by ideologues to spread their message. This wedding was a variant of the self-respect marriages[3] where parents of the couple from different castes give their approval.

The wedding, which took place on 19 January 2020, had no priest, and the ceremony was very simple, with quite a few guests attending. A few people, mostly from an organisation promoting Periyar's ideals, sat on the stage facing the guests. The couple exchanged vows and garlands without any of the elaborate rituals typically seen at weddings. Everyone present, irrespective of their caste, ideology, or beliefs, was given a small pocket-sized book as a present. The book, titled *Dravidar Ponmozhigal* (loosely translated as Dravidian Sayings), began with the line, "Dignity and intellect are markers of the beauty of a human being." Special guests on the stage received four books: *Ambedkarum Saathi Ozhippum* (a translation of *Dr Ambedkar and Untouchability: Analysing and Fighting Caste*) by Christophe Jaffrelot, *Affirmative Action in India* by Ashwini Deshpande, and *The Strangeness of Tamil Nadu: Contemporary History and Political Culture in South India* and *Interpreting the Dravidian Movement*, both by M.S.S. Pandian.

The practice of giving books as gifts is common in self-respect marriages, albeit with minor modifications. During this ceremony, the wedding administrator spoke about Periyar's ideas of social justice, women's empowerment, and marital life, engaging the audience with humour and wit. She ended by presenting her address as an alternative view—something the audience could agree with, or challenge after giving it a thought.

Attending this wedding helped me make sense of the responses I collected from the visitors of reading rooms in the Virudhunagar region. Weddings, as we know, are usually sites where social hierarchies related to gender and caste are reinforced. So, using such an event to spread messages of gender equality, women's empowerment, and the annihilation of caste is a powerful way to politicise people. Sarah Hodges (2005) points out that self-respect marriages are a powerful way to radically reform society by challenging traditional, caste-based, patriarchal, and Brahminical norms.

These marriages sought to break down oppressive social structures by rejecting religious rituals, the financial burden of dowry, and promoting gender equality, inter-caste unions, and women's rights—including the right to divorce and use birth control. Hodges emphasises that such marriages were not just a matter of personal choice but political acts of defiance, public spectacles meant to provoke conversation and transform society by promoting a modern Dravidian-Tamil family based on self-respect and rationalism.

An Overture to the Emergence of Padippakams

> *I assumed office a year ago. Along with naming our motherland as 'Tamil Nadu', I have undertaken a few other activities. Seeing all this, a few are angry.*
>
> *'Can we spare them?' they ask.*
>
> *'The government needs to be dismissed!' they say.*
>
> *Can you do that? I will not challenge them in response.*
>
> *Of course you can!*
>
> *However, after dismissing the government, after someone else takes over, when that person thinks of undoing my work, 'Won't people vehemently retaliate?' a small fear would strike.*
>
> *Until such fear lingers around, irrespective of who is in office, it would mean that Annadurai is still in office.*
>
> —Annadurai, 1968, in Asokan K. 2019: Cover Page (Own Translation Lit.).

An assertive statement like the one cited above, coupled with the dominance of the Dravidian parties for over fifty years since 1967, brings up two questions in line with those posed at the beginning of this chapter. First, what did Annadurai accomplish in his one year in office, and in the years leading up to it? I answer this in later chapters. And second, what role did the DMK, the party he founded, play in spreading the Dravidian-Tamil ethos?

The 1944 Salem Conference was a major turning point for the Justice Party, the predecessor of the DMK. The most significant changes were the party's decisions to rebrand itself and not participate in elections. Instead, it would transform into a social reform organisation with a new name, Dravidar Kazhagam, or DK. To emphasise, while there are many instances of socio-political movements transforming into political parties,[4] the reverse is a rare occurrence in contemporary Indian political history.

Defending the decision, Periyar said that electoral compulsions would overwhelm the objective of the Dravidian-Tamil ethos—awakening society and engaging with people on the ideas of self-respect and social justice. Annadurai, too, was a key figure at the Salem Conference. However, he and a few others would disagree in later years, arguing that social reform can be lasting only with participation in electoral politics. The difference of opinion simmered and the conflict went public in 1947, at the time of Independence.

Periyar, as we have already discussed, viewed Indian independence as a transfer of powers from the British to Brahmins, and observed Independence Day as a day of sorrow, while Annadurai saw in it a moment of showing respect to Dravidian lives lost in the fight for freedom. (Saraswathi, 1974: 110 & 68). While Annadurai concurred with Periyar on Brahmin or Aryan domination,[5] he also opposed British rule. However, the two disagreed on the approach towards creating a separate Dravida Nadu. Periyar's approach was more militant[6] while Annadurai sought to emulate the Congress's approach towards the British (Annadurai, 1947 in Barnett, 1976: 68).

Ultimately, Periyar and Maniammai's[7] marriage, followed by his decision to elevate her as his successor in the DK, spurred the Annadurai faction[8] to break away and form the DMK on 17 September 1949. This was a severe blow to the DK, as around 50,000 of its 75,000 cadres allied with the DMK (Barnett, 1976: 75). However, the DMK continued to align itself ideologically with the DK and Periyar. Annadurai took on the role of General Secretary of the DMK, symbolically leaving the party president's post vacant (Barnett, 1976: 76).

The DMK's journey began in Robinson Park in Madras, where around 50,000 supporters turned up, responding to Annadurai's call. It was almost a cinematic moment. To understand how the party gained such a large following, we need to look at the factors behind the party's growth, which also help understand the surge in reading rooms in subsequent years.

After the 1944 Salem Conference, Annadurai played a pivotal role in reshaping the Justice Party and expanding the DK. In a personal interview, K. Rajendran[9] (Personal Communication, 30 January 2020) remarked that after the transformation from Justice Party to DK, the profile of its followers changed significantly. He noted that the DK shed the elite image of the Justice Party and, instead of the older or middle-aged, many younger people—some educated, with little or no political experience—joined DK. To support this, one can look at the remarkable growth in DK's membership.[10] From 1944 to September 1945, the party's membership grew 361% from 7,369 to 33,984. Between September 1945 and July 1946, it expanded a further 45% to 49,574 members.

Finally, there was a 50% spike in membership by September 1949 to 75,000. The growth rate of membership was 917.7% from 1944 to September 1949, while the State's decadal population growth rate was far behind at 14.66% (1941 to 1951). This comparison determines the party's growing influence, based on whether its expansion is faster, slower, or apace population growth.

A higher growth rate in party cadres relative to population growth suggests increasing influence and mobilisation capability, potentially leading to greater electoral success and political power [Refer to Figures 1 and 2].

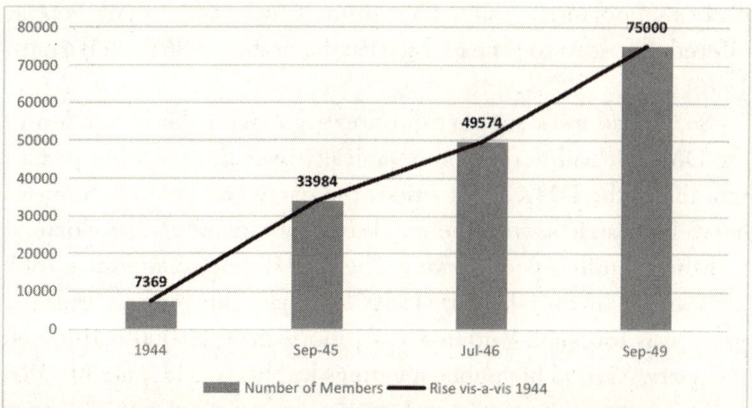

Figure 1: Membership of Dravidar Kazhagam between 1944 and 1949

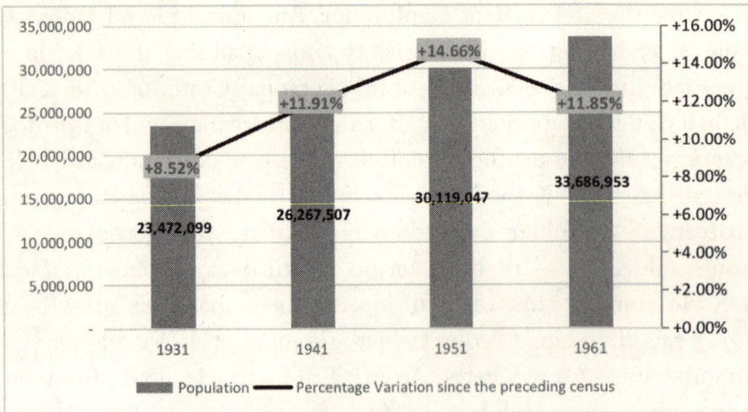

Figure 2: Decadal Variation in Madras State's Population between 1931 and 1961

The resolutions adopted at the Salem Conference deserve credit for putting forward ideas of egalitarianism, such as encouraging people to give up titles and caste references in their names. Annadurai was the face of the conference, even though Periyar presided over it. From that point until the split in 1949, Annadurai's popularity steadily grew among the cadres. In fact, most of the new members who joined the DK were drawn to it because of him. Periyar was aware of this and, at the 1948 DK Erode Conference, he acknowledged that Annadurai had 'captivated' the party's supporters. Despite their simmering disagreement, Periyar offered his seat to Annadurai (Parthasarathy, 1961 in Barnett, 1976: 70).

So, Annadurai's support did not begin with the formation of the DMK. It had developed organically over time. Within just 17 months of the DMK's formation, the party had held conferences in twelve districts, with thousands of party members, supporters, and their families participating. The first district conference took place in Trichy on 1 January 1950, less than four months after the party was founded. Within a year, more than 35,000 had joined the party,[11] 2,035 big public meetings had been held, and 505 *kilai kazhagams* (branch offices) and twelve *maavatta kazhagams* (district offices) had been established (Thirunavakkarasu, 2019: 314–15).

Emergence of Padippakams

Periyar's argument that a social organisation would be more effective than a political party in uplifting the Tamils was persuasive. Keeping in mind Periyar's concern that electoral compulsions could sidetrack reform activities, the DMK held numerous public meetings in its first year on its core issues—seven conferences on women's empowerment, especially seeking reforms in Hindu laws across Madras State, and one conference on the Tamil language in Coimbatore.

The DMK went beyond just public meetings to deepen its engagement with both the people and its cadres regarding the Dravidian-Tamil identity, as well as to expand its organisational base. A key initiative in this effort was the establishment of *padippakams* (reading rooms) alongside the branch offices (*kilai*) of the party. Annadurai saw these reading rooms as vital tools for fostering engagement, spreading political ideas, and strengthening the party's support and cadre base. A host of other activities, such as the publication of journals, pamphlets, and books, and street plays, dramas, and films took place in the reading rooms.

H.V. Hande's[12] (Personal Communication, 28 January 2020) remark to me that Annadurai was the last man in Tamil Nadu who "repaired the heads of people" highlights his profound impact on political consciousness through ideological and intellectual efforts. It is also important to remind ourselves that the culture of publishing and reading rooms in Tamil Nadu has a long-standing history that dates back to the nineteenth century. During this period, the printing press became a critical means of disseminating ideas aimed at challenging the cultural oppression of Brahminism.

As outlined by A.R. Venkatachalapathy (1994), reading practices in colonial Tamil Nadu underwent significant transformations, reflecting the socio-economic changes in the region. Initially, reading was primarily oral, often taking place in communal activities of a religious or scholarly nature. Palm leaf manuscripts, delicate and requiring skilled recitation, served as the primary medium. Access to these manuscripts was limited, and reading was typically guided by scholars or teachers in public spaces such as temples.

By the mid-nineteenth century, the arrival of print culture—following the removal of restrictions on Indian-owned printing presses in 1835—made printed books more accessible. However, traditional scholars viewed printed texts with suspicion, and they coexisted with palm leaf manuscripts. There was reluctance to accept printed books as authoritative, leading to conflicts between the oral tradition and the burgeoning print culture. Despite this, printed books gradually penetrated into Tamil society, though oral culture remained predominant.

The tensions between traditional and print-based reading intensified in the late nineteenth century when scholars reliant on oral traditions felt challenged by the authority of printed texts. Standardised printed texts undermined their mastery over manuscripts. Nonetheless, oral recitation and memorisation retained influence, as many traditional scholars remained uncomfortable with the shift to print.

The rise of the middle class in the early twentieth century made silent reading, largely driven by the popularity of novels, popular for the first time. This was a new mode of reading, and associated with leisure, departing from public, oral practices. Younger readers, particularly students, began reading novels privately, away from the moral scrutiny of elders. Silent reading, providing an immersive and solitary experience, became linked to middle-class lifestyles.

Despite this, oral and group reading continued to thrive, especially among the lower classes during the 1920s and 1930s. Popular literature, such as in chapbooks and ballads, were still consumed in communal settings, with audiences gathering in marketplaces or homes to hear recitations. Group readings during religious or social occasions, such as funerals, also sustained the oral tradition. While middle-class readers embraced silent reading, they could not impose this practice on the broader population.

By the mid-twentieth century, silent and oral reading coexisted in Tamil Nadu. The lower classes continued to engage in communal reading, particularly of popular texts, and newspapers became integral to this dynamic. A literate person would often read aloud for others in public settings like tea shops or village squares.

Table 1: Literacy Rate in Madras State

Year	Total	Male	Female
1951	21.9%	32.4%	11.5%
1961	31.4%	44.5%	18.2%
1971	39.5%	51.8%	26.9%

Source: Census of India Reports

Around a third (30.9%) of the State was literate (42.9% of males and 18.8% females) as per the average of three decadal censuses between 1951 and 1971 (Table 1). As a result, the reading rooms fulfilled two primary objectives: the first was to train cadres on the principles of the party and enable them to become able spokespersons for its ideology, who would then engage with the public.

Secondly, Annadurai conceived reading rooms as debating forums and learning spaces. Senior leaders of the party were made responsible for conducting monthly public-speaking workshops at branch offices to help groom the young cadres. Many reading rooms also served as night schools for children and middle-aged non-literates (Thirunavakkarasu, Personal Communication, 27 February 2020).

Over time, the DMK became a party of writers and orators, and writing and public speaking were considered basic qualifications of a quintessential party member, emulating their founder, Annadurai. (Sivasubramanian, 2019: 301) Apart from writing for the consumption of the general public, Annadurai wrote a series of letters primarily meant for his party's cadres, titled *Thambikku Annavin Kadithangal,* which loosely translates to 'letters to brethren'. Recalling Hande's remark, Annadurai himself flooded the local regional sphere, or the Tamil ecumene, with a range of oral and written messages for people's consumption.

The second objective of the reading rooms was to spread the Dravidian-Tamil ethos of social justice, self-respect, and the greatness of Tamil language and the Sangam civilisation to the public who frequented the reading rooms. Often, this took place on a daily basis. The reading rooms housed reading material, pamphlets, newspapers, books, and other publications run by Periyar, Annadurai, Karunanidhi, and other senior DMK leaders. At times, popular sub-regional periodicals, mostly in the Tamil language, were included. A few English dailies, like *The Hindu*, were also kept.

There were no entry barriers, making the social background of the visitors diverse, encompassing all non-Brahmin lower castes and Dalits who lived around the reading room (Thirunavakkarasu, Personal Communication, 27 February 2020). In a personal interview, Tamil scholar Suba Veerapandian[13] (Personal Communication, 5 February 2020) recalls his experience with reading rooms during his school days in the early 1960s. He says they were easier to access than a library, which would have rules or admission procedures. He describes two reading rooms: one, a hundred-square-foot room down the street from his home called Thannermalai Thirunellai Padippakam, which he regarded as a general reading room for newspapers and weeklies. The other, located in the street behind his home, functioned in the car-shed of the house of DMK leader C.T. Chidambaram, who would be elected MLA from the Karaikudi constituency in 1971.

The second reading room housed material on the Dravidian movement, where he was introduced to *Samaneedhi* (Equal Justice), a journal run by M.G. Ramachandran, who would later break away from the DMK to launch the AIADMK. He said that the two reading rooms gave him knowledge about his society and exposure to the world in Tamil, the language he was comfortable in. Veerapandian's remark about Tamil being the principal language of discourse will be discussed in detail in the next chapter on DMK's responses to political developments in Madras State and the subsequent politicisation of Tamils.

Thirunavakkarasu[14] told me about a network of reading rooms in the northern areas of Madras city, frequented by supporters and colleagues of N.V. Natarajan, one of the founders of the DMK. From the late afternoons and early evenings through late at night, the reading rooms became sites of politicisation, knowledge-sharing, information dissemination, and cadre training (Personal Communication, 27 February 2020).

Figure 3[15] shows the density of the reading rooms in 1957 when the DMK contested the Assembly elections and in 1967, when the party won the elections across Madras State.

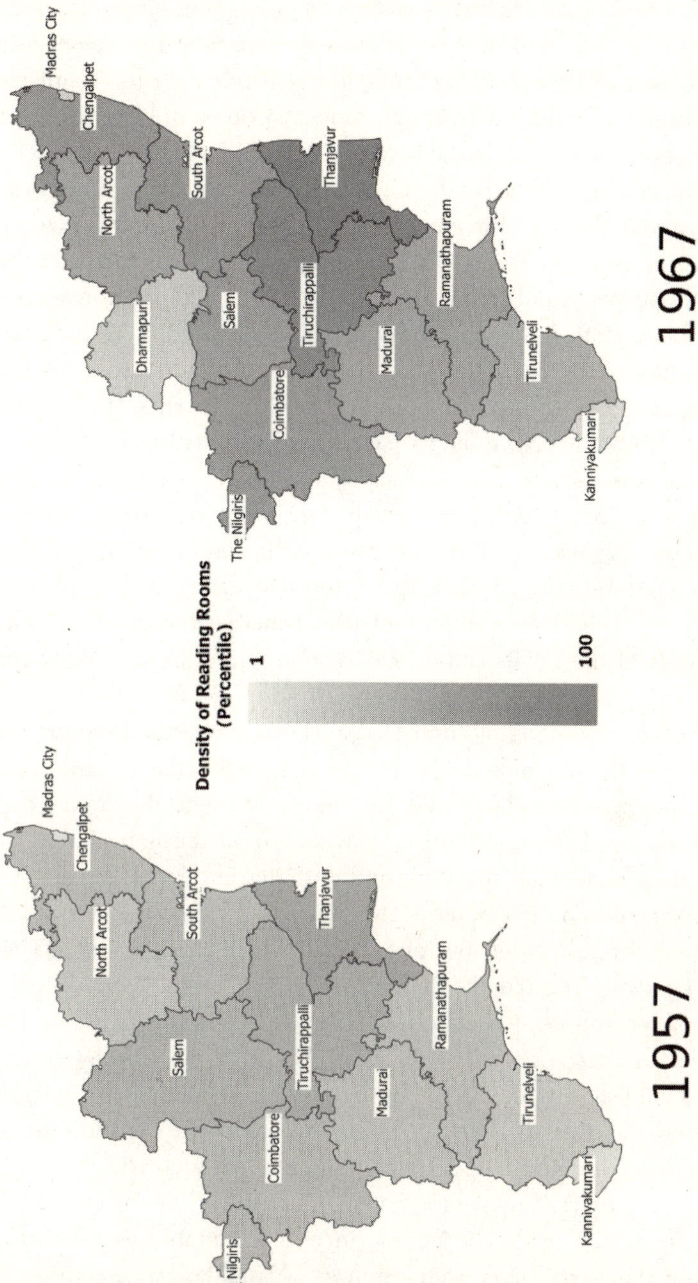

Figure 3: Comparison of the Density of Reading Rooms in 1957 and 1967

The reading rooms had a party member—generally from a non-Brahmin middle or lower or depressed caste who had passed the senior secondary school examination—responsible for regularly reading aloud from newspapers, journals, or pamphlets, in most cases, every day (Thirunavakkarasu, 2019: 315–16).

The reading room run by C.T. Chidambaram exemplifies how they paved the way for the DMK to grow. Establishing reading rooms in the name of the DMK or its members helped expand the party's outreach and create healthy intra-party competition among members. Both the young and old visited the reading rooms, but while older visitors participated in newspaper reading sessions and discussions; the younger visitors, comprising students, studied and did their homework, aided by party members in charge.

The same space that was a business in the daytime, be it a petty shop or a mill or a teashop, became a reading room and homework space, and also served as a night school for local adults. The reputation and popularity of the organisers among parents enhanced over time, and eventually translated into votes. The students of the 1950s and 1960s became voters in the 1960s and 1970s (Virumbi,[16] Personal Communication, 2 March 2020).

At times, the reading rooms helped DMK cadres and supporters engage with the public in personal ways. Viduthalai Virumbi told me that while he and his colleagues taught at night, during the day, they managed the distribution of water to all the households—a task they performed smoothly and without conflict. He said, "We gave tokens and distributed water according to the token system, so that no one was left out or received water twice," (ibid.). That the residents trusted the supporters of the DMK with water, a precious resource also associated with notions of purity, shows the extent of the rapport that those in charge of the reading rooms had established with the public in day-to-day affairs. In Freitag's framework, the activities in public arenas were expanding and shaping a community of people within a larger identity.

Setting up reading rooms was seen as a means of engaging with people, which made the person in charge suitable for elevation within the party or consideration as a candidate in elections. It was also seen as an act that would be appreciated by the DMK leadership at the sub-regional and State levels. Party members who ran reading rooms could negotiate with the local leadership to secure their dues and to ensure against possible favouritism.

Reading rooms spread beyond the formal party organisation as well. They organically expanded across regions, often being set up in salons, cycle-rent shops, and teashops. A class of people, predominantly followers of Annadurai and sometimes Periyar,[17] carried out these activities with great conviction and commitment to the principles of social justice, self-respect, and the promotion of the Tamil language. Their standard qualification was a secondary school certificate, a few of them having also completed a typewriting course. The funds to run reading rooms came from a variety of sources, including the personal income of those in charge, contributions from relatives of party members, government servants, and people working for upper caste and/or wealthy employers. Several school teachers actively promoted Dravidian-Tamil ethos among their students by organising essay writing and elocution competitions centered on these themes.[18]

Thirunavakkarasu (Personal Communication, 27 February 2020) remarked, "They had social justice and DMK in their hearts but they could not openly say it, so they helped in the conduct of reading rooms and thrived as the party's unofficial *saarbu mandrams* (allied groups)." The fact that the reading rooms operated in or alongside salons, cycle-rent shops, and teashops suggests the subaltern sociology of the participants as well as organisers.

The proliferation of reading rooms was neither uniform nor did they adhere to a rigid structure. An archetypal reading room operating outside the formal party office setting would often be found on benches outside a teashop or a salon. Meetings took place periodically, as determined by the group members, with reading material generally including *Dravida Nadu* and *Murasoli*. After the designated reader finished, there would be a discussion on the subject, following by plans for future meetings (Subagunarajan, 2019: 321).

In essence, the *padippakam* or *mandram* in Madras State evolved into any space defined more by its activities and objectives than its physical setting. Recalling a reading room that functioned alongside a salon in Pollachi, a town in western Madras State in the 1960s, Umapathy[19] (Personal Communication, 27 February 2020) noted, "The cartoons in DMK-run newspapers were pasted on the inside of the ceilings, so that they would be visible to the customers when they sat back in their chairs for a shave."

Caste associations, too, set up reading rooms. The Nadar Association-run reading rooms are still functional across Virudhunagar. The connection between the party and caste associations can be traced back to the positive turn of such associations (Rudolph & Rudolph, 1960 and Hardgrave, 1969) and Periyar's work with them (Subagunarajan, 2018) in the late 1920s and early 1930s, which focused on addressing the issues posed by the caste system in Tamil Nadu.

Periyar worked with caste associations leaders through the Self-Respect Movement, advocating for the social and educational uplift of the people belonging to these castes. His continuous engagement with the people in the meetings organised by caste associations created an environment conducive to establish schools, community centres, and libraries across Madras State.[20] The Nadars' involvement with the Self-Respect Movement (Rajadurai, 1992) to rid themselves of the 'un-seeable caste' label is pertinent.

In this context, Thirunavakkarasu (Personal Communication, 27 February 2020) said, "The Self-Respect Movement's public meetings would have the Nadars cook food for the public, and people who opposed it were not allowed to attend the meeting. A section of the Nadar community was, therefore, very loyal to and supportive of the DMK... The other neglected castes like the Vannan (washermen), Pallar (farm labourers), and Ambattan (barbers), too, were loyal to the party due to the progress they achieved, and a sense of equality they enjoyed because of Periyar..."

There was significant development in the material circulated in reading rooms. Following Annadurai's lead, the second-tier leaders of the party took to publishing newspapers, and those who were already publishing expanded their reach. *Murasoli* (Drumbeat) by M. Karunanidhi, *Mandram* (Hall) by V.R. Nedunchezhiyan, *Vidivelli* (Morning Star) by E.V.K. Sampath, *Por Vaal* (Battle Sword) by Sathyavani Muthu, *Thani Arasu* (Separate State) by A.V.P.

Asaithambi, *Ina Mulakkam* (The Cry of a Race) by C.P. Chitrarasu, and *Thendral* (Breeze) by Kannadasan were some of the widely circulated newspapers.

Regional historians estimate that between three hundred and four hundred newspapers and magazines were run by DMK cadres and leaders in the 1950s and 1960s (Thirunavakkarasu, 2019: 316–17). Additionally, if one includes numerous smaller local publications and one-time compilations, their numbers likely reached into the thousands. Publishing was not a one-sided endeavour, as periodicals presenting opposing views were also read and taken seriously. In this context, two events—*Ezhuthuppor* (essay competition) and *Swarppor* (elocution competition), became popular, providing a platform for people with differing opinions to engage in battles of views. These debates were recorded and published in an impartial manner, either as books or issues (ibid.).

It is worth noting that the DMK did not contest the 1951 General Election or the 1952 Legislative Assembly elections as the party felt it was not yet ready. However, DMK cadres supported the Common Weal Party and the Toilers Party in the 1952 elections when these parties agreed to back the DMK's cause, including the demand for a separate land for Dravidians—Dravida Nadu (Barnett, 1976: 78). More significantly, during the 1950s, the DMK took up protests that attracted increasing numbers of people, becoming more organised in the process.

The growing participation and success of these protests cannot be understood without accounting for the steady politicisation facilitated by the reading rooms. Electoral success was reaped to an extent in 1957[21] and to the fullest in 1967. The following Assembly election figures[22] show the correlation between the prevalence of the reading rooms and regions that the DMK alliance contested in and won in 1957, 1962, and 1967. Figure 4 shows the seats where the DMK fielded candidates and won in the 1957 and 1962 elections. It did not contest all seats in these elections. In 1967, the DMK-led alliance put up candidates for all constituencies across Madras State. Figure 5 shows the wins secured by the DMK alliance and the Congress party. Figures 4 and 5 also show the positive

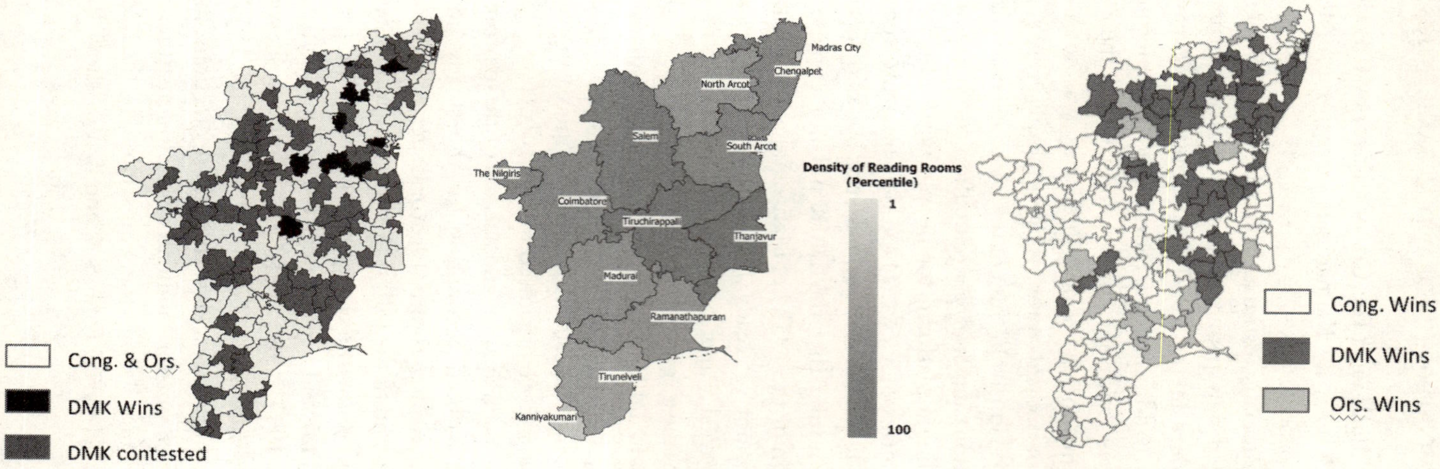

Figure 4: Correlation between the Electoral Participation of DMK in 1957 (L) and 1962 (R) Assembly Elections and the Density of Reading Rooms in 1957 (M)

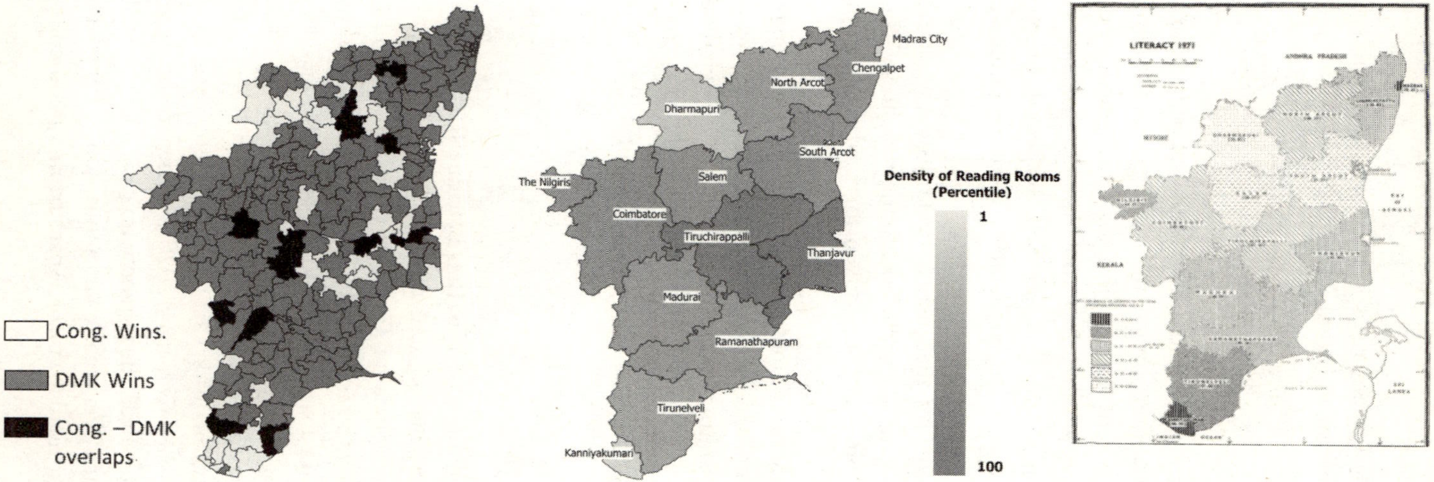

Figure 5: L–M: Correlation between the Electoral Success of the DMK Alliance and the Spread of Reading Rooms in 1967 M–R: Positive correlation between the density of reading rooms[23] *and district-wise literacy rates in Tamil Nadu*[24]

correlation among literacy rates in the State, the proliferation of reading rooms, and the electoral success of the DMK.

Virudhunagar and its Reading Rooms

After my initial research on the functioning of *padippakams* across Madras State, it was interesting to unpack the role of reading rooms in Virudhunagar, where Kamaraj lost the 1967 Assembly election. Broadly, fieldwork revealed the strong influence of the principles of the Justice Party and Periyar's Self-Respect Movement like socio-economic equity, social justice, women's empowerment, and so on.

The work done by the Justice Party leaders and the self-respecters, who were mostly non-Brahmin elites—Nadars in the case of Virudhunagar—was taken forward by Annadurai and the DMK.

Annadurai crafted a mass movement by involving people from all castes and classes (Swamy, 1996:159–74), which then became a strong political movement. This section briefly narrates my experiences from the field, talking mostly to octogenarians and nonagenarians, and visiting the reading rooms that are still functional in Virudhunagar.

A Library from 1918

The hundred-year-old Poraiyar Rao Bahadur Rathinasamy Nadar Memorial Library, inaugurated on 18 January 1918, belongs to the Hindu Nadar Association, and is currently managed by a girls' school, also run by the association. The library is flanked by a shop on either side and runs on the rent they generate, thereby making it a self-sustaining entity. The library is not a reading room in the DMK's framework of a political arena.

Unfortunately, the library had not been functional for close to two months (January–February 2020), owing to the death of the then librarian. However, the person who gave me the details of the library, Kandasamy (Personal Communication, 6 February 2020), happened to be a regular visitor. Apart from a good collection of books, the library houses all the regular newspapers and magazines. The library did not have any entry barriers and the reasons for footfall were similar to that of the Ariviyal Mandram—a similar library which was a reading room in the DMK's framework of a political arena that I will discuss next—the availability of all magazines and newspapers in one place, free of cost. Older newspapers, too, are made available for reference.

The library is a landmark in the area. However, when questioned about the practice of reading out loud—a practice prevalent in the Dravidian reading rooms—Kandasamy said, "That practice takes place in Ariviyal Mandram and not here," hinting at the pro-Congress party nature of the library[25] as against the anti-Congress tilt of Ariviyal Mandram.

Ariviyal Mandram – A Caste Association-run Reading Room

The most popular and functional reading room in the town is the Ariviyal Mandram (science hall). It is both a library and a reading room and was opened to the public on 8 November 1953. V.P. Selvarajan (Personal Communication, 6 February 2020), in-charge of the reading room, said the premises, built in 1950, was previously called the Nadar Paripalana Sabha. In the 1950s and 1960s, the reading rooms witnessed a host of newspaper-reading sessions, discussions, public-speaking workshops, and debates.

Ariviyal Mandram was an example of the social pluralism concept at work. Talking about the current state of the reading room, Selvarajan said that the reading room was refurbished on the eve of its golden jubilee in 2000. It can accommodate sixty people. The hall has four long tables stacked together in the middle with eight chairs per table. The tables can accommodate two additional chairs each, if needed, and there are benches along the walls for extra seating. Towards the end of the hall there are locked bookshelves.[26]

Pictures of Periyar, Annadurai, and several affluent people from the community hang on the walls. Drinking water is kept in pots. The reading room is open seven hours a day, between 9 am and 1 pm before lunch, and then between 3.30 pm and 6.30 pm. The land currently belongs to the Hindu Nadars' Devasthanam, and is managed remotely by an affluent family. Visitors need to sign their names in a register to access the reading room and its facilities.

The practice of issuing books on rent has been temporarily stopped owing to borrowers not returning the books. Selvarajan said around thirty people, who are mostly old and retired, visit the reading room every day. Younger people mostly spend their time before TVs or on mobile phones, and they have access to all kinds of information a lot more easily, he said. However, he acknowledged that a few students and younger people, too, came to the reading room.

Since funds are available, the reading room has almost all leading newspapers like *Dina Thanthi*, *Dinamalar*, *Dinakaran*, *Dinamani*, *The Hindu* (English), *Viduthalai* (the DK's newspaper), *Murasoli* (the DMK's newspaper) and *Janashakti* (the Communist Party of India's newspaper), and many Tamil magazines such as *Kumudham*, *Anandha Vikatan*, etc. Selvarajan said he had heard stories about the reading room being utilised for community activities like debating contests, to read out news to people sitting on the benches and, at times, outside the hall.

A daily visitor, Dharmarajar (Personal Communication, 6 February 2020), who was born in 1938, told me that he had been visiting the reading room for ten years, and reads all the Tamil newspapers and magazines available, except the ones run by political parties. When asked which party he prefers, he smiled and showed on his palm the election symbol of the Congress.[27] He told me he has always been a Congress supporter. Asked why he came to the reading room, he responded, "Everything is available here, I cannot possibly buy all magazines and papers, so I come here to read...It is close to my house too..."

Another daily visitor, Vairamuthu, born in 1941 had been using the reading room for more than ten years for similar reasons. But along with the regular newspapers and magazines, Vairamuthu (Personal Communication, 6 February 2020) read *Murasoli* every day. I asked, "Are you in the party (DMK)?" and he said, "No." When I asked why he read *Murasoli* every day, he said he was inspired by the DMK's *Sudar Manaadus*[28] (flame meetings) of the late 1950s and 1960s, and had been reading *Murasoli* ever since. He described his feeling for the party as *anbu,* or affection.

The reading room has shed its overt political purpose, and is now a space that accommodates people of all age groups and varying degrees of inclination and preference for political parties. I got the opportunity to quickly review the titles and found close to two hundred fifty books on diverse topics such as history, culture, politics, Western political thought, and so on. I learnt that the students who visited the reading room referred to these books. On my way out, I saw a photograph of Kamaraj with V.V. Ramasamy Nadar, who had played a key role in the setting up of reading rooms in Virudhunagar.

A Paper Mart-cum-DMK Town Office[29]

The search for the DMK's town office where I was to meet my respondent, S.R.S. Dhanabalan, the party's town secretary, led me to a small shop that deals in old newspapers and magazines. The shop is in a market area, and belongs to the temple trust of the Sri Parasakthi Mariamman[30] temple, run by the Virudhunagar Hindu Nadars' Devasthanam. The shop has been functional since at least the 1950s.

Studying why and how Hindu Nadars supported the DMK provides valuable insight into the diverse set of aspirations that the party was able to accommodate. The Nadars, historically regarded as an 'un-seeable' caste group, came under the influence of various belief systems since the early nineteenth century—Christianity, promoted by the London Missionary Society, the Ayyavazhi[31] sect, the Saivism of the early Dravidianists, and the deities of Tamil folklore.

A section of the Nadars embraced the worship of folk deities like Mariamman, establishing temples in the southern regions. Given the distinctiveness in the practices—which often contrasted with Vedic traditions and the use of Sanskrit—the temples dedicated to Mariamman and other Tamil folk deities served as appealing alternatives for believers within Tamil civil societies.

The DMK, which promoted the idea of 'One Community, One God', effectively integrated worshippers of Tamil-folklore deities into its fold. This inclusivity was strategic, as it helped the party counter the hierarchical Veda-based Hinduism while strengthening the distinction between Dravidian/Tamil civil society and Aryan/Brahmin civil society.

By the time Dhanabalan arrived, signed forms brought by his colleagues had caught my attention. The party was holding a signature drive seeking people's support against the Citizenship (Amendment) Act, 2019 and any move towards a country-wide National Register of Citizens. Dhanabalan is a second generation DMK politician, his father and elder brother are party members. His elder brother, late S.R.S. Rajakani, was known for his contribution to party-building activities such as organising public meetings with party leaders and non-party personalities, the upkeep of functional DMK-run reading rooms, organising periodic membership drives, etc., and was personally appreciated by 'Kalaignar' M. Karunanidhi, the late DMK leader and former Chief Minister of Tamil Nadu, in 2009.

After hearing a brief on my research and a question on *padippakams*, he said there were many of them. Pointing to the market area, he said that the place was called Deshabandhu Maidanam, where Sankaralinganar[32] undertook his fast unto death. "There was a strong anti-Congress sentiment among a section of people," he said.[33] On reading rooms, Dhanabalan recalled his father's weekly exercise of making children sit on tarpaulin or jute sacks and listen to speakers from the DMK, or holding newspaper- or journal-reading sessions. "We were taught that we are no less than anyone else," he said.

"V.V.R. Ayya[34] asked us to wear shirts and *chappals*, and the women to be strong and to not depend on a man. He asked us to study and prosper," Dhanabalan recalled his father often telling him and others. "Those words still hold relevance," he said, and I was reminded of the wedding vows at the self-respect wedding I attended in January 2020, where education, self-respect, and women's empowerment were underlined. He also said that every *theruvu*[35] had at least one reading room, run either by the DMK or by private individuals or caste organisations.

Private reading rooms to promote education, established in pre-independence times by caste organisations and private individuals, coincided with the expansion of the Justice Party and Self-Respect Movement. Those formed around the time of the emergence of the DMK were run by party members, supporters, and Justice Party leaders. Once the DMK was established, reading rooms spread to every district, proliferating with the party's rise. While most of the privately-run reading rooms have been demolished, due to new building regulations or the absence of caretakers or for other reasons, a few still function.

Only one party-run reading room now exists in Virudhunagar town. Called the Udhaya Suriyan[36] Mandram (Rising Sun Hall), it was built in 1962 by DMK workers with their own savings and without employing construction workers. "Go see the reading room. Do not miss it," Dhanabalan told me.

A DMK-run Reading Room and One Man of the Many Who Built It

Seeni Nadar is a ninety-three-year-old DMK partyman. When young, he backed the Justice Party and referred to himself as a green-box supporter.[37] The Justice Party lost the 1937 provincial elections, renamed itself the DK, and did not contest the 1946 provincial elections. Seeni, fascinated by Annadurai, joined the DMK three years later in 1949. From his memories of the 1950s and 1960s, he clearly recalled one occasion when he defended a flagpost[38] raised to commemorate a fellow partyman who belonged to the Mukkulathor[39] community.

Seeni could recall only the partyman's second name, Thevar. "So what if he is a Thevar?" he told me, "He worked for the party. And so what if the government says 'bring down all the flag posts?' I resisted and guarded it," he said, speaking passionately. When asked his views about Kamaraj, he reiterated that he was a green-box supporter, which meant the Justice Party. I could also trace Seeni's anti-Congress feelings, for he considered it a party of the Brahminical elite who oppressed the lower castes. He was among the many DMK workers who built the Udhaya Suriyan Mandram reading room.

"A group of us constructed one [reading room] back in the day and we did not believe in any entry restrictions—we were open to all," he said. At the end of a short walk was a simple, single-room structure opposite a temple. Built in 1962, it is said to have buzzed with activity at the time—people reading newspapers, discussing party affairs, and hosting occasional competitions and training sessions on public speaking. The old structure was revamped twenty-five years ago by the DMK's then town secretary. Later, the room was partitioned in two. The current caretaker of the reading room is a tailor whose workshop occupies one half of the room. The other half has a table, a bench, a pot with drinking water, and newspapers.

Seeni was once a regular visitor, though he still visits the reading room occasionally. "There used to be four [news]papers a few years ago; the number has come down to two," he complained. *Murasoli*, the DMK's official paper, and *Dinakaran* are the two papers available now.

Two or three people can sit at the table. "I am trying to get two more papers to the *mandram*. I will use my old-age pension scheme money to buy two more papers, and they should be there by the time you visit again," Seeni said, as I took his leave. This interview gave me first-hand experience of how group activities like erecting and defending flag posts for fellow partymen, building reading rooms and frequenting them, and other such activities, allowed people from different social groups to come together under a wider shared identity (Freitag, 1989: 6).

Sankaralingam,[40] Ward Secretary and Public Speaker

Sankaralingam's first-hand account of the activities of the party at the ground level in the 1950s and 1960s is equally fascinating. He joined the DMK in 1952, and is one of the party's oldest members in Virudhunagar. Sankaralingam was appointed *Medai Pechalar* (public speaker) and *Vatta Seyalaalar* (ward secretary) prior to the 1967 elections. "Anna (Annadurai) spoke, gave a call, and we all joined him," he said.

When asked about Kamaraj, in particular the schools he built and the popularity he achieved, Sankaralingam paused, then said, "Yes, he did good work and helped people study, but...Congress was not our party...The DMK represented common people... Tamils...Anna spoke about people's problems and fought for their emancipation. Kamaraj left us and went to Delhi."

I asked Sankaralingam about *padippakams* and if he went to any, and he said, "Yes," listing a few he visited. A few of them are no longer functional, including the M.S. Periyasamy Padippakam in Paarapatti, two Kalaignar Mandrams (named after Karunanidhi) in Kattyapuram and Kaaraichavadi, and one Congress party *mandram in* Kasaapu Theruvu. Sankaralingam was trained to be a public speaker at these *padippakams* and, in the run-up to the 1967 elections, he participated in elocution competitions on Hindi imposition and the non-availability of food grains.

Asked about the Congress party's reading room, Sankaralingam said that there was a Kamaraj Valibar Sangam (Kamaraj Youth Association) too, and both the reading room and the association worked in tandem to promote Kamaraj and the Congress party[41]. "There was an anti-Congress *padippakam* next to Kamaraj's house...V.V.R. helped us set it up," he said with some glee. I learnt that the *padippakams* were just places that had a *koorai* (thatched roof), and where newspapers and magazines were available. A few people around him were excited to hear our conversation, and mentioned Amudhan, Kalimuthu, and Seenivasan, students who played a momentous role in the 1967 election against Kamaraj.

"I worked shoulder to shoulder with them," he said. On how the funds to run the reading rooms were secured, he said it was their own savings, which they pooled. In addition, party members regularly went to the 'Bazaar Nadars' (merchants or traders) for *vasool* (collection). V.V. Ramasamy and M.S. Periyasamy donated regularly for the reading rooms, he recalled. Interestingly, Sankaralingam's son was able to study and finish his MA using a grant from the 'Bazaar Nadars'.

On the impact this had in households, a local resident in his sixties who was in the room said: "...my father would narrate the discussions of the reading rooms to my mother almost every day.

This led to my mother also going to a Self-Respect Movement-run reading room which had quite a few women coming together. Over time my parents would attend public meetings and speeches together…This led to my mother becoming more assertive and thoughtful in family and financial matters. My parents were in an equal relationship…"

Dravida Nadu, *Murasoli,* and *Nam Naadu* were mainly the papers that were read out loud and discussed in the DMK-run or non-Congress reading rooms, although other papers were also subscribed to. Every *padippakam* and *mandram* had dozens of daily visitors, which led to many more *padippakams* opening up in Virudhunagar town.

How the Dravidian-Tamil Ethos Spread

The Dravidian-Tamil ethos spread gradually, with reading rooms as an important channel to spread its message and to sustain its engagement with people. As the previous chapter explains, it was an inclusive political identity, motivating new membership through an eclectic repertoire of ideas.

The frameworks of 'social pluralism' and 'organisational pluralism' suggested by Narendra Subramanian are useful in analysing why multiple reading rooms could exist, run by diverse stakeholders ranging from former Justice Party members to private individuals to the DMK itself, and others. Indeed, Congress cadres used the same methods to reach out to people (Ryerson, 1988: 128), which fostered an atmosphere of all parties undertaking similar political activities.

As previously discussed, not all reading rooms functioned uniformly, and not all those in charge of them made similar appeals as the DMK's leadership. This lack of uniformity helped the party simultaneously raise a wide range of grievances. Each issue was unique, but it could be subsumed within the broad contours of the Dravidian-Tamil ethos. For instance, in Virudhunagar, socio-economic equity, social justice, and anti-Congressism had greater appeal than some other aspects of the Dravidian-Tamil repertoire. Therefore, the reasons to back the

DMK or even join the party were different in Virudhunagar from those in other regions.

The motivations were equally wide ranging—the party's adherence to rational thought, atheism, social justice, anti-Brahminism, anti-casteism, criticising one's own caste, federalism, belief in a singular God, provincial autonomy, equality, socio-economic progress, women's empowerment, the fight against landlordism, access to temples, primacy of or preference for Tamil language, opposition to the imposition of Hindi and/or Sanskrit, the two-language policy (mother tongue plus English) in schools, social welfare, pro-Justice Party narrative, anti-Congress Party narrative, and so on.

That the Dravidian-Tamil ethos appealed differently to different people diversified the party's support base, and the party knew it, making sure to hold public meetings on each theme it espoused across Madras State. Subramanian calls this process supporter autonomy, which means they had the autonomy to "appropriate party appeals in ways different from the explicit appeals and preferred programmes of party leaders" (Subramanian, 2002: 126).

The rise in public participation in public meetings and protests provides evidence of the impact of reading rooms. In Virudhunagar, anti-Congress sentiments among the Justice Party elites, mostly Nadars, propelled them to provide financial support to the reading rooms. Right from the party's inception, they saw the Congress as a party of Brahmins—recall that the Justice Party was formed as an outcome of the Non-Brahmin Manifesto of 1916. The Justice Party elites also vigorously campaigned seeking non-Brahmin representation in positions of power and improved access to education and employment for these communities.

Hardgrave notes that the shift of a section of Nadars in favour of the Congress party in the late 1930s and 1940s irked the Justice Party Nadars. The growing influence of those who had drifted away over two decades (1969: 37) sparked tensions within the Nadar community, pushing those who backed the Justice Party to vigorously extend help to the DMK. Sankaralingam's frequent visits to the 'Bazaar Nadars' for financial collections were a part of this effort. The Justice Party Nadars entertained frequent requests from the DMK cadres as they were motivated to keep the Congress out of power.

The lasting influence of the Justice Party and the entrenchment of anti-Congress sentiments was observable in my respondents unselfconsciously declaring themselves as 'anti-Congress', 'pro-poor', and 'supporters of social justice'. The Justice Party elites' support for Annadurai when he was still struggling to spread the DMK's ideology helped Annadurai's mission to democratise political participation and give people a voice in politics on a daily basis. All of this served to amplify the Dravidian-Tamil clarion call. Some Justice Party elites sacrificed their own political careers in their effort to intimately and effectively convey the need to support a movement for social justice and socio-economic equity.

A testament to the effectiveness of the reading rooms could also be located in the passage of the Modified Scheme of Elementary Education in 1953 by the Rajaji-led Congress government that sought to make students learn their parents' occupations. It was dubbed as *Kula Kalvi Thittam* (Caste/Hereditary Education Scheme) by the DMK (Anandhi, 2018), a straightforward reference to its promotion of caste-based occupation, and to this date people remember the scheme by that name—which I discuss at length in the next chapter.

The exuberant culture of reading rooms and the activities around them waned over time. Both the DMK and AIADMK governments in the 1970s and 1980s made efforts to formalise the reading room culture through government-run libraries across Tamil Nadu, which I discuss in the last chapter. While the channels of engagement between leaders, cadres and the public have changed with time, both parties still periodically hold workshops (*pacarais*) and debating forums (*pechu mandarm*), in which party members and the general public participate.

Conclusion

This chapter argues that the middle, lower, and depressed caste backgrounds of both those in charge of reading rooms and their visitors help explain the growing electoral strength of the DMK.

The prevalence and spread of the network of reading rooms testified to a committed cadre that constantly politicised people at the grassroots. It also allowed for a continuous flow of information from the leadership to the public through newspapers.

The Dravidian-Tamil identity that the political class built and then spread through reading rooms was a subaltern project, at the level of the idea itself and how it was popularised. This identity sought to flatten the internal conflicts among the marginalised castes and keep the antagonism against the upper castes alive. To ensure this, the Dravidian-Tamil ethos accommodated a multitude of grievances.

Therefore, voting in favour of Dravidian parties was not just a transactional act in return for promises made by the political parties. It was also an expression of commitment to the ideals and the political vision built by and for that same voter. A related question in this context is how the DMK responded to political developments in Madras State.

The next chapter discusses the issues that prevailed at the time in the region, and how the party's leadership conceived them, and spread their ideas through the network of reading rooms and other means. I argue that the DMK chose issues and framed responses, which it then effectively spread among the people, helping it consolidate its political repertoire, ultimately gaining electoral successes.

3

THE DMK'S MANOEUVRES IN MADRAS STATE

POLITICAL OPPORTUNISM REVISITED THROUGH THE PRISM OF THE DRAVIDIAN-TAMIL REPERTOIRE

The 1950s and 1960s were very tumultuous for India. Political activities intensified as a result of how the country was formed in the late 1940s (Stepan, 2005: 258), leaving many specific demands of social groups unfulfilled. In broader social category terms, Faisal Devji (2013: 197) contended that the creation of Pakistan fulfilled the political aspirations of Muslims but quashed the Dalits' and the Dravidians' pursuit of Dalitsthan and Dravidsthan that Ambedkar and Periyar conceived. In other words, Devji argued that while the Dalits and Dravidians could not realise their own objectives, they saw the Muslims' political style as the key to fulfilling their aspirations.

After the Muslim League's 1940 Lahore Resolution, Ambedkar initially supported the creation of Pakistan, as he opposed Hindu majoritarianism and its effects on Muslims in undivided India. Moreover, he believed that the creation of Pakistan would create an opportunity to foreground the plight of the Dalits in India, instead of the Hindu-Muslim dichotomy that had prevailed thus far. However, Pakistan's majoritarian tendencies—favouring majority Muslims against the minorities—had him chastise the

Muslim League. Nor did the Hindu-Muslim divide resolve in India, largely owing to the violence of Partition. Therefore, Dalit aspirations had to be pursued alongside the Hindu-Muslim binary, eventually leading Ambedkar to demand separate electorates, Dalit settlements, and other reforms (ibid., 196–97).

Oliver Godsmark (2018: 4) identifies regional aspirations in places like Travancore, Bhopal, Hyderabad, and Kashmir, where leaders wanted to form their own nations. Even though non-Brahmin movements arose to address specific grievances, the political landscape in Maharashtra, Andhra Pradesh, Goa, and other places evolved into extensions of the larger caste-Hindu-elitist ethos that the Indian Union later upheld. There were two main reasons for this. First, while these movements were non-Brahmin in theory, they were led by the ritually higher-caste groups who did not democratise power but instead wanted to replace the existing elite.

For example, the Samyukta Maharashtra Movement was Maratha[1]-led (Godsmark, 2018: 169) and the Visalandhra Movement was led by communists from the ritually higher castes in Andhra Pradesh. In other words, they didn't represent the full spectrum of subaltern groups and still carried caste-Hindu elitist tendencies. Besides, where the movements were democratised and the lower castes did enter, they did not consolidate into a sustainable political force. Take, for example, the Maharashtrawadi Gomantak Party that gave Goa Dayanand Bandodkar, its first non-Brahmin lower caste chief minister. This happened despite the rise of self-aggrandised Goud Saraswat Brahmins who actively rewrote history to create new genealogies to elevate themselves in the social order (Parobo, 2020: 3). But after the death of Bandodkar, the party faced a leadership crises, weakening its subaltern political offering.

The Dravidian-Tamil assertion was somewhat easier to pursue than the Dalit assertion Ambedkar envisioned, largely because the Dravidian people were more concentrated regionally. While Annadurai supported India's independence from the British, the Dravidian cause really gained momentum through mobilisational politics in the 1950s and 1960s. During this time, Periyar's DK and the DMK both challenged the Indian Union and the Brahminical identity of India. The DMK worked within the scope of the Indian Constitution, whereas the DK pushed the boundaries, even subverting it.

While chapters 1 and 2 discussed the accommodative nature of the Dravidian-Tamil identity and the creation of a counterpublic sphere that the marginalised carved out, this chapter shows the correlation between the agitational politics of the DMK and the gradual subaltern shift within both the movement and the legislature, avoiding majoritarian tendencies.

In his comparison of the political cultures of Uttar Pradesh (Lucknow) and Madras State (Madurai) during the 1962 elections, Joseph Elder (1966: 268) pointed out that the scale and frequency of political activities by the DMK—rallies, public meetings, and discussions on a wide range of issues—were unmatched in contrast to the rather subdued political environment in Uttar Pradesh, where parties like the Congress, the Jana Sangh, the Lohia Socialists, and Praja Socialists showing little distinction between them.

Applying the resource-mobilisation theory to social movements, the Dravidian movement so far checks almost all the requisite boxes: a charismatic leader, organisational base, resources to sustain the movement, and the Dravidian-Tamil identity. To expand its supporter base and mobilise the people around this identity, the DMK had to conduct a series of manoeuvres in the 1950s and 1960s.

A comment from Sitrarasu, an autorickshaw driver and DMK member since 1971, who gave me a tour around Chennai is relevant here. He said that the DMK is essentially a reform movement disguised as a political party, and that it is the most fierce and effective when it is in opposition. When I asked him why, he said that he and his father Arivarasu[2] had fond memories of attending public meetings, participating in protests, and spending evenings at the reading rooms: "DMK means endurance and resilience. We have not been in power as much as the AIADMK but we are nevertheless a cohesive party and we have effectuated maximum change. We are responsible for the political discourse of Tamil Nadu" (28 Jan 2020, Personal Communication). I will discuss and analyse the last point in this chapter and the preceding ones in the concluding chapter.

This chapter takes a closer look at how the DMK managed and responded to key political developments from its inception up until the 1967 election. These developments include the Constitution (First Amendment) Act, 1951 (which solidified the existing system of affirmative action), the Modified Scheme of Elementary Education in 1953, the passage of the States Reorganisation Act in 1956, the Constitution (Sixteenth Amendment) Act of 1963 (also called the Anti-Secession Act), the anti-Hindi protests of 1965, and the government's inability to contain the rising prices of essential commodities, primarily rice, starting in 1965 across Madras State. The DMK's reactions to these events were pivotal in shaping the Dravidian-Tamil identity.

This chapter will explore how the DMK leadership, especially Annadurai, used widely read newspapers to circulate their responses to these events, fostering discussions through the party's network of reading rooms. It demonstrates how the DMK, under Annadurai's leadership, was able to both mobilise people by tapping into identity-based predispositions and highlight the fault lines in the government's political and social structure. The issues they raised were not just about the welfare of subalterns; they also positioned themselves against the hegemonic aspirations of the political and socioeconomic elites.

Dravidian-Tamil Tryst with India's First Constitutional Amendment Act, 1951

The Madras Presidency has a longer and more complex history of affirmative action policies compared to much of the rest of the Indian subcontinent, barring a few Princely states.[3] Irschick (1969:14–19), described the tension between the Brahmin and the non-Brahmin communities in the late nineteenth century, which stemmed from the Brahmins' dominance in government positions.

The 1871 Census revealed a stark contrast: between 1857 and 1871, 815 Brahmins graduated from the Madras University, while only fifteen non-Brahmins earned their degrees (Gopanna,

2008: 115). By the 1901–1911 period, the disparity had increased significantly, with 4,074 Brahmin graduates (Brahmins made up only 3% of the population) compared to 1,635 graduates from other communities—1,035 non-Brahmins; 306 Indian Christians; 69 Mohammedans; 225 European and Eurasian (who were 97% of the population).[4]

Non-Brahmins were not exposed to formal education and lacked English proficiency, which marred their chances of securing government positions. This led to growing discontent, ultimately resulting in the movement against the Brahmins and the drafting of the Non-Brahmin Manifesto in 1916. The Justice Party, after coming to power, passed the first Communal Government Order (GO) in 1921, followed by the second one in 1922, both seeking to collect data on the communal composition of government employees.

While the first order concerned new employees, the second order concerned the then existing employees as well (ibid., 113). The second Communal GO set specific 'quotas' for government recruitment from mid-1921: Brahmins (22%), non-Brahmin Hindus (48%), Indian Christians (10%), Mohammedans (15%), Europeans and Anglo Indians (2%), and others (3%).

To promote inclusion and representation, a staff selection board was announced on 15 August 1922 (Irschick, 1969: 368–78). The GOs were seen as a step towards securing representation in jobs and educational institutions, as well as establishing a proportional representation system. However, due to resistance from the Brahmins, the GOs could not be implemented, diminishing the influence of the Justice Party and its leaders. The Congress Swarajists who were elected to office used Gandhi's disobedience tactics (ibid., 114) to ensure the GOs were never implemented.

The 1926 provincial elections failed to produce a clear winner, leading the governor to appoint Paramasiva Subbarayan as Chief Minister. On 15 December 1928, Subbarayan along with Education and Excise Minister Muthiah Mudaliar, passed a third modified Communal GO (dated 1927) that introduced quotas for communal groups. Out of every twelve positions, five were allotted for non-Brahmin Hindus, two each for Brahmins,

Mohammedans and Anglo Indians and Christians, and one for Adi Dravidars (Scheduled Castes).

A college students' selection committee was also set up to ensure better representation of communal groups in educational institutions. On 21 November 1947, just months after independence, Omanthur P. Ramaswamy Reddiar[5] (Omanthurar) modified the quota system (GO: MS 3437), responding to pressure from the non-Brahmin Congress party members, caste association leaders, and Periyar. Now, out of every fourteen positions, two were allotted for Brahmins, one each for Indian Christians and Mohammedans, two each for Adi Dravidars and Backward non-Brahmins, and six for non-Brahmins.

A section of the Brahmins ridiculed this GO, taunting the Congress, claiming that it was not they who were in charge but "beardless Periyar". They reached out to Gandhi for help (Gopanna, 2008: 116) with reversing the order. The quota system also came under pressure after the Indian Constitution adopted in 1950 ushered in a rights-based framework.

C.R. Srinivasan, an engineering student admitted to Government Engineering College, Guindy, and Champakam Dorairajan, another student, challenged the Communal GO's quota system in the High Court of Madras in the same year. They claimed that it violated the fundamental rights guaranteed under Article 15, which prohibited the state from discrimination on grounds of religion, race, caste, sex or place of birth, and Article 29(2), which specifically deals with a citizen's right to not be denied admission into a state-run educational institution only on grounds of religion, race, caste, or language.

The High Court of Madras struck down the Communal GO in its judgment dated 27 July 1950. Fearing a backlash, the State government moved the Supreme Court,[6] where Alladi Krishnaswamy Iyer argued for Champakam Dorairajan and C.R. Srinivasan. The government proved that Champakam Dorairajan did not have any locus standi[7] in the case and defended the GO under Article 46, the Directive Principles of State Policy. On 9 April 1951, a seven-judge bench of the Supreme Court upheld the High Court order that quashed the GO (Sitapati, 2016: 753).

As soon as the High Court order was passed, Dravidian collectives and caste association leaders embraced their agitational spirit. Annadurai said that the High Court's ruling would undo three decades of hard work by numerous stakeholders towards achieving social justice. Already, over 1950 and 1951, he had written a series of articles in his Tamil weekly, *Dravida Nadu* (compiled in 1953 as *Pon Vilangu,* 'Golden Handcuffs'). He now wrote creative and persuasive articles appealing to Kamaraj, Kumaraswamy, Bhaktavatsalam, Omanthurar, and other senior Congress leaders. He compelled them to respond to the situation. "Are you going to fight or are you going to run away?" (Annadurai, 1953 in Gopanna, 2008: 117) was his question, and it resonated with the people.

On 14 August 1950, school and college students staged a massive protest across Madras State. In December 1950, Periyar organised a large public conference on the Communal GO being struck down in Trichy. It was co-hosted by caste associations and leaders like Muthiah Mudaliar, Rathnasamy, and S.S. Ramasamy Padayatchi participated in it. The massive conference pushed for amending the constitution and bringing in a proportional representation framework. A section of the non-Brahmin Congress party, made up of leaders like K.T. Kosalram and Kakkan supported the cause as well, persuading the Congress Legislative Party to bring back the Communal GO.

The DK and caste associations tried to forge an alliance of backward class leaders across States to appeal to the Prime Minister and the President through letters. Sustained protests by numerous groups in Madras State persuaded then Prime Minister Jawaharlal Nehru to reach out to Kamaraj. On his advice, Nehru moved to amend Articles 15 and 29 of the Constitution to allow quotas for socially and educationally backward classes, Scheduled Castes, and Scheduled Tribes. States had the right to earmark quotas for the aforesaid communities. The First Constitutional Amendment Act came into force on 18 June 1951 after it was passed in Parliament on 2 June 1951.

The First Constitutional Amendment steered an effective middle course between the court-ordered repeal of the Communal GO and Periyar's agitation for proportional representation.

Periyar, however, was unrelenting in his advocacy of proportional representation, while Annadurai integrated the contents of the First Amendment into the Dravidian-Tamil repertoire. In an article published in *Dravida Nadu* on 24 June 1951, he wrote that the new system of reservations was an outcome of support of non-Brahmins across parties in Madras and across the country. We created a wave, he observed, which attracted people irrespective of party affiliations.

The article's appreciation for Congress leaders (apart from other collectives) who supported the agitation drove a wedge within the Congress. Those who supported and opposed the reservations were now firmly divided. Thanks to the pro-Dravidian newspapers, the discourse was abuzz with Annnadurai's narrative. Pro-Congress newspapers like *Dhinasari* and *Kandeepan*, too, published articles supporting reservations that conveyed an anti-Brahmin sentiment (Gopanna, 2008: 120).

The Story of the 1951–52 State Assembly Election

Despite Chief Minister P.S. Kumaraswamy Raja's GO reserving 25% seats for Other Backward Classes and 16% seats for Scheduled Castes in 1951, the Congress party could not secure a clear victory in the 1951–1952 State Assembly polls. Despite not participating in the elections, the DK and the DMK emerged as popular collectives among the people. They became key influencers behind the success of a considerable number of candidates in the elections, which were fought against the ruling Congress.

This spoke to an evident aspect of their politics: they were ready for the long haul in their struggle to create a more resilient society, and eventually, a more stable power structure. Even before the first elections held after independence, the Justice Party had seen its fair share of electoral failures in provincial elections. However, the struggle was always kept alive, with the knowledge that politics was a means to alter social relations. There was also a recognition that elections could transform society, but only if the masses were considerably politicised and that meant having a strong grassroots presence.

Around two years after its formation, the DMK decided not to contest in the State Assembly elections due to it lacking a committed cadre base and a weak party organisation. The DMK supported non-Brahmin caste parties like the Tamil Nadu Toiler's Party (TTP), Commonweal Party, and independents, eventually playing a key role in the victory of forty candidates.[8] The Commonweal Party (four candidates were supported by DMK) and the TTP (twelve candidates supported by DMK) won six and nineteen seats, respectively. Five independent candidates belonging to the Kongu Vellala Gounder community also won thanks to DMK support.

Notably, in the 1952 elections in Madras State, Periyar supported the formation of the United Democratic Front government led by the Left parties, which were the primary opposition outfits at the time, rather than Rajaji's Congress coalition. Selig Harrison (1960: 183) demonstrated that the communist candidates who won in the Tamil-speaking region did so largely because of the Dravidian movement and the DK. Out of the fifty fielded, sixteen Communist Party candidates actively backed[9] by the DK won twice the percentage of vote share per constituency (37%) compared to the other thirty-four candidates (18.4%). The communists won fifteen seats, of which thirteen were supported by the DK. In November 1951, Periyar called the alliance of the DK with the communists a partnership of convenience to defeat the Congress Party.[10]

Shortly thereafter, on 14 December 1952, when asked about having supported the communists in the context of his animosity towards the DMK, Periyar categorically refuted the idea. He said, "...the Communists have their office at a foreign place, Bombay or Delhi...and they are just as interested in exploiting our country as any of the other foreign-controlled parties. Besides, most of the communist leaders are Brahmans. Ramamurthi is a *pucca* (grade A) Brahman. The editors of *Janashakti* (Tamil Communist Party weekly) are Brahmans. Wherever a Brahman goes, into the Communist Party or anywhere else, he wants to support caste distinctions" (ibid., 186).

As I argue elsewhere (Karthik & Vasanthakumar, 2022: 118) Periyar's consistent criticism of the Indian communists was akin to that of Ambedkar, which is that Indian communism was indifferent to caste inequalities, largely due to upper caste men occupying leadership positions in Indian communist parties. The result of the 1952 elections legitimised the electoral relevance of DMK and DK.

As mentioned in Chapter 1, going by administrative categories, the population composition of the Tamil speaking regions of the Madras State was: upper castes 2.79%, Scheduled Castes 20.01%, Scheduled Tribes 1.1%, and Other Backward Classes 76.1%. However, a few caste groups had a higher social standing than others. In this context, after studying elections in the State across six decades and the classifications by sociologists and political scientists, Andrew Wyatt and I (Karthik & Wyatt, 2025: x) categorised Brahmins, Reddiars, and some Chettiyar and Vellalar caste groups as upper caste in Tamil Nadu. Though small in number, they have enjoyed high social standing and high economic status. The intermediate castes include Pillais, Rajus, Udayars, Kongu Vellala Gounders, and Naidus.

It's important to recognise that while the Other Backward Classes list is meant to reflect the administrative recognition of socially disadvantaged groups, it doesn't always capture the full complexity of their social status. A good example of this is the Kongu Vellala Gounders. Though many see them as an intermediate caste group, they are officially classified as backward. They were originally considered an upper caste but were moved to the backward classes list in the 1970s following a demand from the community. In 2008, some Kongu Vellala Gounders demanded inclusion in the list of Most Backward Classes[11] after Muslims and Christians were granted sub-category quotas. For the purposes of this book, I count the Kongu Vellala Gounders as a backward community. While no single caste dominates numerically across the State, castes like the Gounders, Mukkulathors and Vanniyars tend to dominate electorally in certain constituencies. These three castes also make up the largest portion of the Other Backward Classes—29% numerically—while the Nadars make up 7.5%, coming in right after the three.

In terms of political preferences, the upper castes had a 17.3% share in the seats, of which 5.23% were Brahmins and

12% non-Brahmins. More than half of the upper castes were in the Congress party, followed by 13.1% share for intermediate castes. The Other Backward Classes secured a larger 39.8% share of seats, but still significantly lower than their share in the population. Of this, the share of Muslims and Christians was low, although a section of Nadar Christians is counted as Nadar and not Christian.

The Kongu Vellala Gounder-Mukkulathor-Vanniyar combine had a 31.4% seat share in the legislature with all other backward communities left with an 8.4% share. The Vanniyars had a larger share of 14.7% seats in the legislature. That said, the 1952 election outcome set in motion the process of shifting the Madras State legislature towards a more subaltern structure (Refer to Tables 2 and 3).

Table 2: Caste Composition of MLAs – 1952 State Assembly Elections

Caste/Category	Relative Shares	Supported by DMK
Upper Caste	17.3%	2.6%
Intermediate Caste	13.1%	1.6%
Other Backward Classes	39.8%	11.5%
Kongu Vellala Gounder	8.4%	2.6%
Mukkulathor	8.4%	0.0%
Vanniyar	14.7%	8.9%
OBC Other	8.4%	0.0%
Scheduled Caste	20.4%	3.7%
Christian	0.5%	0.0%
Muslim	1.0%	0.0%
Unidentified	7.9%	1.6%
Total	100.0%	20.9%

Table 3: Partywise Caste Breakdown of MLAs – 1952 State Assembly Elections

Party[12]	UC	IC	OBC	SC	Christian	Muslim	Unidentified	Total
CPI	2.1%	0.0%	2.1%	2.1%	0.0%	0.0%	1.0%	7.3%
CWP	0.0%	0.0%	3.1%	0.0%	0.0%	0.0%	0.0%	3.1%
FBL(MG)	0.0%	0.0%	1.0%	0.5%	0.0%	0.0%	0.0%	1.6%
INC	9.4%	8.9%	14.7%	11.5%	0.5%	1.0%	4.7%	50.8%
IND	3.7%	2.1%	11.5%	2.1%	0.0%	0.0%	1.6%	20.9%
JUSP	0.5%	0.0%	0.0%	0.0%	0.0%	0.0%	0.0%	0.5%
KMPP	1.6%	1.0%	0.5%	0.5%	0.0%	0.0%	0.0%	3.7%
SCF	0.0%	0.0%	0.0%	0.5%	0.0%	0.0%	0.0%	0.5%
SP	0.0%	1.0%	0.0%	0.0%	0.0%	0.0%	0.5%	1.6%
TTP	0.0%	0.0%	6.8%	3.1%	0.0%	0.0%	0.0%	9.9%
Total	17.3%	13.1%	39.8%	20.4%	0.5%	1.0%	7.9%	100.0%

Source for tables 2, 3: Fieldwork – Vignesh Rajahmani

Modified Scheme of Elementary Education; the Infamous Kula Kalvi Thittam: Caste in the Name of Vocation?

At the heart of the Dravidian Movement were two key ideas: dignity and socioeconomic mobility for the marginalised, with education being central to the vision. At the time, the school enrolment ratio in Madras State was below 50%, and of those, only 40% (which is less than 20% of the total population) could finish five years of schooling. In this context, the Modified Scheme of Elementary Education (MSEE) was introduced by then Chief Minister Rajaji in 1953, aiming to improve education in the State. However, this scheme made him highly controversial and unpopular among the Tamils, a sentiment that lingers even today.

The failure of the scheme—and its unpopularity—reflects the shifting political sensibilities in Madras State. So, what led Rajaji to introduce it? This is a crucial question, and Rajmohan Gandhi, his biographer, sheds light on it.

As a child, Rajaji didn't like the six-hour school day, spilt into two shifts with a lunch break in between—it felt like too much effort. In fact, as a young man in the 1900s, he was critical of primary school teachers, regarding them as "angry and ill-educated" men who stifled children's curiosity (Gandhi, 1984: 245). Gandhi also notes Rajaji's fascination with the artisanal communities in rural India. His educational vision had some similarities to the Wardha Scheme of Education of 1937, championed by Mahatma Gandhi, as both shared a suspicion of standardised education.[13]

Rajaji tried several times, both as Chief Minister of Madras Presidency in late 1930s and as the Governor General of India in the late 1940s, to promote school education that revolved around vocations and crafts. As Governor General, he praised the village system, even linking its effectiveness to the caste system. He saw families engaged in caste-based education as 'trade schools' with children as apprentices of their parents (ibid., 245).

The MSEE scheme aimed to overhaul school hours in around 32,000 schools across Madras State. It reduced school hours from five to three hours in a single shift, while the remaining hours were dedicated to an out-of-class programme where students were expected to learn a trade or occupation specific to their family or village, tying into and supporting the village polytechnic. Government data showed that fewer than 11,000 out of the 32,000 schools actually needed help finding craftsmen to teach these skills, while the rest had occupational families who could manage the out-of-class activities (ibid., 246) on their own.

Essentially, the scheme tried to double the enrolment ratio (and subsequently, the literacy rate) without incurring any costs or expenditure. It was launched without the approval of the legislative assembly, but it did get support from leaders like Zakir Husain. However, the public consciousness in Madras State was in transition. The Dravidian-Tamil movement was on the rise, and there was growing emphasis on primary education in the mother tongue and English, as well as technical education for first-generation learners, as key to empower the marginalised communities. This vision clashed with the MSEE, and both the DK and DMK staged numerous protests, labelling the scheme as *Kula Kavi Thittam* (Caste/Hereditary-based Education Scheme)—a term that sticks to Rajaji even today.

The protests saw support from social reform groups, civil society organisations, and other collectives like the South Indian Teachers' Union, the Federation of Madras State Panchayat Union, the Federation of Depressed Classes, and the Tamil Nadu Toilers' Party.

The DK's agitation, led by Periyar, was rooted in strong anti-Brahmin sentiments. Periyar framed it as a conflict between Aryans and Dravidians, seeing the scheme as a barrier preventing non-Brahmins from accessing modern education. He criticised the DMK for not sticking firmly to the principles behind their protests and instead praised the Congress leaders who opposed the scheme, calling them "Congress-Dravidians". While Annadurai had already driven a wedge into the Congress party over the First Constitutional Amendment, Periyar took the division further. The DMK's focus, however, was less on anti-Brahmin rhetoric and more on the socioeconomic empowerment of the marginalised communities.

The protests against the MSEE scheme became part of a broad wave of unrest known as the *Mummunai Porattam*, or the

Three-Cornered Protests, which began on 15 July 1953. The anti-MSEE protests were led by E.V.K. Sampath,[14] who staged a picket in front of Rajaji's house. The second protest involved rail blockades, sparked by Nehru's "childish nonsense" remark about the people of Madras State, who had been frequently defacing name boards (mostly at railway stations) that featured Hindi [Devanagari] text.[15] The third protest, led by Karunanidhi, also on 15 July, was directed against the renaming of Kallakudi, a town in Trichy district, to Dalmiapuram after the business magnate Ramakrishna Dalmia.[16]

The three-cornered protests brought Madras State to a standstill despite numerous arrests, including those of DMK leaders. The simultaneous agitations and the backlash the DMK faced struck a chord with people across different caste groups. The DMK's moderated anti-Brahmin stance did not seem to hurt the support for it. For instance, Annadurai's argument in *Dravida Nadu* on 30 August 1953 is worth noting. He pointed out that if Brahmins could leave their caste occupations and enter modern education to secure government jobs, why were lower castes being denied the same opportunity?

Modern education, Annadurai wrote, allowed the poor and marginalised to succeed and improve their lives, which the MSEE scheme was trying to prevent. Essentially, he was reiterating the argument he had made two years ago in support of the reservation system. As Shanmugasundaram Anandhi (2018) pointed out, Annadurai managed to rally support not just from first-generation graduates from non-Brahmin communities but from Brahmin youth as well.

At the time, anything Rajaji said seemed to backfire, no matter what his intentions were. While Periyar framed it as a battle between Dravidians and Aryans, Rajaji described it as a conflict between *Asuras* (Demons) and *Devas* (Gods). This was a distasteful comparison, both metaphorically and substantively. A section of the Dravidians worshipped *Asuras* from Indian epics (Jaffrelot, 2008: 26) such as Raavana and Naragasooran—whose deaths are actually celebrated in North India as Dusshera and Diwali, respectively (Arivazhagan, Personal Communication, 3 March 2020).

Much like Periyar, Rajaji was also opposed to rote learning, and he expressed a desire for upper-caste students to work alongside artisans in their workshops. But the problem was that segregated neighbourhoods made such interactions impossible without government intervention, which the MSEE scheme failed to address. When he praised the washermen in Madras city, he invoked *kuladharmam* (the duty of a caste or community to society), which is a core concept of the caste system. Rajaji's comments and responses during this period only hurt his reputation (Gandhi, 1984: 248). Eventually, it wasn't his lack of knowledge but his stubbornness in pushing forward with the scheme that led to his downfall, costing him both his reputation and the political position he had been so proud of just about a year earlier.

Dissent within the Congress party started to show in more obvious ways. The creation of Andhra State, shortly after the MSEE scheme was launched, weakened Rajaji's support base. The scheme was put on hold in the legislature and sent to a committee for review. Even before that, in May 1953, Rajaji was aware of Kamaraj's moves against him.[17] In his diary on 4 May, he wrote, 'It happens [that] I am reading Julius Caesar...Kamaraj is stabbing Caesar, I fear, just the same way. God forgive him' (ibid., 248). At that time, Kamaraj couldn't follow through fully because Nehru was still firmly backing Rajaji. But the first signs of intra-party opposition came when Varadarajulu Naidu made a play for the Chief Minister's post, prompting a swift rebuke from Nehru.

Gandhi suggests that if Rajaji had backed down and called off the scheme, he could have quelled both the intra-party opposition and the protests from Periyar and the DMK. But Rajaji did not yield. The reason behind Varadarajulu Naidu's move is unclear, especially since, in 1954, he would go on to propose Kamaraj for the Chief Minister's position when the political climate was more favourable. One could argue that Kamaraj had a hand in Naidu's move—an astute move that allowed Kamaraj to stir the pot in Madras State without risking his own position in Delhi or damaging his relationship with Nehru.

As the time for Rajaji's exit from office approached, the Congress leadership urged him to abadon the scheme. Omanthurar, for example, pointed out that the growing influence of the DK (who wore black shirts) was seriously damaging the party's reputation among the public. But, as expected, Rajaji did not back down. His confidant, C. Subramaniam, who was the minister in charge, presented data showing increasing school attendance and argued for the continuation of the scheme. On 24 March 1954, the MLAs convened a meeting. Rajaji, who was suffering from bronchial pneumonia, offered to step down for health reasons—but only on two conditions: that the scheme be kept in place, and that Subramaniam be made the Chief Minister (ibid., 251).

Kamaraj, ever the strategist, sidestepped Rajaji's offer by asking him to stay on and repeating Omanthurar's advice to give up the scheme. When Rajaji remained firm about stepping down, Kamaraj agreed not to scrap the scheme immediately. Kamaraj then swept the intra-party elections against Subramaniam but kept Subramaniam in his Cabinet, only to drop the MSEE scheme in May 1954. Rajaji finally stepped down on 13 April 1954, and this time, Nehru didn't intervene.

The final scene of the iconic movie *Seven Samurai* directed by Akira Kurosawa, released in 1954, shows peasants returning to their fields after a bloody battle between samurai and bandits. Interestingly, the peasants aren't shown as either revering the samurai or hating the bandits—they are portrayed as floating somewhere in between. Kurosawa seems to be making a central point: it's the common people, not the heroes and villains, who are at the centre of the plot. Similarly, the MSEE scheme episode saw the DK pushing its Aryan (Brahmin) versus Dravidian (non-Brahmin) narrative, while the DMK focused on socioeconomic empowerment and dignity for the marginalised.

The Congress party, under Kamaraj's leadership, reorganised itself with a clear non-Brahmin, and even anti-Brahmin stance. This shift was evident when they gave election tickets to former DK members in the 1957 elections, a point I discuss in later sections. The public discourse in Madras State was coalescing around the ideas of dignity, social justice, and socioeconomic empowerment of Tamils—core principles of the Dravidian-Tamil identity. Gandhi (1984: 252) summed it up by writing, "Once more his Tamil country had rejected CR (Rajaji)." But I would argue that Rajaji's rejection, his return to prominence within a decade, and Kamaraj's eventual defeat demonstrate that it is the power of ideas—and people's alignment with them—that prevails over any leader's personal charisma—which is an important element, nevertheless.

State Reorganisation 1956: One Step Back and Two Steps Forward

The rejection of language as the primary basis for dividing States, as suggested by the Linguistic Provinces Commission[18] in 1948 (chaired by S.K. Dhar and established by President Rajendra Prasad) was also supported by the JVP Committee (comprising Nehru, Vallabhbhai Patel, and Pattabhi Sitaramayya), set up shortly after the Dhar Commission submitted its report. However, the death of Potti Sreeramulu in 1952, followed by the creation of Andhra State as a breakaway region from Madras State with Kurnool as its capital in September 1953, rekindled the debate on State reorganisation.

This led Nehru to form the States Reorganisation Commission (SRC) in December 1953. The SRC, chaired by Fazal Ali with H.N. Kunzru and K.M. Panikkar as its members, began collecting feedback from various parties and submitted its findings in September 1955. The States Reorganisation Act came into force on 1 November 1956. I'll break down the events of this period through four key interventions—from the communists, Periyar, Rajaji, and the DMK—to highlight the political agility and strategic flexibility of the DMK.

The Communist Party of India backed the reorganisation of States along linguistic lines, but with the condition that there was geographic congruity (Arunan, 2008: 171). More importantly, the communists in Andhra as well as then Hyderabad backed the Visalandhra (Greater Andhra) movement, which wanted to unite Telugu-speaking regions from the Hyderabad State with Andhra State. The popularity of communists in the Telangana region was due their noteworthy role in backing the peasant agitations. Rajaji, who lost his popular support and party backing due to the formation of Andhra State was wary of the rise of communists.[19] He, therefore, supported the Dakshina Pradesh idea, which sought to merge Travancore-Cochin with Madras State.

Arunan (2008: 174) claims that Rajaji's version of Dakshina Pradesh also included the Mysore and Kodagu regions, which a section of the Congress leadership favoured, but could not materialise (Balan, 2012: 1414–15) since it lacked popular support. Rajaji believed that Dakshina Pradesh would check the rise of the Communist Party as well as the Dravidians.

Periyar's involvement in the creation of Madras State based on linguistic lines was driven by his broader idea of non-Brahmin sovereignty, which he saw as a challenge to Brahminism disguised as nationalism. When Periyar started using the term 'Tamil Nadu' in 1927, he was not referring to a specific region with clear boundaries, but rather to an identity rooted in Tamil ethnicity. This identity was based on rational thinking and egalitarianism (Ganeshwar, 2022: 103–04). As Rajendran (Personal Communication, 30 January 2020) remarked, "Periyar was happy with any portion of land where the values of self-respect, social justice, and rational thought prevailed."

Like Pandian (2009: 65), Rajendran also argued that for Periyar, the importance of identity and ideology overweighed the need for geographic borders.[20] In contrast, one of Periyar's contemporaries, Mylai Ponnuswamy Sivagnanam (Ma Po Si henceforth), the leader of the Tamil Arasu Kazhagam (Federation for Tamil Autonomy), was very keen on securing the physical boundaries of the State. He was working towards making Madras city[21] the capital of Madras State and pushing for the inclusion of Peermedu-Devikulam (from Travancore) and Chittoor (from Andhra State) into Madras State.

It might seem counterintuitive, but the DMK didn't oppose the States Reorganisation Commission (SRC) or the idea of reordering States along linguistic lines. Instead, the party blew hot and cold on reorganisation and its secessionist claims. On 3 May 1954, Annadurai said Madras State has the right to self-determination, and that it had everything a nation would need—namely, cultural antiquity and historical uniqueness. The DMK, meanwhile, supported the merger of Chittoor with Madras State.

In response to the building waves of the Visalandhra movement, Annadurai and DMK leaders proposed a federation of States including Visalandhra, Samyukta Karnataka, Aikya Kerala, and Tamil Nadu (Arunan, 2008: 171–72). The DMK's leadership argued that while these four States would be divided based on language, the federation would reflect their unity as an ethnic group. But this position seemed to water down DMK's earlier call for secession.

In fact, veteran communist leader Jeevanandham pointed out that the DMK's support for the States' Reorganisation Act suggested that the DMK had given up on the idea of secession (ibid., 173). Interestingly, both the DMK and the communists agreed on one thing: rejecting the idea of Dakshina Pradesh. While the communists saw it as an anti-democratic move to undermine linguistic reorganisation, the DMK was trying to secure as much federal autonomy as possible within the framework of linguistic reorganisation (ibid., 174).

The death of veteran Congress leader Sankaralinganar, after his protest fast demanding, among other things, that Madras State be renamed Tamil Nadu (Tamil Country), gave the DMK a chance to shift the focus away from its earlier secessionist stance. Sankaralinganar, a Gandhian, had long called for prohibition on alcohol and for leaders to lead simpler lives. On 27 July 1956, he began his fast unto death with twelve demands, one of which was for the renaming of Madras State. Kamaraj, the Chief Minister of Madras State and a fellow Congress member, ignored the demands despite making efforts, along with other leaders, including Annadurai, to persuade Sankaralinganar to end the fast. Sankaralinganar died on 13 October 1956. Annadurai wrote an obituary in *Dravida Nadu* vowing to fulfill his demand.[22] Subbu, the DMK's Madurai District Secretary, helped organise his widely attended funeral procession (Thirunavakkarasu, 2015: 1065–72).

Overall, the episode had three key outcomes for the DMK—one negative and two positive. First, the party's move away from secession became clearer, which would evolve further over time. On the plus side, Rajaji's push for Dakshina Pradesh was effectively shot down, and, most importantly, the DMK emerged as a serious contender in the 1957 Assembly elections—far more formal and organised than the secessionist party that had backed a few candidates in the 1952 elections.

As the 1957 elections drew nearer, the DMK became more aware of a couple of key issues. First, its leadership realised that the DK's support for the Congress, combined with Congress maintaining a Dravidian identity in a somewhat accommodative style, was weakening the DMK's claim to be the true representative of Dravidian politics. The DMK also started recognising the growing economic challenges within Tamil society, especially with the Marwari dominance of trade, industry and, therefore, capital in Madras State. However, the DMK wasn't ready to entertain the idea of aligning with Tamil capitalists. The Party understood that simply shifting the monopoly of trade from Marwari, Baniya, or northern communities to their Tamil counterparts wouldn't necessarily end oppression and exploitation of non-business-oriented communities. As early as in 1951, Annadurai (in Vedaratnam, 1951: 34) had pointed out:

> *It is very easy to secure the support of the capitalists and industrialists to our cause by giving them a blank cheque. They will be only too willing to support us because of their natural desire to step into the shoes of their North Indian counter-parts. In the Dravida Nad which we envisage, we will not countenance capitalism of any sort, be it North Indian or Dravidian. And this is the reason why the Dravidian capitalists are not with us.*

Unlike their communist counterparts in Tamil Nadu, the DMK intuitively grasped that caste struggles couldn't always unite different class struggles or undo class antagonisms or vice versa. Annadurai's efforts to form an alliance with Rajaji's Swatantra Party and the business elites who supported the DMK need to be seen in this context.

But merely recognising issues wasn't enough for the DMK; it also needed to find a way to talk about them politically. So, at the 1956 Trichy Conference, the party decided to run in the elections with a clear manifesto. It wasn't just about making abstract promises—it listed out issues of material significance to people's everyday lives: land reform with a ceiling on land holdings, minimum wages, free secondary education, limiting the Union Government's power to tax States, nationalisation of industries, healthcare benefits for working classes, a casteless and classless society, promotion of Tamil language, renaming the State, and opposing the imposition of homogenising national narratives or the overreach of the Union Government institutions.

The manifesto showcased a mix of pragmatism and idealism in the DMK's politics. While it pushed for the lofty goal of a casteless and classless society, it also recognised the need to tap into the very same castes and class aspirations to achieve that vision. Caste and class were not merely political categories for the DMK but essential tools for understanding the society they wanted to create, uplift, and transform. This meant that the DMK was committed to creating laws and policies to bring about real structural change, rather than just hoping that social consensus would be enough to fix the deep inequalities of caste and class. As we've seen, Dravidian politics and identity were always shaped by active political and legislative labour; they never were just handed down.

The DK continued to support Kamaraj, but its more conciliatory approach forced Kamaraj to make it clear that he was not actively seeking their support—they had volunteered it. I'll go into more detail on this in the next chapter. Still, this clarification did not sit well with a section of the older Congress members, who could not tolerate any kind of support from the DK. To make matters worse for the Congress, the party gave tickets to 45 former DK members, prioritising them over its own party members. This led to a split, and those Congress members went on to form their own party called Congress Reform Committee, which also contested the 1957 elections (Hardgrave, 1965: 57).

Meanwhile, the communists criticised Congress for allegedly bowing to demands for the disintegration of the Indian Union, given the DK's earlier secessionist stance. Annadurai, however, took a different and relatively mild approach. He saw the alliance between the DK and the Congress more as a political move, recognising that it reflected the changing demographic profile of the Congress party, particularly its MLAs' increasing non-Brahmin profile. He suggested that this alliance was both DK's and Kamaraj's way of consolidating power—essentially working together to weaken Congress from within.

Unlike in the previous elections, Kamaraj's Congress victory in 1957 was decisive. More than one-sixth of the members of the Madras legislature came from upper-caste backgrounds (3.9% Brahmins and 13.6% non-Brahmins), while 10% were from intermediate castes. The Other Backward Classes made up a significant portion of the Assembly at 42%, with the three largest and politically dominant communities—Kongu Vellala Gounders, Mukkulathors, and Vanniyars—forming 28.3% of MLAs (about 29% of the population). The Other Backward Classes made up 13.7%, half of whom were Nadars, another influential backward class group.

After achieving an ideological victory with the withdrawal of the MSEE and the reorganisation of states, the DMK's leaders contested 112 seats as independents, since the party was not fully registered, nor did it have a constitution, etc., and won fifteen seats. The DMK's vote share was 14.6%, the second-largest after the Congress's 45.3% (151 seats). It made significant inroads, winning three seats in Chennai district, four each in South and North Arcot, one in Chengalpattu, two in Salem district, and one in Trichy. Notably, none of the DMK candidates or winners were from the Brahmin community.

The election results marked a significant shift in the political landscape, with both major parties adopting more Dravidianised positions and the DMK growing its influence, particularly in the northern and central parts of Madras State (Refer to Tables 4 and 5)[23]. In a surprising twist, the following year, V.P. Raman, a Brahmin, joined the DMK and took on a prominent role within the party.

Table 4: Caste Composition of MLAs – the 1957 State Assembly Elections

Caste/Category	Relative Share
Upper Caste	17.6%
Intermediate Caste	10.7%
Other Backward Classes	42.0%
Kongu Vellala Gounder	*10.2%*
Mukkulathor	*8.3%*
Vanniyar	*9.8%*
Others OBC	*13.7%*
Scheduled Caste	18.0%
Scheduled Tribe	0.5%
Christian	1.5%
Muslim	2.0%
Unidentified	7.8%
Total	100.0%

Source: Fieldwork – Vignesh Rajahmani

Table 5: Partywise Caste Breakdown of MLAs – 1957 State Assembly Elections

Party	UC	IC	OBC	SC	ST	Christian	Muslim	Unidentified	Total
CPI	0.5%	0.0%	0.0%	0.0%	0.0%	0.0%	0.0%	1.5%	2.0%
INC	12.2%	7.8%	30.2%	13.7%	0.5%	1.5%	2.0%	5.9%	73.7%
IND	3.4%	2.0%	7.8%	2.4%	0.0%	0.0%	0.0%	0.5%	16.1%
PSP	0.0%	0.0%	1.0%	0.0%	0.0%	0.0%	0.0%	0.0%	1.0%
IND (DMK)	1.5%	1.0%	2.8%	2.0%	0.0%	0.0%	0.0%	0.0%	7.3%
Total	17.6%	10.7%	42.0%	18.0%	0.5%	1.5%	2.0%	7.8%	100.0%

Source: Fieldwork – Vignesh Rajahmani

Dravida Nadu: Crucified De Jure, Enkindled De Facto

In the 1940s, Periyar, alongside Jinnah's push for Pakistan and Ambedkar's call (2019: 425–26) for separate settlements for Dalits to escape caste discrimination, worked towards the idea of an independent Dravida Nadu (Kannan, 2017: 70). While all three were challenging majoritarian politics in their own ways, Jinnah was focused on fighting religious majoritarianism, while Periyar and Ambedkar were confronting ethnic, social, and economic Brahminical majoritarianism.[24] Although Periyar's attempt to create Dravida Nadu did not succeed, his disagreement with Annadurai over India's independence played a crucial role in the founding of the DMK. Notably, DMK's constitution still featured the demand for Dravida Nadu.

The 1956 linguistic reorganisation of States triggered a ripple effect, reshaping the DMK (both in terms of its organisation and public stance), Madras State, and even the Indian Constitution. This shift was gradual and well-thought-out, and ultimately, it worked to the DMK's advantage that it let go of one of its foundational aims.

At first, Periyar dismissed the idea of Dravida Nadu as something hollow, comparing it to an onion with no substance beneath layers of peel[25] (Kannan, 2017: 265). Annadurai, on the other hand, even though his stance had softened after the States Reorganisation Act of 1956, still made fervent interventions on the issue, sometimes even seeming to extend beyond India's borders. In June and July 1958, he criticised the Ceylon [now Sri Lanka] government's high-handed approach towards Tamils following the anti-Tamil pogrom of 1956. He also condemned India's inaction, and called for international attention on the issue. On 22 June, which was declared Ceylon Tamils Freedom Day, a large public meeting was held in Madras city that drew significant support.

On 10 August 1958, Annadurai appealed to both Ceylon and Indian Tamils, saying, "…that does not necessarily mean demanding a Tamil Raj comprising Tamil Nadu and that portion of Ceylon wherein Tamilians are in a majority. The task immediately ahead is to focus public attention on the problem. World opinion should be harnessed to the cause of justice and fair play. The plight of the

Tamilains in Ceylon should be placed before the discerning public all over the world…" (Annadurai, 1958 in Eelaventhan 2018).[26]

Annadurai's words made it clear that in the DMK's imagination of Dravida Nadu, they weren't seeking territory outside Indian borders. However, the DMK shared a strong feeling of solidarity with Sri Lankan Tamils and their fight for equal citizenship.[27] For instance, the DMK passed a resolution in a public meeting on 13 March 1961, backing the Ceylon Tamils' protest against the introduction of Sinhala as the official language in the Tamil-majority regions. More importantly, almost all political parties in Tamil Nadu have extended and continue to extend their support to the cause of Sri Lankan Tamils.

The DMK's success in the local body elections of 1959 in Madras and Coimbatore rejuvenated its cadres and helped the party grow and consolidate its organisation. With post-poll support from the Communist Party, the DMK was able to secure the Mayor's position in Madras Corporation, where the DMK had the majority, while the communists took the Mayor's position in Coimbatore Corporation, where they held the majority (Barnett, 1976: 105). The incremental victories in both the 1957 Assembly elections and these elections indicated the formalisation of the party organisation. This allowed the DMK to participate more actively in policymaking and to have a greater impact on the people of Madras State. That said, it also limited the party's free-spirited approach, particularly on matters challenging the Indian Union.

In 1960, senior DMK leaders gathered in Madras to discuss the viability of pursuing an independent Dravida Nadu. Karunanidhi, Mathiazhagan, Nedunchezhian, Sampath, and the party's lawyer, V.P. Raman,[28] told Annadurai that dropping the demand would greatly benefit the party's growth and effectiveness (Kannan, 2017: 266). While Annadurai was open to this suggestion, he hesitated to bring it to the party cadres, fearing a backlash. However, when the Finance Minister of Madras State, Subramaniam, questioned the DMK's loyalty to the Constitution of India in December 1959, Annadurai's response in July 1960 provided a clear statement of the party's position. He argued that North Indian domination symbolised the imbalance of power between the Union and

State governments, with the Union wielding disproportionate influence. In response, he said, the DMK wasn't looking to subvert the Constitution but wanted an amendment to prevent such a subversion.[29]

These two points—rejection of subverting the Constitution and the demand for constitutional reform—became the bedrock of DMK's stance within the Indian Union. The years 1961 and 1962 were marked by three significant developments that further influenced the DMK's position on Dravida Nadu: factionalism within the party, which led to Sampath's departure; the DMK's success in the 1962 elections, which paved the way for the passing of the anti-secessionist law in the 1963 Sixteenth Constitutional Amendment; and the Indo-Chinese war of 1962.

Sampath's decision to leave the DMK stemmed from at least four key differences with the party. First, there was his ongoing conflict with Karunanidhi, which dated back to the early 1950s. At the time, Sampath had criticised Karunanidhi's idea of creating a strong communication between the headquarters and the party's district, circle, town, and village offices[30] (Karunanidhi, 2017: 257). Kannan (2017: 201) described Sampath's possessiveness towards Annadurai and the DMK as "legendary". Karunanidhi, on the other hand, had significant influence over the lower-level leadership and cadres of the party (Barnett, 1976: 108), as well as strong connections with veteran Tamil film industry artistes. This combination gave Karunanidhi a powerful infrastructure for spreading the party's message. He was widely regarded as an exceptional organisation builder.[31]

In contrast, Sampath's clout was restricted to the party leadership and the General Council, along with a few student groups (ibid.). Over time, the tension between them grew, reaching a breaking point after a scuffle between their factions during a General Council meeting in Vellore in January 1961.[32]

Second, Sampath was deeply critical of Annadurai's stance on Dravida Nadu in 1960. He felt that Annadurai's approach was weak and lacking in conviction, labelling it as frivolous.[33] Sampath argued that achieving Dravida Nadu required "strife and sacrifice", not just speeches and legislative procedures (Hardgrave, 1965:

66). However, after breaking away from the DMK in 1961, he quickly reconsidered his position, admitting that the demand was not feasible if secessionist claims were made unconstitutional or illegal (Barnett, 1976: 109).

Third, Sampath believed that the DMK should abandon its dual identity as both a political party and a social reform outfit. He felt that the party should focus on hard-nosed politics, like the Congress did, and distance itself from the cultural activities it was involved in, reducing its dependence on the network of artistes and film industry figures (ibid., 108–09).

Fourth, Sampath was inspired by the Communist Party's structure and wanted to model the DMK's organisation along the lines of its tightly-knit structure (Kannan, 2017: 263). He also believed that the DMK should ally with the communists, while Annadurai was exploring an alliance with Rajaji's Swatantra Party (Hardgrave, 1965: 69). An alliance with Rajaji's party was more beneficial for the DMK, as the Swatantra Party in Madras State didn't have many popular leaders but did include affluent figures who could help the DMK with both resources and taming its anti-Brahmin image.

Thirumaran (8 February 2020, Personal Communication) suggested that Annadurai's deal with the Swatantra Party was made on DMK's terms, and that the Swatantra Party's shared goal of defeating the Congress helped keep the alliance strong. The claim makes sense because, after Sampath's departure, the DMK began to lose the Communist Party's support but did not damage its reputation during the Indo-Chinese war. More importantly, it gave the DMK the freedom to shape its own distinct socialist framework for development, which aligned more closely with the communists' ideology, even while the DMK was negotiating with the Swatantra Party.

On 9 April 1961, Sampath, along with leaders from the DMK's General Council, the Mayor of Madras Corporation, and six councilors, left the DMK to form the Tamil Desiya Katchi (Tamil Nationalist Party or TNP). Although Sampath had previously dismissed the Dravida Nadu demand as farcical, his new party's manifesto for the 1962 elections included the right to secede from the Indian Union as one of its demands. The TNP defined India as a federal republic made up of linguistic States, challenging the prevailing idea of the Indian Union (Hardgrave, 1965: 71).

Sampath's departure effectively tamed DMK's belligerence regarding the Dravida Nadu demand. However, the TNP didn't last long. In 1964, it merged with the Congress party in a move engineered by Kamaraj, at which point it gave up the Dravida Nadu demand entirely. Meanwhile, the DMK stayed largely intact between 1961 and 1964. Many of the leaders who had defected to the TNP returned to the DMK, partly because the TNP's position on Dravida Nadu lacked clarity and Sampath's popularity was waning among both his party members and the people of Madras (Hardgrave, 1965: 71 and Barnett, 1976: 113–14).

The DMK's success in the 1962 elections forced the party to reflect on both the losses of some of its key leaders[34] and the overall win in comparison to the 1957 polls. The party secured 50 seats out of the 142 seats it contested (27.1% vote share) in 1962, compared to just 15 (14.6% vote share) in 1957. This outcome signalled to the national leadership in Delhi that Madras State might be heading towards secession, which Kannan (2017: 278) suggests was one reason for the Constitution (Sixteenth Amendment) Act of 1963. We'll discuss this further later in this chapter.

The result caught Kamaraj off guard, especially since, in August 1961,[35] he had predicted that the DMK would fade away after the 1962 elections. But interestingly, Annadurai, who had been uncertain about the future of the Dravida Nadu claim, began to push for it more passionately from July 1961. He argued that India's idea of national integrity was really a way of keeping the unequal power dynamics between the north and the south alive, where the north was exploiting the south. In other words, the Dravida Nadu claim was about self-determination and challenging the rule of a Brahminical, centralised power in Delhi.

Subramaniam challenged Annadurai to make Dravida Nadu the central issue in DMK's election campaign, but Annadurai chose not to take that route. Recognising that people's disenchantment with

Congress carried more weight than support for the Dravida Nadu idea, DMK's 1962 manifesto focused on addressing immediate issues concerning the people, while placing the Dravida Nadu claim as a longer-term goal (Kannan, 2017: 284).

The Congress party comfortably formed the government. The upper castes saw a final spike in their share of the legislature, reaching 18.9%, mostly coming from Congress, before their influence started to decline. The intermediate castes held a 15% share, while the Other Backward Classes remained steady with a 42.2% share. The alliance and merger of the Vanniyar caste parties with the Congress had made the Vanniyars prominent in the 1957 Congress government but the cost they paid was political autonomy that they enjoyed as caste parties (Rudolph & Rudolph, 1969: 89). Moreover, by 1962 the community was marred by intra-caste-class differences and rivalrous conflict among the leaders (ibid.), thereby resulting in the share of Vanniyars falling to 5.3%, while Kongu Vellala Gounders and Mukkulathors were at 11.7% and 9.7%.

Therefore, the share of the remaining Other Backward Classes saw a marginal spike of 15.5% which was a better ratio in relation to their population. The election also exposed DMK's inability to make inroads in western Tamil Nadu among the Kongu Vellala Gounders community (Tables 6 and 7).[36] The 1962 election results brought to the fore the ramifications of fragmentation of choice among numerous opposition parties vis-à-vis the voters, which enabled Congress to get a 139-seat victory out of 206 seats and also increase its vote share marginally. The DMK, on the other hand, unsettled the Congress hegemony but could not pull through fully owing to the absence of alliance partners. The party could not send enough Vanniyars to the legislature despite having a good sway, owing to lack of alliance parties. The inability of Annadurai to form an alliance with Rajaji's Swatantra Party deprived the party of both upper caste votes and resources to fight the elections.

Table 6: Caste Composition of MLAs – 1962 State Assembly Elections

Caste/Category	Relative Share
Upper Caste	18.9%
Intermediate Caste	15.0%
Other Backward Classes	42.2%
Kongu Vellala Gounder	*11.7%*
Mukkulathor	*9.7%*
Vanniyar	*5.3%*
OBC Other	*15.5%*
Scheduled Caste	18.0%
Scheduled Tribe	0.5%
Muslim	1.9%
Unidentified	3.4%
Total	100.0%

Sources for tables 6 & 7: Fieldwork – Vignesh Rajahmani

Table 7: Partywise Caste Breakdown of MLAs – 1962 State Assembly Elections

Party	UC	IC	OBC	SC	ST	Muslim	Unidentified	Total
CPI	0.5%	0.0%	0.0%	0.5%	0.0%	0.0%	0.0%	1.0%
DMK	3.4%	3.4%	12.6%	3.9%	0.0%	0.5%	0.5%	24.3%
INC	13.6%	10.2%	25.7%	13.1%	0.5%	1.5%	2.9%	67.5%
IND	0.0%	1.0%	1.5%	0.0%	0.0%	0.0%	0.0%	2.4%
SWA	1.5%	0.5%	1.0%	0.0%	0.0%	0.0%	0.0%	2.9%
SOC	0.0%	0.0%	0.5%	0.0%	0.0%	0.0%	0.0%	0.5%
FB	0.0%	0.0%	1.0%	0.5%	0.0%	0.0%	0.0%	1.5%
Total	18.9%	15.0%	42.2%	18.0%	0.5%	1.9%	3.4%	100.0%

Madras State to Dravida Nadu via Rajya Sabha: One Last Attempt

After the DMK secured a considerable number of seats, Annadurai lost in the State Assembly Elections, but this opened the door for him to be elected to the Rajya Sabha in 1962. In April of that year, he gave his first speech in the Rajya Sabha—one that's still widely cited. In the speech, Annadurai argued that Dravida Nadu could bring about two key improvements: economic regeneration and social progress (Annadurai, 1962 in Ramachandran, 1975: 11). Although Nehru outright rejected these ideas, the Chinese invasion of India in October 1962 led Annadurai to respond in a surprising way. At the time, he was in Vellore jail for protesting against rising prices. Despite his earlier stance, he said that it was the DMK's responsibility to support the Indian government and do everything possible to 'protect and safeguard the sovereignty' of India (ibid., xix). Much like Periyar, who paused his protests during World War II, Annadurai called for a halt to the DMK's activities.

On 7 October, in Madras, Annadurai said, 'Only if we have the house can we change the shingles. Only if there is a country, can we run a party. When the country is in danger, for us to advocate separation would be to give way to the foreigner. If we do so our future generation will curse us' (Annadurai, 1962 in Kannan, 2017: 291). Ironically, both he and Periyar were still labelled separatists by the elitist and puritanical nationalists.

Even with the embargo on DMK's activities, Annadurai remained skeptical of and concerned about the Indian government's actions. As expected, the Government of India introduced the Sixteenth Constitutional Amendment Bill in the Lok Sabha in January 1963.[37] This bill would bar individuals or groups advocating secession from contesting in elections. It also sought to change the oath taken by elected representatives to emphasise their duty to protect the sovereignty and integrity of India.[38]

Some Congress Members of Parliament from Uttar Pradesh, like Mahavir Tyagi and Pandit Krishan Chandra Sharma, as well as Manoharan Krishnan from the DMK, opposed the bill. The Congress members argued that it was unnecessary, as the Constitution already had enough provisions. However, Manoharan argued that it was a direct attack on the DMK. He urged the treasury benches in the Lok Sabha to address the matter politically and with constitutional fairness, instead of resorting to legal weapons (Rao, 1963: 154–55). Despite the opposition, the bill passed with a thumping majority and was sent to Rajya Sabha for consideration.

When the bill was discussed in the Rajya Sabha on 25 January 1963, Annadurai delivered a passionate speech against it. He framed his opposition to the bill around two main points, both of which led him to predict an undesirable outcome—which still hold relevance today.

First, he argued[39] that the committee behind the bill didn't consult the DMK before submitting its report. The committee claimed that they couldn't reach out to the DMK leadership because they were Vellore jail. But Annadurai exposed the claim, pointing out that party leaders like N.V. Natarajan, the Organising Secretary, and Manoharan were not in jail at the time. He said: "We are very small men. I do not want such a show of generosity from a committee of such stalwarts, but they could have taken the trouble to contact some people who were outside. Did they take that trouble?" (Annadurai, 1963 in Rajya Sabha: 4893). The phrase "small men" signified both the marginalisation of the DMK and their underlying frustration. He argued that the bill, coming from a non-consultative committee report, was an undemocratic move.[40]

The second point Annadurai raised had to do with the question of sovereignty. Referring to the Indian Constitution, he explained that political sovereignty belongs to the people, while legally, power is divided between the States and the Union. He made a strong case for giving States more autonomy within India's federal system, arguing that this would make them more effective. He criticised the highly skewed power balance between the Union and the States, pointing out that the States were forced to depend on the Union for approval on projects and development plans. He even suggested that the Congress leadership in the Madras State would feel the same way (ibid., 4898).

He asserted, "...many of the members of the ruling party in Madras may swear by the sovereignty and integrity of India, but whenever they find one of their proposals brushed aside, whenever they find one of their projects not taken up, whenever they find that they are not allotted the amount they need, they think about me.... That is why Annadurai is demanding support. Deny me a steel plant in Salem, I rise up there. Deny Tuticorin its development, the DMK comes in. Therefore, you should take the DMK as the spearhead of the opposition to the unitary nature of the federal structure of this Constitution. As elder members of Parliament, why should you take this into the jungle? Lift it up to the highest political arena and allow it free play; make the Federation become a real Federation..." (ibid., 4900).

Annadurai's words gave new life to the slogan "*Vadakku vaazhkirathu, therku thaeikirathu*" (The North is thriving, the South is diminishing) that was popular in the 1950s and had become deeply etched in the minds of the people of Madras State and still resonates today. The "undesirable outcome" that Annadurai had predicted was the transformation of a clear, tangible grievance—one that could be addressed—into a more abstract and unresolved feeling of resentment. This, he argued, would be far more dangerous.

When his fellow Member of Parliament, Bhupesh Gupta, suggested that the DMK might go underground if the law were to be enforced, Annadurai responded that the DMK would not go underground, but the "sullen discontent will go underground". He warned the house that there was no political solution for this kind of intangible discontent among people. Instead of addressing it, the bill would make it invisible and worse, increasing resentment without doing anything to solve it (ibid., 4898). To offer a solution, Annadurai proposed that States should have the right to secede, similar to the Soviet Constitution (ibid., 4900).

On 9 May 1963 after the bill had been referred to a Joint Parliamentary Committee and its report had been submitted on 14 March 1963[41]—the Rajya Sabha took it up again. In his speech, Annadurai called for the bill to be dropped. He argued that if it came into force, States would effectively become colonies—something that contradicted what Nehru had said in 1945. On 29 August of that year, Nehru had backed the right to secede or self-determination, stating that it was the Congress party's responsibility to persuade any seceding groups to abandon that idea. Annadurai believed that denying the right to secede would leave Madras State economically backward and vulnerable to "language imperialism" (Annadurai, 1963 in Rajya Sabha: 2846).

Annadurai wasn't alone in his views. Before Independence, in his 1946 Congress Presidential address, Acharya J.B. Kripalani (1948: 51) argued for greater autonomy for the States, claiming that centralisation was a threat to liberty. However, Louise Tillin (2021: 161–81) outlined four reasons why India chose a centralised federal structure. First, the violent partition of the country left its leaders unsettled. Second, there was a desire to build a unified national (civic) identity to overcome communal differences. Third, they wanted to build a strong welfare state to address the country's socioeconomic challenges. And fourth, they needed to distribute investments across the country to combat the growing economic inequality across regions.

While Annadurai did not agree with the Congress's approach, he wasn't completely rigid about Dravida Nadu as an imminent secessionist goal either. He urged the government to address the issue politically instead of imposing legal measures.

The Sixteenth Constitutional Amendment Bill was passed by the Rajya Sabha in May 1963. Soon after, Annadurai set off on a tour across Madras State before the DMK's General Council meeting in June 1963. He argued that the amendment was an attempt to wipe out the DMK by changing the rules. As he put it, "When people in power could go to the extreme of changing the Constitution and have no shame about it, why should the DMK shy away from amending its constitution to stay afloat in changing times?' (Karunanidhi, 2015: 483). While this shift in the party's stance drew criticism, the DMK's adaptability and resilience fuelled its actions more than negative reactions.

By the end of 1963, the party amended its constitution, changing its goal from an independent Dravida Nadu to a Union of South Indian States within the bounds of the Constitution. In Narendra Subramanian's (1999: 39) framework, this is described as "leadership flexibility", in the sense that the DMK had always pursued long-term goals centered on social justice, equal opportunity, and empowering marginalised groups. In doing so, the leadership altered its core objectives to better align with the interests and aspirations of both their supporters and those who were not yet on board. Annadurai, frustrated with the Union's insipid engagement with the Dravida Nadu claim, famously said, 'I have given up the Dravida Nadu claim, but the reasons for the claim persist.'[42] This slogan still resonates today.

The DMK's vision of Dravida Nadu almost became a reality with the linguistic reorganisation of States—one of the key reasons for the Dravida Nadu vision was the desire to preserve the common language and culture. Over time, as the party grew electorally salient and formalised its functioning style, the DMK became more involved in policymaking, creating real impact. However, two apprehensions remained. One was the fear of Hindi imposition due to constitutional requirements, and the other was the Union's lack of support for development in the South.

While the centralised federal structure was adopted in response to Partition, though it contradicted what Nehru or Kripalani had advocated, the process got a further impetus from the Chinese invasion. The Union's unilateral pursuit of the Sixteenth Constitutional Amendment Bill[43] amplified the fears among a considerable section of people in Madras State.

Annadurai's claim for Dravida Nadu and his plea for the right to secede were, in essence, bargaining chips—used to counter the excesses of the Union. In the light of the evidence gathered so far, arguably, if the right to secede had been recognised, or at least addressed politically, it could have eased the concerns of the people. In other words, recognising the right to secede could have helped balance out the Union's excesses and the demands of the Madras State. Refusing to engage with the issue only fuelled edgy apprehensions, leading to one of the longest and fiercest agitations in Madras State in 1965, sparked the very instant Hindi was announced as the Union's official language. At the same time, widespread social discontent—due to rising prices, scarcity of essential commodities, and low employment rates—dealt a decisive blow to the Congress party in the State, despite the presence of highly revered stalwarts.

The Crucible of Dravidian-Tamil Ethos: Madras State and the 1965 Anti-Hindi Agitations

After the Sixteenth Constitutional Amendment was passed and the DMK officially renounced its claim for Dravida Nadu, the party's relationship with the Indian Union evolved in the minds and actions of the people of Madras State. The public view in Madras State was that Annadurai had become one of the most compelling orators, whether in Madras State or in Parliament.

Through the DMK-run magazines and the growing network of reading rooms, the party's fifty MLAs sparked a ripple effect, influencing the minds of people through their words and deeds in the State legislature. However, the delicate balance of the new equilibrium was rattled when the Official Languages Act of 1963 was passed. There were massive protests in Madras State, unprecedented in scale and boldness, led largely by students and younger people who didn't back down despite facing harsh action from State agencies.

Stalwarts of the Indian freedom movement, from Bal Gangadhar Tilak to Mahatma Gandhi, insisted on promoting a single official language that would also serve as the "link language" for all Indians, and they chose Hindi—or Hindustani, which was Gandhi's preference. In fact, Gandhi set up the Dakshin Bharat Hindi Prachar Sabha (South Indian Hindi Propagation Association), in Madras city in 1918, and Annie Besant inaugurated it. Rajaji also tried to make Hindi compulsory in schools in the Madras Presidency in 1938,[44] and Omanthurar made another attempt in 1948. Both efforts sparked widespread protests.

Despite the pushback, there was a strong consensus in Delhi for Hindi,[45] and the Indian Constitution included provisions to promote Hindi as the official language of the Indian Union,[46] along with encouraging its learning across the country. The Constitution also included a fifteen-year clause, during which both English and Hindi would serve as official languages.

When the Official Language Commission's report was presented in Parliament on 12 August 1957, there were just two dissenting voices: renowned linguist S.K. Chatterji and Subbarayan, who both warned that the recommendations pointed towards the imposition of Hindi. In response, the Government of Madras called for an extension of the fifteen-year timeline. In January 1958, two important meetings took place: one of the chief ministers of the South Indian states of Andhra Pradesh, Madras, and Mysore, and the other of the All-India Congress Committee at Guwahati, to discuss the official language policy.

The Guwahati resolution emphasised flexibility and consensus-building while making Hindi the official language, but left the timeline unchanged. A Parliamentary committee headed by G.B. Pant reviewed the Official Language Commission's report and recommended extending the transition period. It also suggested that English might continue to be used after 1965, provided Parliament passed a law to define its scope. The turning point came when Nehru gave an assurance in Parliament on 7 August 1959, saying English would continue as long as non-Hindi speaking people wanted it. Both Annadurai and Rajaji welcomed this reassurance (Ramasamy, 2020: 17–20).

The relief, however, was short-lived. On 27 April 1960, a Presidential Order instructed the Ministry of Home Affairs to push Hindi as the official language of the Union. The Dravidar Kazhagam escalated the situation by burning a map of India, excluding Madras State, symbolically calling for secession. Thousands of protestors were arrested on 5 June 1960. Annadurai planned protests from 6 August[47] to 16 August, except on Independence Day. But assurances from President Rajendra Prasad and Minister of Home Affairs G.B. Pant, stating that Hindi would not be compulsory in non-Hindi speaking regions, persuaded the DMK to call off the protests.[48]

Then, on 13 April 1963, the Official Languages Bill was introduced in Parliament, allowing English to continue as an official language. The bill stated that "English may continue", implying that it wasn't compulsory, unlike the previous language of "English shall continue" as the official language. Speaking about the bill in the Rajya Sabha on 2 May 1963, Annadurai argued that English should continue instead of Hindi: "In this problem, the DMK occupies only a very small space. It depends upon the future of this Bill whether the DMK is to occupy a greater sphere or occupy [the] same sphere..." (Annadurai, 1963 in Ramachandran, 1975: 72).

Annadurai's opposition revolved around two arguments. First, he argued that choosing Hindi would put non-Hindi speakers at a disadvantage compared to native speakers—a concern echoed by B.N. Das from Orissa (now Odisha) and Avinashilingam Chettiar from Madras State (ibid., 72). English, on the other hand, would create a mutual disadvantage for everyone but would also allow India to engage with the world.

Second, Annadurai pointed out that while the number of Hindi speakers was large, they were concentrated in specific regions, which made the argument of majority valid arithmetically, but not ethically (ibid., 69). He warned in the Rajya Sabha: "If Hindi is imposed, DMK will unfold its relentless fight, its relentless agitation against the imposition of Hindi, whatever be the consequences" (ibid., 72).

In addition, Annadurai cited Gopalaswami Ayyangar's own admission when he introduced the proposal for Hindi as the official language of the Union in the Constituent Assembly in 1949 that Hindi is not a fully developed language (ibid., 65).

While the leaders in the Rajya Sabha did not seem to take Annadurai seriously, they could not have known at the time that just four years later, none of the major parties in Parliament would have a solid, independent vote base and would only manage to secure seats sporadically in the following decades. The DMK, meanwhile, was gearing up for a series of protests against the Official Languages Act of 1963, which came into force on 10 May 1963. Karunanidhi, who had proven himself in the three-cornered protests of 1953, was appointed president of the DMK's Agitation Committee.[49]

From 15 to 23 September 1963, the DMK declared an anti-Hindi week across Madras State. Karunanidhi organised a list of volunteers who were willing to be arrested (Ramasamy, 2020: 22). He leveraged the party's network of reading rooms and enlisted sympathetic artistes to spread Annadurai's arguments against Hindi imposition. "We held multiple workshops in our reading rooms about the problems associated with imposition of Hindi. I learnt the speech by Anna (Annadurai) in Parliament by heart.... Not just me, almost everyone in the State internalised a line or two from the speech.... Many drama troupes that were sympathetic to the cause would also practise near the reading rooms and stage street plays across the town and in villages nearby.... Kalaignar (Karunanidhi) would closely monitor our progress," Sankaralingam told me (Personal Communication, 7 February 2020).

A special anti-Hindi public conference was held in Madras on 13 October 1963. It was the final of numerous anti-Hindi public conferences held in Tirunelveli, Thanjavur, and Salem. Karunanidhi's volunteers were named by Annadurai at the conference, and copies of Part XVII of the Indian Constitution, pertaining to the official language of the Union, were burnt. Union Government offices in Madras State were chosen as sites where DMK volunteers would picket. Consequently, when the arrests began in November 1963, Annadurai himself was among the first to be picked up, along with some other leaders. However, DMK party workers relentlessly volunteered to be arrested, and the cycle of burning copies of Part XVII and getting arrested continued. "My father was imprisoned for a month," said Sitrarasu (Personal Communication, 28 January 2020).

The passing of the anti-secession amendment marked a significant shift in the anti-Hindi agitation. By then, the idea of protecting the Tamil language—as against Tamil country—had become central to the Dravidian-Tamil identity, a cause that had taken root in the minds of people, who believed that it needed to be saved at any cost. Moreover, among the newly educated youth, there was extreme concern about their future career prospects and wellbeing, if Hindi were to be forced upon them, as Thirumaran shared with me (Personal Communication, 8 February 2020). The reading rooms buzzed with discussions about the law, the arrests, and the potential impact of Hindi imposition on their socioeconomic progress. Meanwhile, the constant arrests by the police only deepened the divide that the law had already created.

When Republic Day 1965 was announced as the day Hindi would become the official language of the Union, Minister of Home Affairs Gulzarilal Nanda stated at the Chief Ministers' conference on 13 December 1964 that important circulars would be issued in both English and Hindi (Ramasamy, 2020: 24). This sparked even more unrest.

The DMK responded with two massive anti-Hindi public conferences in Madras city and Trichy on 17 January 1965. In Madras, Annadurai, ever the astute leader, clarified that the DMK would mourn Republic Day, though it had been celebrating the event since 1950, only in opposition to the imposition of Hindi. Meanwhile, the Trichy conference called for English to remain the official language indefinitely. It was also suggested that the protests would include hoisting black flags, wearing black badges, and distributing pamphlets.

On 19 January, Kamaraj challenged the DMK to follow through with its planned protests, while Bhaktavatsalam, the Chief Minister, promised that the state government would come down hard on the protesters. At this juncture, the Congress party unleashed its youth wing and allied student and youth collectives.

In response, Annadurai went on the defensive, likely compelled by the circumstances: it was the aftermath of the anti-Tamil pogrom in Sri Lanka, and protests could trigger responses that went beyond the conventional or expected outcomes (Thirumaran, Personal Communication, 8 February 2020). He urged the volunteers to hoist flags at their homes and party offices and not in public places. He also requested them not to react to state action against them. College students in Madras, Trichy, Madurai, and Coimbatore braced for impact.

Congress party workers led the first physical attack against the students in Madurai on 24 January, which intensified on 25 January. There was retaliation, and the police entered the fray, further inflaming the protest. It spiralled into burning of the national flag and attacks on government buildings, hoardings in Hindi, and public property. The Chief Minister had refused to meet student representatives on 25 January, which worsened matters in Madras city considerably. A. Chinnasamy, a volunteer in Trichy, self-immolated on 25 January 1964 after a failed attempt to convince the Chief Minister Bhaktavarsalam. "*Tamil Vaazhga, Hindi Ozhiga*" (Long Live Tamil, Down Down Hindi), Chinnasamy cried before he died.

Almost all the respondents I interviewed knew of Chinnasamy's death. The fact that someone could take his life for the sake of Tamil language deeply moved students and the youth at the time. Meetings and processions across the State continued to highlight Hindi imposition as a barrier to securing government jobs. In processions in Virudhunagar, Thanjavur, and Coimbatore over 1,500, 5,000 and 6,000 students, respectively, participated (ibid., 32).

Republic Day 1965 in Madras State began with another self-immolation; that of Sivalingam, an office bearer of the DMK in the city. On 27 and 28 January, Ranganathan died by self-immolation, and Muthu consumed pesticide, in Madras city and Trichy, respectively. The DMK beseeched party members not to take their lives.

While the senior leadership courted preventive arrests, and the protesters faced the brunt of police action and the violence of Congress party workers, the Union government issued Bharat Ka Raj Patra (India's Gazette, in Hindi) on Republic Day. In subsequent days, women students, even school students[50] (ibid., 40–42), joined the protests. Hindi exams were boycotted. Educational institutions were closed. Meanwhile, the police shootings, arrests, and the loss of life and property continued.

School students in rural areas like Kovilpatti, Palyamkottai, and Thanjavur participated in the protests, and some were shot at. This, in turn, led students to lead processions in solidarity in Andhra Pradesh, including in Madanapalli, Cudappa, and Tirupathi districts (ibid., 44). There were protests in Assam, West Bengal, Mysore, Kerala, and Andhra Pradesh, as well as agitations by Tamils in Bombay, Bangalore, and even Singapore. February 1965 passed by with the protests moving to railway stations and post offices, and there was heavy state action, including intervention by the army. There were shootings, widespread arrests of students and leaders, and many were booked under the Defence of India Rules. Then came the announcement that the Union Public Service Commission exams would be conducted in Hindi. Attempts to get the Congress leadership to change its stance failed, and finally, people gave up on believing their assurances.

After Annadurai's release from jail in March 1965, he delivered an impassioned speech in the Rajya Sabha, highlighting the Union government's hypocrisy regarding English. He pointed out the irony of the three-language formula prescribed for education (Ramachandran, 1975: 86–87), arguing that if the Union recognised the importance of English by continuing its use in education, then why was it engaging in doublespeak on the official language debate. He made it clear that he was not advocating for English out of love for the language but because it was in the best interests of the people. Annadurai also argued that the Union's lack of confidence in Hindi being accepted as the de facto link language by people was forcing it to unpopular de jure measures (ibid., 88) instead.

His critique squarely focused on how the domination of Hindi would disadvantage non-Hindi-speaking communities, leading to their marginalisation in socioeconomic and cultural realms (ibid., 90). Essentially, Annadurai reframed the concerns about Dravidian-Tamil identity, placing them within the broader context of justice and socioeconomic empowerment.

It was only after the Congress party faced significant electoral setbacks in 1967—despite being unmoved by deaths and destruction caused during the crackdown on the protests—that it passed legislation to recognise English as an associate official language alongside Hindi. This came after significant uproar for Hindi to have primacy in the Hindi-speaking regions. On 8 January 1968, the amendment was passed, formalised as the Official Languages (Amendment) Act. While this new law allowed English to continue, it did not address the demand for Tamil to have primacy in Madras State.

The students who led the anti-Hindi protests were unhappy with the new legislation and planned to resume protests in late December 1967, after the bill was passed by both houses of Parliament. Unlike Rajaji, who chose to ignore protests until they unsettled the leadership's legitimacy, and Bhaktavatsalam, who used state power to suppress them, Annadurai took a different approach—he engaged directly with the student protesters. After a lengthy five-hour meeting on 5 January 1968, he called for a special legislative assembly session on 23 January. He sidestepped the students' demand to pass a resolution urging the Union to adopt all the languages listed in Schedule VIII of Indian Constitution as official languages. He also moved away from the three-language formula (Tamil/mother tongue, English, and Hindi), and instead adopted a two-language formula (Tamil/mother-tongue and English), effectively removing Hindi from state-run schools.

These changes had two goals. First, they aimed to temper the exceptionalist tendencies of the Dravidian-Tamil identity, positioning it to stand on equal footing with other regional identities across the country. Second, they sought to prioritise the socioeconomic empowerment of the people in the State, particularly the marginalised, using cultural and identity concerns as a springboard. The fact that both the protesting youth and the wider people welcomed Annadurai's actions is a clear indication of how deeply the Dravidian-Tamil ethos of pluralism and empowerment had spread within Madras State.

Food Shortages, Increasing Prices, and the Dravidian Campaign

In 1968, Barnett (1976: 209–11) conducted a survey of representative samples from the DMK's local leadership (N=459) and top leadership (N=38), and drew two compelling inferences about how the party perceives State-level problems. First, 26.8% of local leaders[51] and 31.6% of General Council members identified language as the most critical issue. Closely behind was the issue of food—25.5% of local leaders and 26.3% of General Council members ranked it as the most critical issue. While the Congress's mishandling of these issues and the DMK's political response will be explored in the next chapter, this section focuses on the causes, earlier protests by the DMK, and their outcomes.

Ramanujam (1967: 157) argued that the DMK began addressing food shortages and inflation only after abandoning its secessionist demand for Dravida Nadu. He also criticised the party for relying more on catchy slogans than substance. Conventional wisdom aligns with this view. However, it is important to note that the

DMK had raised the issue of rising essential commodity prices as early as 1962.[52] During this period, DMK cadres picketed revenue offices, and leaders like Annadurai and Karunanidhi courted arrest. The protests came to a halt with the Chinese invasion, as the DMK temporarily ceased its activities to prioritise the country's stability and security (Panneerselvan, 2021: 381–88). The skyrocketing prices of rice, reduced ration quotas, and long queues at ration shops—with people often returning home empty-handed—deeply affected the daily lives of people. Not being able to afford basic cooking essentials like oil, lentils, and milk hurt a vast majority of people in the State in a very intimate way.

Notably, the grain[53] self-sufficiency ratio[54] in India in 1961 was 92.8%, along with East Pakistan,[55] which was better than Indonesia (89.7%), the Philippines (87.5%), Japan (69.3%), and Korea (90.8%), and worse than Thailand (140.6%), China (93.2%), and Taiwan (128.9%) (Otsuka 2013: 9). So what caused the food shortage and increasing prices? Annadurai, with a postgraduate degree in economics and some fieldwork experience in the State, addressed these issues in the Rajya Sabha.

Speaking on the Finance Bill in June 1962, Annadurai criticised the government's new taxation structure, which aimed to increase revenue. Of the total revenue, 62% came from indirect taxation and 38% from direct taxation. Annadurai pointed out the contradiction that the government itself claimed that around 95% of the population was living at subsistence level (Annadurai, 1962 in Ramachandran, 1975: 97–98). A large population struggling to survive on such low incomes made the country highly vulnerable to inflationary pressures.

Furthermore, he criticised the political system, noting that within the Congress party, members who disagreed with the government's handling of the economy were unable to voice their concerns openly. Instead, they were forced to defend the government both inside and outside Parliament (ibid., 99).

Barnett's (1976: 212) survey of Congress leaders in Madras State, which mirrored the surveys conducted with DMK leaders, corroborated Annadurai's concerns. Among 120 Congress leaders surveyed, 25% regarded food shortages as the paramount concern in the State.

In his 1964 speech in the Rajya Sabha, Annadurai addressed the food crisis directly. He traced the crisis to three primary factors: production, distribution, and price control. Annadurai argued that production and distribution should occur simultaneously, rather than sequentially. He identified the slow implementation of land reforms and the persistence of absentee landlordism as primary contributors to the crisis (Annadurai, 1962 in Ramachandran, 1975: 111).

To address production, Annadurai suggested reducing land revenue and lowering the cost of electricity and fertilisers[56] to ease the financial burden on tillers. In contrast, he criticised the approach of offering high prices for agricultural produce, which he argued disproportionately benefited landlords (ibid., 120). On the distribution front, he supported setting up a Food Corporation of India, but insisted that the government should take full control of trading to minimise the influence of middlemen[57] (ibid., 116). Finally, he appealed to the government to set fair prices for essential commodities, taking into account the affordability of the majority of Indian consumers (ibid., 119).

From the foregoing, it is evident that Annadurai had a nuanced and meticulous understanding of the issue at hand. The food shortages and the government's failure to control rising prices of essential commodities were central to his argument. He reframed the issue within the Dravidian-Tamil context, where food grain provisions and the welfare of farmers were viewed as the state's responsibility, not acts of charity. "*Moondru padi latchiyam, oru padi nichayam*" (Three portions of rice grains as the goal, one portion of rice grains as the guarantee), became the definitive slogan in the DMK's campaign against food shortage leading up to the elections, galvanising people into action, particularly when the supply of rice to Madras State was halted three weeks before the elections (Bhatia in Ramanujam, 1967: 268). The handling of this issue in the context of the elections will be explored further in the next chapter.

To sum up, two comments made by Kamaraj on 24 February 1967 provide profound insights into the reasons behind the

Congress party's defeat and the DMK's success. First, in response to the challenge of building a committed cadre that would engage with people, he said, "…in those days, the goal was Independence. Now we must have something which could enthuse the people. Otherwise, how can we attract people, young or old?" Second, he pointed out that intra-party factionalism had weakened the Congress party: "… in many States, there was really no opposition worth mentioning but still a number of opposition parties have benefited. The reason is intra-party fights. The hatchet should be buried…"

The DMK, by contrast, devised a political strategy that was dynamic and discursive, yet retained its core values. It raised and responded to issues that resonated with the masses, helping it grow both as a political force and as an organisation. Its philosophy and its potential to deliver on its promises attracted support. The party was not immune to factionalism, as evidenced by Sampath's split. The party's resilience lay in the ability to hold itself together and the leadership's shrewdness to further its aims. These still make for great lessons in how to build a party.

At the same time, the DMK put the relative rigidity of the Congress party and its factionalism to its own advantage, which gave it an edge in becoming an entity that led the discourse, in an electorally sustainable way, in the State. The State unit of the Congress party has since been relegated to the margins of Madras State's (now Tamil Nadu) electoral arena, and the Dravidian parties (including DMK's offshoot and arch enemy, the AIADMK) continue to be largely in control of the political discourse in the State.

Conclusion

The 1944 doctrine of self-respect championed by Periyar gave voice to the Tamil non-Brahmins and marginalised communities, who expressed themselves through the DK. While criticising the Congress party for its predominant Brahmin leadership and its role in the movement for independence from British rule, the DK placed itself firmly within the broader transformation of Dravidian politics in the Madras Presidency. The DMK, emerging from the DK, successfully overcame the limitations that held the DK back.[58]

The three key features of the DMK that helped its surge were its organisational focus, commitment to ideology, and charismatic leaders. However, the DMK could gain political legitimacy and eventually claim electoral victory through a process no less moving than the plot of a Tamil blockbuster, with high stakes and a dramatic climax. To call this development a 'drama' is not an exaggeration, but rather an acknowledgement of the political theatre at play.

The DMK could mould identity-related vulnerabilities—stemming from caste, rural-urban mobility, and class inequalities—into political mobilisations, attracting individuals from non-elite, non-Brahmin, lower-class and lower-caste backgrounds. This included students, traders, workers, and the unemployed. The party could appeal to solidarities beyond all these conflicts and concerns before they could transform into radical insecurities. It created political communities beyond immediate caste/class associations and concerns, not accidentally but through politics, working consciously to build expansive horizontal solidarities.

However, the continued dominance of the Dravidian parties cannot be explained solely by this. Drawing from Narendra Subramanian, I argue that the DMK's agility, dynamism, and success can be attributed to its *strategic flexibility* rather than *tactical flexibility*. Subramanian (1999: 39) defines tactical flexibility as the process of appealing to different groups differently, meeting their needs without changing or modifying the ultimate goals and objectives of the party. On the other hand, strategic flexibility involves modifying ultimate aims and objectives in line with demands of constituents.

The DMK's manoeuvres did not involve abandoning its ideals or ideology. In fact, its strategic flexibility promoted the continued accommodativeness of its political offering. In other words, the DMK could forge a broad counter-hegemonic alliance that was universalist in its formation but attuned to the particular grievances of individual communities.

The next chapter will explore the significance of Kamaraj's defeat as a key turning point, representative of the changes that the DMK brought to the political landscape of Madras State.

4

A METICULOUS UNDERDOG AND A SEEMINGLY LAX STALWART

THE TALE OF THE 1967 MADRAS STATE ASSEMBLY ELECTION IN VIRUDHUNAGAR CONSTITUENCY

Even before the 1967 elections in Madras State, India had witnessed the formation of a few non-Congress governments, such as the multi-party coalition led by Tanguturi Prakasam (1953–1954), E.M.S. Namboodiripad's Communist government in Kerala (1957–1959), and Dayanand Bandodkar's Maharashtrawadi Gomantak Party government in Goa (1963–1973).

In his comprehensive analysis of the 1967 elections in India, Professor Samuel J. Eldersveld identified the reasons for the Congress party's decline in its weakening party organisation, factionalism, rise of regional parties, and increased caste and community mobilisation. While he argued that the electoral shifts marked a gradual change within the framework of the established political and electoral systems—rather than a revolution or forced subversion (Eldersveld, 1970: 1029)—he singled out the DMK as a notable exception. The party's performance represented a distinct case within the broader trend of political transformation in India.

Two personalities towered over the 1967 elections: Rajaji and Kamaraj, both of whom played significant roles in the freedom movement, nation building, and in party activities before independence. The correspondence between Nehru and Rajaji serves as a testament to Rajaji's prominence in national affairs (Gandhi, 1984). On the other hand, Kamaraj played a crucial role at various points in time, from the early electoral successes of the Congress party right—when it was still finding its feet in electoral politics during British rule—to becoming a trusted confidant of Nehru. Following Nehru's death, Kamaraj also became a key member of the ideologically agnostic and conservative Congress Syndicate (Hardgrave, 1970: 259).

The man who suffered one of the most shocking electoral defeats in the history of Madras State represented a political ethos that is still revered today. This is the story of Kamaraj[1], hailed as a 'Trueborn Tamilian' by Periyar (Venkatachalapathy, 2018), and how he was successfully opposed. No other leader possessed the aura of Kamaraj—campaigns were built around him, meetings focused on his accomplishments, people trusted him, and he was key to the Indian National Congress's popularity. It was all about what he could achieve for the State because of his stature within the Congress party. At least, this is how people were expected to imagine Kamaraj. So, what went wrong in 1967? How did a student leader of the DMK defeat him in an Assembly election?

This chapter mobilises evidence to explore the halo built around Kamaraj, and unpacks the reasons for his defeat as well as the Congress party's losses in the 1967 assembly elections—one after which it could never meaningfully revive itself. It also looks at the role of the DMK and its sympathisers in identifying the shortcomings of both the Congress and Kamaraj before the elections, and in preserving Kamaraj's image as a revered icon of the State, albeit within the Dravidian-Tamil realm.

Kamaraj, Rajagopalachari, Satyamurti, and the Congress Party

Kamaraj was a devoted follower of the veteran Congress leader Sundara Sastra Satyamurti, after whom he named the headquarters of the Congress party in Madras. Satyamurti played a significant role in shaping Kamaraj's political career in its early stages. It can also be argued that it was from Satyamurti that Kamaraj inherited his animosity towards Rajaji—another prominent Congress leader and former Premier of Madras Province (1937–1939) and Chief Minister of Madras State (1952–1954). This aspect will be taken up for discussion later in the chapter.

Unlike his mentor, Kamaraj was not from the socially and politically dominant Brahmin caste but was a Nadar. Kamaraj actively participated in all the meetings Satyamurti organised and eventually began organising his own, representing the party. He had a natural ability to draw large crowds, thanks to his relatable and accessible persona. Soon, he rose through the ranks to become president of the Provincial Congress Committee—the first non-Brahmin leader to hold that position in the party.

Being a people's leader did not mean that Kamaraj lacked the ability to manage the internal workings of the party. He could settle internal differences and feuds (Ramanujam, 1967: 187) and worked on building bonds, which grew his influence within the party machinery in the State. His growing power in Madras State made him an important figure in the Congress circles in Delhi. However, it all came at a cost. Settling internal feuds often meant leaving some factions dissatisfied. Inevitable resentments and tensions arose, but there is no evidence that they significantly affected party relationships or overshadowed its leaders.

Kamaraj was fiercely loyal to his party and expected similar commitment from every Congress worker. He disliked open criticism of the party and wanted internal problems to be dealt with on the inside, away from the public gaze. He was also considered a shrewd strategist who was deft at political manoeuvring, which helped him secure a leadership position in the Congress in later years.

The dominance of the faction Kamaraj led, and his own power, depended heavily on his ability to manage his adversaries. One of them was Rajaji. The friction between them dated back to the conflict between Rajaji and Kamaraj's mentor, Satyamurti, in the 1930s. Satyamurti was a member of the Swarajist faction of the Congress party that advocated participating in elections. He gained popularity in 1934 after the Civil Disobedience Movement weakened. That year, a parliamentary board was set up, and Satyamurti secured a win in the 1934 Central Legislative Assembly elections of the Madras Presidency. In 1935, Rajaji stepped down as President of the Provincial Congress Committee, and Satyamurti took over. Satyamurti was reelected as President in 1936 and appointed his protégé, Kamaraj, as the General Secretary.[2]

In the early 1930s, the Justice Party weakened, and the Self-Respect Movement simultaneously gained momentum. The Congress party in the Madras Presidency was focused on winning seats in local bodies. They decided to contest the 1937 elections, even though the party's top leadership was undecided about actually taking on political office if they won. The elections were set for February 1937, and despite many expecting Satyamurti to lead, on 16 January, Sardar Vallabhbhai Patel announced that Rajaji would take charge. Patel claimed that the decision came at Satyamurti's request. Veteran journalist Kasturi Srinivasan of *The Hindu* was the one to pass on the news to Satyamurti. The Congress 'high command' explained bringing Rajaji in would help avoid a leadership challenge from the Andhra region of the Madras Presidency. Although Rajaji praised Satyamurti's role in the party's success, once he took office, he left Satyamurti out of his cabinet—a snub too obvious to go unnoticed (Ramanathan, 2008: xvii–xviii).

In 1940, Kamaraj was elected President of the Madras Provincial Congress Committee, a position he held until 1954.[3] During this time, Kamaraj worked on strengthening the party in Madras and building a strong reputation in Delhi. Meanwhile, Rajaji continued juggling multiple roles at both the provincial and national levels. In the 1952 provincial elections, the Congress party won 152 out of 375 seats in Madras State, including seats in the Telugu, Kannada, and Malayalam-speaking regions.

Tensions were brewing over the demand for a separate Andhra State, and with the Left and two other parties—seen as having the support of the Vanniyar caste group—coming together, they formed the United Democratic Front (UDF), a post-poll alliance lead by Tanguturi Prakasam Pantulu of the Kisan Mazdoor

Praja Party. In response, senior Congress leaders, including T.T. Krishnamachari, turned to Rajaji for a solution, rather than Kamaraj, who believed that forging a broad, weak coalition would anyway make the UDF government ineffective and, in due course, the Congress could gain popularity among people (Kandaswamy, 2001: 50). However, even though Prakasam claimed to have the support of 166 members, the Governor, Sri Prakasa, didn't invite him to form the government. Instead, he invited Rajaji[4] and even nominated him to the Legislative Council. While this move was seen as a breach of constitutional morality,[5] Rajaji engineered enough support and comfortably sailed through a confidence vote.

The creation of Andhra State reduced the size of the Madras legislature. As we saw earlier, the Modified Scheme of Elementary Education, 1953, which the DMK labelled *Kula Kalvi Thittam* (Caste/Hereditary Education Policy), seriously damaged Rajaji's reputation in Madras State. Kamaraj quickly seized this opportunity. He resigned from his seat in Parliament and contested the 1954 by-election for the Gudiyatham constituency, aiming to join the Madras State Legislative Assembly. Kamaraj faced Communist Party candidate Kothandaraman in the election. However, the Congress party's strong grassroots efforts, along with support from Periyar, the DK, DMK, the Tamil Nadu Toilers Party, and the Commonweal Party,[6] helped Kamaraj secure a victory.

With this alliance of subaltern forces backing him, after a long wait and much effort, Kamaraj became Chief Minister of Madras State in 1954. According to James Walch (1976: 162–63), by solidifying his position, Kamaraj essentially reduced the domination of the Brahmin and upper castes[7] within the Congress party.

The factional feud within the Congress gave the DMK an opportunity to grow and strengthen. A section of non-Brahmin elites, who had previously supported the Justice Party, along with ambitious businessmen, saw potential in the DMK and backed it financially. Meanwhile, some Brahmin elites, landlords, and merchants who had joined the Swatantra Party after it was founded in 1959 began to distance themselves from the Congress.

As we saw in Chapter 2, by 1957, a considerable number of DMK branch offices and reading rooms had opened up, and this only grew by 1967 (Thirumaran,[8] 8 Feb 2020, Personal Communication). So, while Kamaraj's astute handling of internal party feuds helped him stay on top, the rivals created in the process helped a resilient opposition emerge.

Periyar's Role: Finding Method in the Madness

The political relationships between figures like Periyar, Kamaraj, Rajaji, and Annadurai make for a fascinating and sometimes unexpected web of alliances. Periyar, who was leading the large socio-cultural organisation—the DK[9]—offered his support to Kamaraj in the early 1950s. This support, which was often unconditional, can be explained by the kind of change Periyar wanted to see in Madras State's political landscape. He believed Kamaraj would stand up to Brahminical oppression and help steer the State towards a better future.

As also mentioned earlier, Periyar had called Kamaraj a "trueborn Tamilian" after his victory in the 1954 Gudiyattam by-election. While Periyar supported Kamaraj fully, he didn't hold back from criticising the Congress party. As discussed in Chapter 1, Periyar was wary of Congress's nationalism and its political stance at the time of independence. Over time, his concerns grew, especially as policies that limited the federal rights of States in the name of the unification of India became more prominent. In this context, Kamaraj appeared to Periyar as the right ally to help empower the marginalised when he emerged as the chief ministerial candidate in 1954.

When Kamaraj stepped into the spotlight in 1954 after Rajaji's resignation, Periyar threw his support behind him and called on all parties to back him too. At that time, the DMK didn't contest the 1954 by-elections but supported Kamaraj instead. The DMK leadership believed that not supporting Kamaraj would indirectly imply that the DMK supported Rajaji, which would have led to criticism from Periyar.

Periyar's calling Kamaraj "Trueborn Tamilian" is key to understanding why he supported him during the 1950s and 1960s. In a speech[10] at a public meeting in Erode on 30 July 1962, Periyar said, "When did we ever get someone like Kamaraj before? Should not a grateful Tamilian support someone who has the welfare of Tamilians in mind and acts confidently? What can we really talk about someone who puts all this aside and seeks to oppose and destroy him?" (Periyar, 1962 in Gopanna, 2008: 201; Original Translation Lit). The opposition Periyar is talking about includes the DMK, which won 50 out of 206 seats in the 1962 elections and became the second-largest party.

Kamaraj often acknowledged the support he received from Periyar. He would fondly recall how, back when Periyar led the Vaikom Satyagraha,[11] he was just a member of the (Congress) party—and how unlikely it was that Periyar would even remember him over twenty-five years later. In 1961, Kamaraj inaugurated an entrance arch for an area he named Periyar Nagar in Trichy. At the event, he said,[12] "The government has inaugurated the Harijan Welfare board (*Ilaaka*). Periyar is supporting the government because his aim is being fulfilled. It is being said that we speak on the phone secretly every night (laughs). We are not engaging like that. It is because good reform measures are being implemented by the government that Periyar is supporting it" (Kamaraj, 1961 in Gopanna, 2008: 203; Own Translation Lit.)

Throughout the 1950s, it was common to see Kamaraj invoking Periyar's name, with Periyar also praising Kamaraj in return. Periyar supported Kamaraj because of various initiatives he introduced, like free school lunches, free education, and ending the '*Kula Kalvi Thittam*'. From Kamaraj's speeches, it was evident that they stood together in the fight against caste oppression. While there were disagreements with the Congress party, Periyar's focus on the welfare of the marginalised resonated in the policies introduced by Kamaraj, which is why their support for each other continued[13] (ibid.).

However, Kamaraj had to be careful whenever he spoke about Periyar's support, since the media was trying to spin a different narrative. In a conversation with Sankaralingam (Personal Communication, 7 February 2020), I was able to better understand Kamaraj's caution. The media, especially the newspapers and magazines linked to the DMK—either run by its members or sympathisers, or those who believed in the Dravidian-Tamil ethos had painted Periyar and Kamaraj as a single unit and the DMK as another. This left little room for other political viewpoints.

DMK stalwart Murasoli Maran once observed that Periyar and DK's agitational and maximalist positions, like the rejection of Congress's brand of nationalism and the Indian Union placed the Congress at the other end of the spectrum, making room for the DMK to forge a middle ground, which was more relatable, practical, and reconciliatory (Panneerselvan, 2018).

In the end, Kamaraj's relationship with Periyar was shaped by Periyar's support, which Kamaraj could neither fully embrace nor completely distance himself from. This complex dynamic was a result of how Kamaraj had consolidated his power within the Congress party, which led to the alienation of some leaders. His dependency was also fuelled by the rapid spread of the Dravidian-Tamil ethos by the DK and DMK, which resonated deeply with the people of the State, leaving Kamaraj with little choice but to engage with it.

The Waning Popularity of the Congress Party and its Ethos

By the 1960s, the Congress party, which had once been associated with Gandhi and Nehru, had slowly became a party for the moneyed. Fancy roadshows and lavish ceremonies, a far cry from how Kamaraj presented himself, became everyday affairs. One criticism against the ruling Congress dispensation was its heavy reliance on patronage. Many influential Congress leaders were also wealthy patrons of the party, and as a result, the disconnect between the party and the people grew over the 1950s and 1960s. The case of Sankaralinganar, which we discussed in Chapter 2 is a good example. While his hunger strike is often remembered for pushing issues like renaming Madras State as Tamil Nadu and alcohol prohibition, it's important to note that one of his twelve demands was for politicians and elected leaders to cut lavish displays.

In the years leading up to the 1967 elections, Kamaraj was focusing on strengthening the Congress party's organisation and cadre. He wanted to prove to the people of India and Madras State that the Congress was not just an elite-driven party with a rigid structure. To do this, he proposed several measures, commonly known as the Kamaraj Plan or K-Plan. It called on senior office-bearers of the Congress party—ministers at the Union and State levels—to resign and dedicate their time to build the party from the ground up. The K-Plan followed India's defeat in the war with China, which had badly damaged the Congress party's popularity. Socialist leaders such as Ram Manohar Lohia, liberal socialists like Acharya J.B. Kripalani, and liberals like Minoo Masani had won important by-polls at the time.

Kamaraj's solution for the slowing momentum was to energise the party cadres and cultivate new leadership from the grassroots level. Along with other chief ministers like S.K. Patil and Biju Patnaik, and Union ministers like Jagjivan Ram, Morarji Desai, and Lal Bahadur Shastri,[14] Kamaraj resigned from his position on 2 October 1963.[15] Just a week later, on 9 October 1963, he was elected President of the Indian National Congress. Periyar, however, had strong opinions about Kamaraj's decision. While he agreed that the Congress party needed an overhaul, he didn't think resigning was the right move. He event sent Kamaraj a telegram, warning him, "Either on your own accord or on the advice of others, your resignation from the chief-ministership will be suicidal to Tamilians, Tamil Nadu and yourself" (Periyar, 1963 in Gopanna, 2008: 204).

When Kamaraj stepped down, he chose Bhaktavatsalam to succeed him as Chief Minister. Bhaktavatsalam was the second most senior in Kamaraj's Cabinet as State Minister for Finance and Education. In the election for the leader of the Congress Legislative Party, Bhaktavatsalam won comfortably with 128 votes against RV Swaminathan's 22 votes.[16] Swaminathan had contested in an attempt to break the "monotony of unanimous elections".[17] Bhaktavatsalam's tenure as Chief Minister came during a particularly turbulent period, with challenges both from outside and within Madras State. His tenure was marked by numerous criticisms, which fuelled the prevailing narrative of a weakening Congress party and a steady erosion of its popularity. On the surface, it seemed like the Kamaraj Plan didn't help the Congress in Madras State—just as Periyar had predicted.

The three key issues we discussed in the last chapter—dropping the secessionist demand for a sovereign Dravida Nadu following the China war, the anti-Hindi agitations, and the severe food shortages and price rise—dealt a decisive blow to the Congress party's prospects in the 1967 elections. Leading up to the election, prices kept climbing, hurting the poorer sections the hardest. The Chief Minister's failure to manage the crisis, combined with the opposition DMK's ability to shape and amplify public outrage, significantly hurt the electoral prospects of the Congress.

Kamaraj and the Humbling of the Halo

In politics in Madras, and subsequently in Tamil Nadu, a few tall leaders were the face of the party across the State. These leaders were expected to be at the forefront, delivering the party's message loud and clear. Kamaraj was the first of this group of leaders, which later included Annadurai, Karunanidhi, M.G.R., and Jayalalithaa. But by the 1960s, Kamaraj was feeling the pressure. While he was away working on the Congress party's organisational issues at the national level, his image was starting to fade in Madras. He had built a reputation with his impressive record in education, industry, and power supply, but in the years preceding the 1967 elections, many saw him as inactive, silent, and indifferent—a perception that cost him and the Congress party dearly.

As Chief Minister, Kamaraj was always out in the field, engaging with people and listening to their concerns. But his national duties took him away from this kind of hands-on leadership. A report in *The Hindustan Times* noted that Kamaraj's work at the all-India level "without a doubt cut him out of detailed confabulations constituency-wise, which, many Congress leaders themselves admit is more necessary this time than in 1962 or 1957".[18]

One example of this disconnect was Kamaraj's birthday celebration in 1964. At a time when the whole country, including the Congress high command, was mourning Jawaharlal Nehru's passing, Kamaraj's grand birthday celebration was seen as a tone-deaf show of extravagance. Ramanujam (1967: 139–40) reported on this poorly thought-out outreach event, which was widely publicised in the State. It didn't even align with Kamaraj's own personality and image. The wealthy organised a procession of hundreds of cars in Madras city and other similar events everywhere in the State. People began to wonder why Kamaraj, a leader of the Tamils who looked, behaved, and sounded like one of them, stayed silent while the lavish spectacle was planned and executed.

Kamaraj's role as a leader in Delhi didn't do much to help the Congress party in Madras State. The State's Congress Committee argued that Kamaraj's increased focus on Delhi would eventually benefit Madras State and the Tamil people. But the question was, could people see those benefits at the time? Kandasamy, who frequently visited the pro-Congress reading room mentioned earlier (Chapter 2), told me that it was a source of pride for people that Kamaraj was handling affairs at the national level. He grew up hearing about Kamaraj's greatness. But when I asked him why Kamaraj lost, he remembered what his father—who was a merchant—said: the trading business wasn't doing well because of the currency devaluation,[19] and Kamaraj, being one of the tall leaders, should have done something about it.

On top of that, the lack of effective help during the famine-like conditions and the failure of the Congress to provide clear answers despite being in power for over two decades, really shook people's trust. Bhaktavatsalam, in response to questions about the grain shortage, suggested people eat the meat of rats. The nonagenarian Thirumaran, who spoke with me, said, "Imagine saying something like that when Periyar and Annadurai were invigorating people with the spirit of self-respect and social justice." Thirumaran also said in his now feeble but firm tone, "Consider the inaction of a party that has been in power for over twenty years in the State and failed to build systems to tackle famine-like situations."

All the positive infrastructure Kamaraj had built didn't matter as much when it came to such a widespread crisis. According to Thirumaran, the party never seemed to acknowledge the severity of the situation or present a solid plan to fix things. Measures beneficial to some regions cannot be compared to a State-wide crisis, impacting everyone but the rich. "Moreover, even if the Congress did try to work out a solution, it did not communicate it effectively enough to create an impact in the minds of people," Thirumaran said (Personal Communication, 8 February 2020).

The rise in everyday prices was a problem across the country at the time. In fact, between 1966 and 1969, India went into a phase known as the 'plan holiday,' where no new plans for economic development were launched with the situation in mind. Trying to sell industrial growth as a success was not going have much appeal in a State where basic food items like rice were not available (Bhatia, 1967 in Ramanujam, 1967: 267–68), creating a starvation-like situation and where women fainted in the scorching heat, waiting in long queues for rations (UNI, 1967 in Ramanujam, 1967: 268–69).

At this time, the opposition's criticisms seemed very relatable to the people, and the way it communicated them to the people was a lot more effective. During the campaign, the DMK's organisational infrastructure was complemented by its reading rooms, workshops, and public meetings with numerous supportive film stars. Top DMK leaders who were playwrights for the film industry joined rallies. Some even staged plays that raised the concerns of people. Satirical questions, like the following, were put in Tamil rhyme: "Brother Kamaraj, what happened to the price of mustard seeds?" "Brother Bakthavatsalam, what happened to the price of lentils?" (Thirumavelan, 2016 loc.: 11646). The opposition knew the ground realities, and understood the Congress had no answers.

Notably, most of the questions raised against the Congress party were perceived as questions asked to Kamaraj, as he was seen as the ubiquitous power centre in Madras State's Congress ecosystem.[20] The perception that Kamaraj was complacent over everyday concerns expanded the void created by his absence from the State. Even when Kamaraj criticised or questioned the state of affairs, it was not heard by the people. This was in contrast to the 1950s, when Kamaraj's criticism of his own government's heavy expenditure struck a chord (Kandasamy, Personal Communication, 6 February 2020).

Two factors contributed to the changed public perception about Kamaraj: first, his engagement with affairs of Madras State had become intermittent rather than consistent, and second, the troika of thriving newspapers, reading rooms, and public meetings and dramas run by the DMK and its supporters. Kamaraj's absence at a crucial moment when he was needed in the State gave space to the Dravidian-Tamil opposition and it grew until it was no longer within his power to control it.

The United Front as the Opposition and DMK's Manifesto

The United Front was an alliance formed by various opposition parties with the goal of unseating the Congress party from power. Although it was dubbed a "rainbow alliance" during the 1967 elections, the United Front initially consisted of only three parties—the DMK, the Swatantra Party, and the Indian Union Muslim League. As the election approached, more parties joined the alliance, including the Forward Bloc, Tamil Arasu Kazhagam, Naam Tamilar Katchi, the Left Communist Party, and the Praja Socialist Party. Considering the growing number of parties, aligning their different ideologies and goals proved challenging.[21]

After the 1962 India-China war, ration shops and the Public Distribution System (PDS) as a whole suffered from poor supply management, while prices and taxes rose. Nehru's death tilted the scales further in favour of the DMK. Of course, it would take a political front that could set the context for the elections to harness all these favourable factors. This was clear to all the stakeholders in the 1967 polls. However, as against the elections held in 1957 and 1962, the stakes were higher in 1967.

Learning from its mistakes of the past, the Tamil Nadu Congress drew up a manifesto dedicated to Dravidian demands, a subtle indication that it would no longer attempt to subsume the Dravidian-Tamil identity in its quest for a uniform pan-national identity. This manifesto stressed on the abolition of land tax and laid out the state's role in trading in food grains. The provincial landed and propertied classes also found a space in the manifesto, indicating that the Congress party was keen to co-opt this class in its quest for electoral salience, and expressed its desire for political and social power.

The opposition's unity in the run-up to the 1967 election would also consolidate votes in swing constituencies (Ramanujam, 1967: 153). The Congress was, therefore, contesting against an alliance with varied core interests, but a unified message. Nowhere was the unity of its opponents more evident than in how it publicised the Congress's failures. The United Front's signal to voters was that a party whose leaders could not handle pressing concerns did not deserve to govern them. The DMK began criticising the Congress soon after the by-elections in 1954 at the grassroots level, and its voice had gradually built up over time,[22] notwithstanding the moments of strategic support to Kamaraj. The issues the opposition raised had a compelling emotional appeal within Madras State.

And as for the Congress, it remained out of tune. During the widespread opposition to Hindi imposition,[23] the Congress government had enforced measures to suppress peoples' protests, costing many lives, and, in the process, intensifying the perception that it was disconnected from popular concerns about an existential threat to the Tamil culture. Kamaraj's silence conveyed ambiguity, which people found disappointing. Meanwhile, ever-larger crowds began to gather at the DMK's meetings, with people anxious to hear Annadurai and Karunanidhi, and to watch stars like M.G.R. enact plays on stage. Stardom worked in their favour, but their command over Tamil, their invocation of everyday problems, and the solutions they proposed made people feel they had found an ally in the political sphere.

Rajaji, a key stakeholder in the run-up to the 1967 elections, helped legitimise the DMK as a responsible political party and the United Front as a formidable opposition alliance. This legitimacy counted for a lot among a section of the elite[24] that had been wary of the DMK[25] due to its anti-Brahmin image and support for secession. The affluent businessmen and merchants of the Swatantra Party, who broke away from the Congress, now also supported the DMK-led[26] United Front financially (Sankaralingam A., Personal Communication, 7 February 2020).

That said, the Congress had significantly more resources at its disposal, and the party spent heavily in an environment of acute shortages, hungry people, and empty granaries (Madras

Correspondent, *Link*, 1967 in Ramanujam, 1967: 178–79). K. Santhanam (1967 in Ramanujam, 1967: 266–67) contended that the lavish expenditures by the Congress party were unimaginable in scale, far higher than all the other parties' election budgets combined. On 24 February 1967, Annadurai expressly acknowledged the support extended by Rajaji and Mohammad Ismail of the Indian Union Muslim League.[27] Both Annadurai and Rajaji decided not to contest, and instead focus on the campaign and crisis management without being tied to a constituency.

It was clear in the camps of the Congress's opponents that their energy must be spent to defeat their rival by highlighting its failures. This helped the DMK for it got the Congress to include some Dravidianist promises in its manifesto, and foreground the utility of the Swatantra Party in non-ideological matters. The propaganda and manifesto of the DMK and its peers had a far-reaching impact. The positive development plans drawn up for the State were quite similar to what the Congress (Ramanujam, 1967: 154) was promising voters, but the opposition's style of communication bridged the gap. The DMK was unhappy that the Congress 'stole' its assurance to abolish land taxes, for instance, but its poll promises catered to every section of society, effectively offsetting one or two assurances shared by its primary electoral opponent.

The DMK capitalised on the growing sense of urgency and frustration among the people of Madras State. After experiencing an arduous phase of food scarcity, they were not prepared to buy the Congress's assurance of industrial development that loomed in a distant horizon. They needed immediate relief. The DMK's manifesto had a mix of short- and long-term deliverables, to first address immediate necessities, thereby gaining time to pursue projects that would take longer to materialise. For instance, it promised to set up small fertiliser plants in several places, instead of larger ones that would take longer to become functional.[28] It sought the nationalisation of banks, transport services, and movie theatres.

The Congress's promises were not very different, but it was weighed down by having been in power for nearly two decades.

The DMK held the Tamil Nadu Congress Committee and Kamaraj accountable for not having fulfilled earlier promises—the iron ore factory in Salem, for instance. Delays increase distrust, and the Congress's fresh set of assurances made voters angrier. In retrospect, the Congress government's performance in Madras State was not bad compared to other states, but it suffered because it could not handle issues and lacked a robust communication network that could counter criticism and reassure voters.

The DMK also promised to pursue the Congress and the Union government to end the dominance and imposition of Hindi, and urge the Union Public Service Commission to conduct examinations in all fourteen languages listed in the Eighth Schedule of the Constitution. This appealed to voters, reminding them afresh of their sacrifices over the years in the agitations against Hindi imposition. The manifesto especially condemned the army being called in to quell agitations. Annadurai's appeal, directed at the youth, to give up their protest and let the party take up their cause on their behalf cemented their faith in the DMK's intentions. Indeed, it is the DMK's leaders and supporters who had borne the brunt of police action during those agitations, and now the DMK members wore their success and courage with pride, even flaunting it on the campaign trail.

On the whole, the DMK's campaign projected two simultaneous images: of a sincere opposition party (Barnett, 1976: 118) that believed in the system and wanted to make it work to empower the marginalised and of a resilient, capable party that could stage massive protests against the government, and not shy away from enduring the repercussions.

Student Leader P. Seenivasan v. Stalwart K. Kamaraj

Kamaraj's electoral defeat in 1967, especially in his home constituency of Virudhunagar, can be viewed as the apotheosis of the Congress's decline in Madras State. However, it was not what set the ball of the Congress's rout rolling. After the 1952 assembly elections, the next election in Virudhunagar constituency was only in 1967. This is because Andhra State was created in 1953, Andhra

Pradesh in 1956, and fresh constituencies were drawn up only on the basis of the 1961 Census.

Virudhunagar was Kamaraj's hometown. Jonathan N. Gnanadason (1969: 1337) and Duncan B. Forrester (1970: 60) have explained Kamaraj's shrewd understanding of caste and religious dynamics in the electoral context as his reason for preferring to contest from seats with a significant Nadar caste presence. The Virudhunagar constituency is one such seat, where the Nadar caste members are numerically dominant, though socially non-dominant. Seenivasan, the student who defeated Kamaraj, on the other hand, was from the Naidu caste, which is socially dominant but numerically non-dominant in the region.[29]

Forrester (ibid.) cited two reasons for Kamaraj's defeat in the elections: first, that his Nadar support base was unsettled by the youth of the district feeling drawn to the DMK emotionally. Second, that the youth across Madras State had come to Virudhunagar to support Seenivasan's campaign. Besides, Seenivasan's relative, the then President of the State Congress Committee, Krishnasamy Naidu, also lost the 1967 election in the neighbouring Sattur constituency.[30] Notably, in the 1962 election, Kamaraj had beaten the Swatantra Party candidate Kota P. Ramamoorthy in Sattur—that, too, had been a Nadar-Naidu contest, similar to Virudhunagar in 1967.

But what if Kamaraj's electoral loss can be better explained by factors other than caste? Why did the youth back Seenivasan, who was otherwise a non-entity? A good place to begin finding answers is the reactions to Seenivasan's victory. For Annadurai, Seenivasan was inconsequential—he called him "The Bullet", as we noted in the Introduction, not the gun. But after he won from Virudhunagar, Seenivasan met Rajaji, seeking a berth in Annadurai's cabinet. Rajaji asked him if he had ever seen or heard of a statue being dedicated to Harvey Oswald, who assassinated United States President John F. Kennedy (Kesavan C.R., Personal Communication, 10 February 2020). But was Seenivasan a fame-hungry maniac like Oswald?

Seenivasan was but a twenty-eight-year-old law graduate when he contested the Virudhunagar election. He had spent three months in jail in 1963 at the same time as Annadurai for protesting against the rising prices of commodities.[31] He had been only twenty-three at the time, and a student at Pachaiyappa College, Madras. It was Annadurai's alma mater. Recall what Sivasubramanian had said (Chapter 2) on how the youth desired immensely to share similarities with Annadurai in those days.

Seenivasan also headed the students' union and the Students' Tamil Association in his college, and had met Kamaraj during a procession to the Chief Minister seeking an assurance against the imposition of the Devanagari script on regional languages. Kamaraj had chided Seenivasan, saying he should raise the issue with the public instead—a suggestion that would ultimately cost Kamaraj dearly.

On 25 January 1965, a day before the officially announced protest against the imposition of Hindi, Seenivasan was one of five student representatives allowed inside the Madras State Secretariat to meet Chief Minister Bhaktavatsalam, though the meeting did not ultimately take place (Ramasamy, 2020: 31). Seenivasan then mobilised students from neighbouring Andhra Pradesh and Mysore under the All-India Students' Anti-Hindi Agitation Council, and was subsequently arrested under the notorious Sino-Indian wartime legislation, the Defence of India Rules, 1962.

The arrest boosted Seenivasan's popularity among the youth, and more than 1,000 came to Virudhunagar to support his election campaign. Thirumaran, who witnessed the campaign, told me about Kalimuthu, Amudhan, N. Kamaraj, and Subbu, Seenivasan's compatriots and key student leaders who managed the campaign. Thirumaran said he saw the DMK's veteran leader Rahman Khan briefly during that campaign.

In those days, colleges were conducive sites for holding meetings, and I was told that Seenivasan had sent Kalimuthu to address gatherings on campuses at night. V.V. Ramasamy Nadar (Chapter 2), a follower of Periyar and a former Justice Party leader who was overseeing the administration of the colleges, supported the DMK at the time. The young men were everywhere, speaking to other students, Thirumaran said. School teachers also joined them, he said. Kamaraj's vague position on the anti-Hindi agitations and his unavailability to student protesters created resentment among teachers. They held positions of dignity and respect in the rural areas, so their displeasure with Kamaraj's attitude struck a severe blow, Thirumaran said.

While Rajaji did not openly comment on Kamaraj, the Swatantra Party leader of the region, who was a wealthy businessman, supported Seenivasan's campaign financially (Elangovan T.K.S.,[32] Personal Communication, 20 December 2019). The image of younger people on bicycles, working round the clock to understand and solve the problems of the region, had an impact.[33] Apart from the language issue, Seenivasan's campaign had focused on the repeal of the 17th Constitutional Amendment that allowed the government to acquire land, even if it was held under the ryotwari system in Madras and Kerala.[34] The seventeenth amendment allowed the lands held by people in his constituency and throughout Madras State to be taken over by the government. One of the few pithy one-liners formulated by the otherwise pensive Thirumaran went as follows: "The architect of the 16th Constitutional Amendment was defeated by a youngster who promised to fight against the 17th Constitutional Amendment."

Seenivasan also stood for the improvement of village infrastructure and living conditions, which resonated with voters' aspirations. Effective door-to-door communication steadily gathered votes into the DMK's camp, transcending the caste boundaries of Virudhunagar's constituents.

Kamaraj was responsible for the entire election campaign and went to the rallies of several Congress leaders. About a fortnight before the election, he hurt his leg in a car accident and could not campaign effectively during the last stretch. It was reported that he was complacent, and believed that he would win Virudhunagar (and many other seats) even with his eyes closed.[35] This comment attributed to him made him appear like the proverbial cat that closes its eyes and then claims the world is dark. Kamaraj needed to adopt a categorical stand on the anti-Hindi agitation, especially then, since in Virudhunagar, the DMK and the United Front were targeting him personally for failures. Arguably, Kamaraj did all he could for Congress candidates across the State, but ended up spending less time on his own constituency. Such a confident approach might seem logical—after all, the result was a big surprise to all.

Annadurai did not campaign in Virudhunagar out of respect for Kamaraj, and said other key leaders would not campaign either. Seenivasan sought an M.G.R. aide's help, R.M. Veerappan, who would become an AIADMK stalwart.[36] DMK was at the time milking the sympathy for its star campaigner, M.G.R., following an incident between him and veteran actor M.R. Radha. After a squabble on 12 January 1967 at M.G.R.'s residence, Radha shot at him, then tried to shoot himself.[37] Both survived with injuries, but eventually, M.G.R. took the post-election oath of office from the hospital.[38] As the incident happened during the campaign, Veerappan sought votes for the DMK with a photo of the injured leader. The same photo was used by Seenivasan in his campaign in Virudhunagar.

Kamaraj's defeat in Virudhunagar can indeed be seen as emblematic of the larger decline of the Congress party in Madras State. The State unit of the party had largely banked on him, and his absence due to national commitments created a significant void, especially felt by the voters of Virudhunagar. People missed their leader in action, even if party workers were among them. Seenivasan used this void—which amounted to the absence of an entire political narrative, not just a leader—to sway public sentiment in his favour. He won by a slim margin, but Seenivasan secured a lead right from the beginning.

The result indicated that the people supported the candidate who stood for their rights, protected their core identity, and promised to work for their socio-economic mobility. After having faced violence from the state machinery for expressing their dissent, the people saw elections as a chance to challenge and unsettle the system (Gopanna, 2008: 244). In public discussions, the story of the election and the surprise victory was trumped by conversations about Kamaraj's shocking loss. All but three ministers had lost their seats in the election, including Chief Minister Bhaktavatsalam. But Kamaraj's defeat captured the imagination. On his part, Kamaraj accepted the verdict, reflected on the problems that needed resolution, and said that to stay relevant, the party would need a course correction.

Hailed as Pioneer of Education and Defeated by Teachers

According to Sankaralingam, even the DMK could not have imagined the spectacular defeat of the Congress in the 1967 elections (Personal Communication, 7 February 2020). In the case of Kamaraj, the loss of support from teachers was a significant factor for his loss. Sankaralingam told me that Kamaraj had even expressed his displeasure at elementary school teachers campaigning for the DMK.

Recall that school students across Madras State had participated in the 1965 anti-Hindi protests (Ramasamy, 2020: 40–41). The DMK's alignment with the Dravidian-Tamil cause made it particularly attractive to teachers, students, and other sections of society that were disillusioned with the Congress party's handling of regional identity issues.

A senior Congress leader remarked that more than 1,50,000 elementary school teachers across Madras State were drawn to the ideals of the DMK, and campaigned like party workers for it. This was despite the teachers holding secure jobs and the government paying them Rs 100 a month—thanks to Kamaraj's policies. In frustration, this leader regretted the Congress government's decision to educate the people of Madras State.[39]

Conventional wisdom, however, would suggest that Kamaraj was an incredible leader who worked towards promoting education. The support that government school students enjoy even today in Tamil Nadu can be traced to initiatives he launched.[40] For him and his colleagues to have expressed their displeasure at the teachers for supporting the DMK reflected poorly on the party, and validated the criticism that the party was not aligned with the sensibilities and aspirations of the people.

Kamaraj: Defeated as Candidate but Conserved as an Idea

By this point, it was clear that Annadurai was a powerhouse campaigner in Madras State. His oratory and leadership made him stand out—he really could capture attention. What made him even more admirable was the respect he showed for other key figures like Kamaraj and Periyar, which spoke volumes about his statesmanship. He was relentless in raising issues about Madras State and its people, never missing a chance to speak up. His role in shaping the communication strategy for the United Front was key to their success. The way he crafted his message, peppered with relatable analogies and witty rhymes, while never reducing the emotional value or seriousness of the issues, contributed immensely to the campaign's strength.

Annadurai did not go to Virudhunagar to campaign for Seenivasan. Instead, he focused his criticism on the Congress party and the administration, leaving it to the people to make their own choice. After 1963, things became easier for Annadurai since Kamaraj moved to Delhi. His criticisms became more direct and he no longer felt he had to hold back. As the situation in the State worsened, the opposition's voice grew louder and its leaders became more popular.

Annadurai's strategy was to unite the opposition, and get all workers on board with a goal of building a better government. As a student of the veteran Congress and Swatantra Party leader N.G. Ranga with hands-on experience from the Madras State in the 1930s, he was determined to make the most informed choices when it came to picking candidates for constituencies. He made sure that no one in the party meetings threw up names without a thorough review of the region and the constituency. Once lists were made, feedback was gathered from party members and alliance leaders to gauge the chances of success. Viewed in this light, it is clear that choosing Seenivasan for Virudhunagar was a carefully considered decision.

After the elections, Annadurai was interviewed by a Tamil newspaper, where he said he felt shocked by Kamaraj's defeat. He explained that one of the reasons he'd picked Seenivasan for Virudhunagar was because Seenivasan had become a prominent leader in the anti-Hindi agitations, which had been violently suppressed. However, Annadurai also admitted that, deep down, he had some doubts about Seenivasan's chances of beating someone as established as Kamaraj.

Annadurai's observations about voters were worth noting. He pointed out that the Virudhunagar result showed how people were able to separate the individual from the ideology. In his view, it was the strength of their ideology that led to Seenivasan's victory and Kamaraj's defeat. Clearly, Kamaraj had lost touch with the people of Madras State and their Dravidian-Tamil values. The Kamaraj who had once been seen as the voice of the subalterns within the Congress party in the 1950s, and a champion of social justice, had become complacent. He had gotten too caught up in his national responsibilities and had drifted away from the very things his people had once looked up to him for.

Annadurai's shock over Kamaraj's defeat was not an ephemeral feeling. In fact, just after the election, Annadurai, while unveiling a portrait of Kamaraj at Pachaiyappan High School in Kanchipuram on 23 April 1967, said: "...a diamond is a piece of charcoal that has been under the ground for ages under high pressure. Kamaraj is like a diamond that has emerged from those sections of the society that have been oppressed for very long..." (Annadurai, 1967 in Gopanna, 2008: 311; Own Translation Lit.).

Even today, the DMK holds Kamaraj in high regard, considering him one of the tallest leaders in Tamil Nadu. DMK governments mention his name in the same breath as giants like Periyar, Annadurai, and Karunanidhi. He is affectionately referred to as *perunthalaivar* (great leader) and *karmaveerar* (warrior of deeds). When Kamaraj passed away in 1975, Karunanidhi immediately arranged for a state funeral, even though both he and Kamaraj were opposing Indira Gandhi's Emergency at the time.

When I asked Thirumaran about the DMK leaders' fondness for Kamaraj despite their campaign against them, he recalled what his brother, the veteran DMK leader K. Anbazhagan, had told him: Annadurai and Karunanidhi saw Kamaraj as a bridge between the Congress and the Dravidian-Tamil political vision. According to Anbazhagan, Kamaraj, the Dravidian movement, and the DMK all gained from each other. So, preserving the idea of Kamaraj was essential for carrying forward the Dravidian-Tamil ethos. Both ironically and unsurprisingly, the stories we hear about Kamaraj today, especially from self-proclaimed chroniclers, are filled with hagiographical details about him.

The Social Composition of Representatives at the Time of the Consummation of the Movement's Transition into Party Politics

In addition to Seenivasan, there were three important DMK candidates in the 1967 elections. First, there was Rajarathnam, a brick-kiln owner and bus operator who took on Chief Minister Bhaktavatsalam. Then, Ponnambalam, a school teacher, who ran against Food Minister Ramiah. Finally, there was T. Thangappan, a shopkeeper who took on Shanmuga Rajeswara Sethupathi, the ruler of the Ramnad kingdom and Minister of Public Works. The selection of these candidates shows how the movement didn't just appeal to diverse caste and class communities, but also how it turned more grassroots or semi-political movements into focused political demands and campaigns. On the other hand, the Congress's reliance on millionaire candidates and its internal squabbles worked in favour of the United Front campaign (Nathan 1967: 2138).

Table 8: Caste Composition of MLAs – 1967
State Assembly Elections

Caste/Community	Relative Share
Upper Caste	10.3%
Intermediate Caste	10.3%
Other Backward Classes	47.4%
Kongu Vellala Gounder	*9.8%*
Mukkulathor	*11.5%*
Vanniyar	*11.5%*
OBC Other	*14.5%*
Scheduled Caste	18.4%
Scheduled Tribe	0.9%
Christian	0.9%
Muslim	1.7%
Unidentified	10.3%
Total	100.0%

Source: Fieldwork – Vignesh Rajahmani

Table 9: Partywise Caste Breakdown of MLAs – 1967 State Assembly Elections

Party	**UC**	**IC**	**OBC**	**SC**	**ST**	**Christian**	**Muslim**	**Unidentified**	**Total**
CPI	0.0%	0.4%	0.0%	0.4%	0.0%	0.0%	0.0%	0.0%	0.9%
CPM	0.9%	0.9%	0.4%	0.9%	0.0%	0.0%	0.0%	1.7%	4.7%
DMK	6.4%	5.6%	27.8%	13.7%	0.4%	0.0%	0.4%	4.3%	58.5%
FBL	0.0%	0.0%	0.4%	0.0%	0.0%	0.0%	0.0%	0.0%	0.4%
INC	1.7%	2.6%	10.7%	2.1%	0.4%	0.9%	0.0%	3.4%	21.8%
IND	0.4%	0.4%	0.0%	0.4%	0.0%	0.0%	1.3%	0.0%	2.6%
PSP	0.0%	0.0%	0.9%	0.0%	0.0%	0.0%	0.0%	0.9%	1.7%
SSP	0.0%	0.0%	0.9%	0.0%	0.0%	0.0%	0.0%	0.0%	0.9%
SWA	0.9%	0.4%	6.4%	0.9%	0.0%	0.0%	0.0%	0.0%	8.5%
Total	10.3%	10.3%	47.4%	18.4%	0.9%	0.9%	1.7%	10.3%	100.0%

Source: Fieldwork – Vignesh Rajahmani

The DMK-led United Front alliance swept the elections with 182 out of 233 seats, securing a 54.02% vote share. The DMK secured a simple majority on its own with 138 wins out of the 173 seats it contested in. It contributed 41.21% of the United Front's combined vote share. The Swatantra Party secured twenty of the 27 seats it contested, with 4.98% of the alliance's vote share, the CPI(M) secured 11 of 22 seats and 3.89% of the total vote share, the Praja Socialist Party won all four seats it contested (0.89% vote share), and the Samyukta Socialist Party won two seats out of the three it contested (0.55% vote share). Seven alliance-backed independent candidates also won (Nathan, 1967: 2138).

On the other hand, the Congress party contested 234 seats and won only 49, though with an impressive 41.43% share of the total votes. Among the parties that did not join any alliance, the CPI bagged 2 seats. The share of seats of upper castes dipped to 10.3%, while the intermediate castes had a 10.3% share. The Other Backward Classes had a 47.4% seat share, within which caste groups other than the numerically dominant Mukkulathors, Vanniyars, and Kongu Vellala Gounders had a 14.5% share.

The Mukkulathors, Vanniyars, and Kongu Vellala Gounders won 32.9% of the seats, slightly over their proportion in the population. The DMK had a higher share of Vanniyars and MLAs belonging to the non-dominant backward caste groups. Since the Congress did not win this election, the share of Kongu Vellala Gounder candidates, whose community were its traditional voters, fell in the Assembly. However, the DMK had a few winners from this community (Tables 8 and 9).

DMK's MLAs and Representativeness of the Legislative Assembly

After the 1952 election, DMK-supported MLAs had a 20.9% share in the Assembly, of which 2.6% were upper castes, 1.6% were intermediate castes, 11.5% were OBCs and 3.6% were SCs. In 1957, the DMK had a 7.3% of seats in the legislature, of which 1.5% were upper castes, 1% were intermediate castes,

2.8% were from the Other Backward Classes and 2% were from a Scheduled Caste.

In 1962, the DMK had one-fourth of the seats in the legislature (24.3% seat share) of which 3.4% were upper castes, 3.4% were intermediate castes, 12.6% were from the Other Backward Classes category, and 3.9% were from the Scheduled Castes. Now, after the 1967 elections, the DMK had a 58.5% share in the Assembly with 6.4% upper castes, 5.6% intermediate castes, 27.8% Other Backward Classes, and 13.7% Scheduled Castes [Table 10].

It was clear that the DMK's rise deepened the democratisation among subaltern communities, which steadily reflected in the changing composition of the elected representatives sent to the legislature by voters. To be sure, the DMK's success did not reduce the representation of the regionally dominant lower-caste groups. The regional dominance of lower-caste groups, and the social unrest that came with it due to the presence of numerically and/ or socially dominant caste groups, was tackled by spreading the politics of social justice among the public as a whole.

Moreover, the broader, anti-caste Dravidian-Tamil identity, which people needed to be aligned with in order to be electorally relevant—especially given the organisational strength of the DMK and the prevailing conventional wisdom at the time—ended up weakening the casteist influence of such dominant lower-caste groups.

The Not-So-Representative Cabinets?

Let's take a look at the caste composition of cabinets under different leaderships. The Congress cabinets include the one Rajaji cobbled together in 1952, the 1953 cabinet after the bifurcation of the Madras State and formation of the Andhra State, the 1954 cabinet put together by Kamaraj, the 1957 and 1962 cabinets following Assembly elections, the one in 1963 after Kamaraj's resignation following the Kamaraj Plan, and the 1967 post-election DMK cabinet led by Annadurai.

In the 1952 and 1953 cabinets, more than 50% of the berths were allotted to upper and intermediate caste members—nine

Table 10: Election-wise Breakdown of Caste Composition of DMK MLAs

Year	UC	IC	OBC	SC	ST	Christian	Muslim	Unidentified	% of seats in Assembly
1952 Supported by DMK	2.60%	1.60%	11.50%	3.70%	0.00%	0.00%	0.00%	1.60%	20.90%
1957 IND (DMK)	1.5%	1.0%	2.8%	2.0%	0.0%	0.0%	0.0%	0.0%	7.3%
1962 DMK	3.4%	3.4%	12.6%	3.9%	0.0%	0.0%	0.5%	0.5%	24.3%
1967 DMK	6.4%	5.6%	27.8%	13.7%	0.4%	0.0%	0.4%	4.3%	58.5%

Source: Fieldwork – Vignesh Rajahmani

out of 15 (six to upper castes and three to intermediate castes) in 1952, and eight out of 12 (five to upper castes and three to intermediate castes) in 1953. The backward castes and Scheduled Castes together had a two-fifths share in the 1952 cabinet (four berths to OBCs and one to an SC), and a one-third share in 1953 (four berths to OBCs and zero to SCs). The bifurcation of Madras State freed up some space for lower castes in Tamil-speaking regions who were more politicised compared to the lower castes in Andhra State.

Kamaraj began the subalternalisation and Dravidianisation of the cabinet. Over the next four cabinets—three formed by Kamaraj and one by Bhaktavatsalam—there was a noticeable shift. The representation of upper and intermediate castes dropped to an average of just 30% (10 out of 33 seats). Meanwhile, the share of backward castes (17 berths) and SCs (four berths) rose to 63% on average. Muslims also gained representation in the 1962 and 1963 cabinets, with their average share across the four cabinets standing at 6%.

The composition of the 1967 DMK cabinet mirrored the average of the four previous cabinets—one-third to upper and intermediate castes, more than half (four) to Other Backward Classes and Scheduled Caste (one), and one berth out of nine to Muslims. Among the Other Backward Classes, across all six cabinets, the Kongu Vellala Gounders, Mukkulathors, and Vanniyars together held three-fourths of cabinet berths (23/30). The remaining backward castes held seven out of thirty berths.

The allotment of less-sought-after berths like Finance, Public Works, etc., to lower or depressed-caste groups—a criticism levelled again later Dravidian cabinets—does not apply to the cabinets discussed here due to indomitable leaders like Sanjivayya and Kakkan in the Congress party and Sathyavani Muthu in the DMK, who belonged to Scheduled Caste groups but held important portfolios. However, the criticism about lower average share (8.69%) of such communities across these cabinets is valid and of concern (Table 11).

Table 11: Caste Composition of Madras State Cabinets (Fieldwork Findings)

Category	1952	1953	1954	1957	1962	1963	1967	Total
Upper Caste	6	5	2	2	2	2	1	20
Intermediate Caste	3	3	0	0	1	1	2	10
Other Backward Classes	5	4	5	5	4	3	4	30
Kongu Vellalar Gounder	*2*	*2*	*1*	*1*	*1*	*1*	*1*	*9*
Mukkulathor	*1*	*1*	*1*	*1*	*1*	*1*	*0*	*6*
Vanniyar	*1*	*1*	*2*	*1*	*1*	*1*	*1*	*8*
Other OBC	1	0	1	2	1	0	2	7
Scheduled Caste	1	0	1	1	1	1	1	6
Muslim	0	0	0	0	1	1	1	3
Unidentified	0	0	0	0	0	0	0	1
Total	15	12	8	8	9	8	9	69

Due to unavailability of data, the educational profiles of Members of the Legislative Assembly from 1952 to 1957 remains a lacuna in the research into that period. However, we do know that the elections held in 1957, 1962, and 1967 produced no unlettered elected representative. Also, the share of elected representatives in the lowermost category of literacy dipped from 39.02% in 1957 to 8.25% in 1962, and to zero in 1967. The education level of elected candidates kept rising in this period—the data show that MLAs who completed middle school rose by 73%, those who completed secondary school 59%, and those who had completed their intermediate education in the arts or sciences more than doubled, rising by 134%.

In 1957, one-fourth (24.88%) of Legislative Assembly members were degree or diploma holders, including graduates and postgraduates. This dipped slightly to 24.27% in 1962 and shot up to 35.19% in 1967. The reduction in the number of postgraduate legislators and the rise of graduates in the Assembly between 1957 and 1967 is in line with the lower median age of members of the Assembly after the 1967 elections. This reveals the upwardly mobile but subaltern backgrounds of the new class of legislators joining the Assembly (Table 12).

Table 12: Education Profile of MLAs (TN Assembly Archive)

Educational Qualifications	**1957**	**1962**	**1967**
Literate	80	17	0
Middle School	43	71	85
Matriculate or Secondary School-Leaving Certificate	26	55	47
Intermediate in Arts or Science	5	13	19
Degrees and Diplomas			
Graduates in Arts or Science	15	21	21
Post-Graduate in Arts or Science	10	6	8[41]
Teaching	1	3	4
Engineering	0	0	1
Agriculture	0	0	0
Veterinary	1	0	0
Commerce	2	2	0
Legal	19	18	35
Medical	2	0	3
Others	1	0	10
Total	205	206	233

Evaluating the Outcome of Salem Conference's Resolution against Usage of Caste References

The DK's Salem Conference of 1944 called on people to drop caste titles, references, and honorifics from their names as a way to forge a fraternal and secular bond with the people. Along with this, the creation and spread of the Dravidian-Tamil ethos led to new naming practices in the region. Names given to children, and even stage names for adults and youngsters, began to reflect a shift towards assertiveness and dignity. Before this, names associated with marginalised castes were often easily identifiable and considered sub-par to those from other groups.

The new naming conventions had four key sources: first, figures from Western Enlightenment; second, icons of Tamil culture and references from the Sangam era; third, the Self-Respect Movement, which encouraged words associated with desirable qualities—like 'Arivu' (intelligence) as names. Sometimes, these trait-based names were combined with titles like 'Arasan' (king) or 'Arasi' (queen), resulting in male names like Arivarasan and females named Arivarasi. Many of these names are still common today. Fourth, the socio-political movements in the West, and most importantly, the communist ideology and the Bolshevik Revolution, were admired in the Madras region. Periyar even named children Moscow and Volga. However, more commonly used names were Lenin, Marx, and Stalin.

School teachers, many of whom were influenced by the movement, played a key role in ensuring that caste names were dropped when students were registered. This effort continued from the 1950s to the 1980s, with teachers either using the father's name as a surname or giving students new Tamil names. Today, having a caste reference in your name is considered an oddity, as opposed to a state like Uttar Pradesh, where research (Kumar, 2024) indicates that the ascendance of marginalised-caste-led socio-political movements has led to the inclusion of caste references in people's names.

The rise of the DMK also had an impact on the use of caste titles by candidates from all parties. After the 1952 elections, 42.4% of MLAs had caste references in their names (Table 13). Of the 21% MLAs that the DMK supported, 10.5% had caste references in their names (Table 14). The 1957 MLAs list registered a slight dip, with 41.5% having caste references in their names. Of the 7.4%

seats that the DMK candidates won, 2% had caste references in their names, and 5.4% did not (Table 15).

The increased presence of the DMK in the Assembly in the 1962 elections decreased the percentage of MLAs with caste titles to 36.9%. Of the DMK MLAs, a mere 3.9% had caste references in their names (Table 16). The 1967 results saw a definitive trend: only 18.8% of MLAs had caste references in their names. The DMK had a 58.6% share in the Assembly, of which 6% MLAs had caste references in their names (Table 17).

Table 13: Tracking Caste References/Titles in Names of MLAs – 1952

Party	Caste Title Present	Caste Title Absent
INC	20.4%	30.4%
CPI	0.5%	6.8%
CWP	2.6%	0.5%
FBL(MG)	1.6%	0.0%
IND	11.5%	9.4%
JUSP	0.0%	0.5%
KMPP	1.6%	2.1%
SCF	0.0%	0.5%
SP	1.0%	0.5%
TTP	3.1%	6.8%
Total	42.4%	57.6%

Source: Fieldwork – Vignesh Rajahmani

Table 14: Tracking Caste References/Titles in Names of MLAs Supported by DMK – 1952

Party	Caste Title Present	Caste Title Absent
CPI	0.00%	0.50%
CWP	1.60%	0.50%
IND	6.30%	3.70%

Party	Caste Title Present	Caste Title Absent
KMPP	0.00%	1.00%
SCF	0.00%	0.50%
TTP	2.60%	4.20%
Total	10.50%	10.50%

Source: Fieldwork – Vignesh Rajahmani

Table 15: Tracking Caste References/ Titles in Names of MLAs – 1957

Party	Caste Title Present	Caste Title Absent
CPI	0.0%	2.0%
INC	30.2%	43.4%
IND	9.3%	6.8%
IND (DMK)	2.0%	5.4%
PSP	0.0%	1.0%
Total	41.5%	58.5%

Source: Fieldwork – Vignesh Rajahmani

Table 16: Tracking Caste References/Titles in Names of MLAs – 1962

Party	Caste Title Present	Caste Title Absent
CPI	0.00%	1.00%
DMK	3.90%	20.40%
FB	1.00%	0.50%
INC	28.20%	39.30%
IND	2.40%	0.00%
SOC	0.00%	0.50%
SWA	1.50%	1.50%
Total	36.90%	63.10%

Source: Fieldwork – Vignesh Rajahmani

Table 17: Tracking Caste References/ Titles in Names of MLAs – 1967

Party	Caste Title Present	Caste Title Absent
CPI	0.00%	0.90%
CPM	0.00%	4.70%
DMK	6.00%	52.60%
FBL	0.40%	0.00%
INC	7.70%	14.10%
IND	0.40%	2.10%
PSP	0.40%	1.30%
SSP	0.00%	0.90%
SWA	3.80%	4.70%
Total	18.80%	81.20%

Source: Fieldwork – Vignesh Rajahmani

Assemblies and Cabinets as Almost All-Male Clubs

The Justice Party had a woman member of the Legislative Council in the 1920s—Muthulakshmi Reddy—when voting rights were limited by both gender and class. However, when universal suffrage was introduced, the first Assembly election in Madras State didn't result in any representation for women. Twenty-four women (13 Congress, one DMK, 10 Others) were fielded in 1957, with 12 being elected (11 Congress and one DMK). The seat share was 5.9%.

In 1962, 23 women candidates were fielded (15 Congress, two DMK, and six Others) of which 13 were elected (11 Congress, one DMK, and one Others). The seat share was 6.3%. And in the 1967 elections, women's representation dipped: sixteeen candidates were fielded (10 Congress, three DMK, three Others) of which four were elected (three DMK, one Others; Table 18).

Only three women got cabinet berths across all cabinets between 1952 and 1967—Jothi Venkatachalam (1953, 1962, 1963) and Lourdammal Simon (1957) in the Congress cabinets, and Sathyavani Muthu (1967) in the DMK cabinet. While Jothi belonged to an intermediate caste (Naidu) and married a Dalit, Lourdammal belonged to a caste included within the Other Backward Classes category (Mukkuvar), and Sathyavani belonged to a Scheduled Caste (Paraiyar). To sum up, the seat share was abysmally low at 1.7% and the average share of cabinet berths to women was low at 7.24%.

Table 18: Women Candidates and Women MLAs between 1957 and 1967

Year	Contested Women			Elected Women		
	Congress	**DMK**	**Others**	**Congress**	**DMK**	**Others**
1957	13	1	10	11	1	0
1962	15	2	6	11	1	1
1967	10	3	3	0	3	1

Source: Fieldwork – Vignesh Rajahmani

Conclusion

The 1960s saw the DMK and its allies changing how political mobilisation and communication were done in Madras State. The DMK's mobilisation techniques were about giving people agency. The leaders were ordinary people who echoed the concerns of the public—concerns which resonated across the State. The DMK's leaders and workers always had an ear to the ground, and that enabled them to forge even closer ties with people. Being able to relate to their issues, in turn, helped calibrate the Dravidian-Tamil vision. As the people's dissatisfaction grew against the style and substance of the ruling Congress party's governance, the DMK could channel it in ways that threw the government off-balance.

The DMK and its United Front allies could effectively communicate to the people that the prevailing politics of patronage could not address their day-to-day issues. While a leader like Periyar stood with Kamaraj for the positive measures he took for welfare and development, the DMK was also a responsible opposition to the Congress.

The schemes of the Congress had their limitations: talking up plans for industrialisation in remote districts—which meant that welfare was relegated to the distant future—proved counterproductive among people starving from acute food shortages, including of staples like rice.

The decentralisation of electioneering, with a focus on regions and constituencies, turned the election into a series of small battles rather than one big war. But the DMK was ready for both—fighting those smaller battles and the larger war. This strategy helped ensure Seenivasan's victory in Virudhunagar, and also boosted the United Front candidates across Madras State. Seenivasan emerged as a representative of a new generation of young leaders, and his campaign showed there were many committed younger people in Virudhunagar who could tap into the region's potential and drive change.

The DMK's reach in Virudhunagar was significant, thanks to the combined efforts of various groups—students, former Justice Party leaders, Swatantra Party leaders, sympathisers, and caste associations. The Dravidian-Tamil identity successfully challenged the prevalent power structures, and the Dravidian movement's transition into party politics created a space where new, marginalised groups could find expression, get politicised, and gain power.

Kamaraj's sudden shift in 1963, which he thought was necessary to strengthen the party, made sense in theory—it seemed like a selfless and noble decision. But his absence revealed how much the Tamil Nadu Congress Committee relied on his persona. They needed him much more than he may have realised.

CONCLUSION

This book set out to explore and explicate how the DMK played a crucial role in transforming the Dravidian movement—a socio-cultural movement centered on anti-caste politics and the uplift of marginalised sections—into electorally viable party politics. This shift, which took time and tremendous effort, involved building a solid party structure with a coherent organisation and dedicated support base, and it reached its finest hour in 1967 when the DMK won the Assembly elections in the Madras State.

The first chapter traced the conception of the Dravidian-Tamil identity as a broad political concept with universalist appeal that challenged prevailing hegemonies of caste, class, and religion, at local as well as national levels. It argued that Periyar was key in bringing together the ideologies of social reformers like Iyothee Thass, Maraimalai Adigal, and others, forming the 'Dravidian-Tamil' identity as an ethnic group. As the aggregator of these ideologies, Periyar drove what are called 'horizontal solidarities' among backward and depressed caste groups under the Dravidian-Tamil ethos, shaping a vital counter-hegemonic alliance to the graded inequality of the caste system.

The chapter also discussed the role of Annadurai and the DMK in making the Dravidian-Tamil identity relatable and open to hitherto excluded groups like theists and Brahmins. This allowed the identity to be embraced by a wider range of people, rather than being seen as something rigidly defined by caste. The chapter also highlighted the tension within the identity around gender, which was more openly acknowledged by the DK. Additionally, it discussed the limited ability of the Dravidian-Tamil ethos to penetrate the private lives of individuals from different caste groups.

The second chapter focused on the often-overlooked networks that helped spread the DMK's ideology, particularly the network of reading rooms established and managed by the DMK and its sympathisers. These reading rooms played a crucial role in getting the people of Madras State politically engaged. Run by a range of stakeholders—the DK, the DMK, caste associations, and individuals or collectives sympathetic to the movement—they became hubs where content and ideas flowed freely between the DMK and the general public.

In addition to serving as associational spaces for reading, these rooms evolved into training centres where a new generation of fiery cadres were nurtured. These cadres often stood out as charismatic public speakers during elections. The reading rooms often became public spaces where people could come together for collective action, bond over shared goals, and invest themselves in the movement. The DMK's approach to organisational pluralism, allowing autonomy for both its cadre and supporters, helped unite different stakeholders and build a powerful public sphere. The growing spread of political messages and the cultivation of dedicated cadres gave the DMK a significant edge as it ventured into electoral forays.

Building on the analysis of this dynamic dissemination network, the third chapter explored six key developments that were either sparked by the DMK or affected it—in some cases, both—and how the party's response to these events helped it gain ground in the electoral arena. One major turning point was the protests by Dravidian collectives, caste associations, and some Congress leaders against the Union government's decision to abolish the Communal GO. This led to the Constitution First Amendment Act, which reinstated affirmative action quotas for marginalised groups, albeit in a different form. The controversy caused a split within the Congress party, setting the stage for the Madras State unit of the Congress party to begin its shift towards a more subaltern-focused identity.

The underwhelming performance of the Congress party in the 1952 Assembly elections and the subsequent intervention by Rajaji in the form of an unsustainable coalition government enabled the DK and DMK to develop into formidable political and electoral forces. The DMK's persistence in advocating for mobility of the marginalised groups—especially against policies that either denied equality or reinforced caste—became a driving force behind both the socioeconomic rise of the marginalised and political ascendence of the DMK.[1]

The formation of Andhra State in 1953 and the subsequent linguistic reorganisation of States in 1956 created a Tamil-speaking region that was increasingly dominated by people from marginalised caste groups, as many from the dominant caste groups moved to other States including Karnataka, Kerala, and Andhra Pradesh. This shift weakened Rajaji's position in the political arena due to the moving away of a section of elites and landlords from Madras State and simultaneously contributed to the dilution of DMK's secessionist demand. However, the Congress party's knee-jerk reaction in 1963 with the Sixteenth Constitutional Amendment compelled the DMK to officially abandon the demand for a separate Dravida Nadu. All the same, the DMK continued to keep the spirit of federal autonomy alive and warned the people about centralising tendencies of the Indian Union.

The Union's push to impose Hindi as the sole official language and a mandatory language in schools became a pivotal moment for the restiveness brewing in the Madras State. Mass agitations by people from all walks of life, along with the tragic deaths during the agitations—whether through self-immolations or State violence—tarnished the Congress party's reputation. Chief Minister Bhaktavatsalam's high-handed and inflexible approach to the agitations and the DMK's mobilisations cost the Congress party dearly.

Meanwhile, the effects of price rise and the Congress government's failure to deftly manage the difficult economic situation left large sections of people disgruntled, irrespective of caste, class, language, or gender. All these factors made the Dravidian ideologies of social justice, socioeconomic mobility of the marginalised, and federal autonomy, combined with its promise to help the marginalised realise their aspirations, resonate more deeply with the people. They increasingly sought to adopt the ideology. The DMK's strategic flexibility—its ability to adapt its long-term goals to fit within the evolving framework of the Indian Union—ultimately played a crucial role in consolidating the party's power.

The final chapter focused on the defeat of Kamaraj at the hands of Seenivasan, a student leader, marking a pivotal moment in the Dravidian movement's transition into an electorally successful political force. Several factors contributed to Kamaraj's downfall: factionalism within the Congress, the party's reliance on powerful and wealthy elites to secure votes, the absence of Kamaraj in the State owing to his K-Plan starting in 1963, and the DMK-led United Front's well-organised campaign. All these factors contributed to Congress party's rout and Kamaraj's defeat.

Rather than celebrating Kamaraj's loss, the DMK took a different approach. The party acknowledged his significance as a great leader, which allowed it to preserve the idea of Kamaraj as a subaltern leader of Madras State. By separating Kamaraj's personal stature from his party affiliation, the DMK effectively maintained his legacy while positioning itself as the political force of change.

The book also explored the changing composition of the legislature and cabinets throughout the 1950s and 1960s, highlighting the growing dominance of the marginalised castes over the upper caste groups. While anti-Congress alliances were being formed in states like Bihar, West Bengal, and Gujarat during this period, there were two key differences in Madras State. First, unlike the other states, the alliances in Madras were built on large-scale social movements.

Second, unlike in other states where anti-Congress alliances were led by upper-caste leaders, Tamil Nadu (then Madras State) saw lower-caste leadership play a crucial role in challenging upper-caste dominance and later spearheading the formation of anti-Congress alliances in the State.[2] In addition to examining the changing caste composition in the legislature and cabinets, Chapter 4 tracked the practice of dropping caste titles and references from the names of members of the Legislative Assembly between 1952 and 1967. This move was part of an effort to secularise public life and establish horizontal solidarity among the State's diverse caste groups.

The DMK and Periyar's DK, though both were rooted in self-respect and non-Brahmin assertion, operated fundamentally differently. The DK was known for its dramatic tactics, such as burning Hindi books, the Indian flag, and sometimes even copies of the Constitution of India. Through these, it sought to denounce Aryan oppression, a term used to symbolise both Brahminism and the dominance of the elite in the Union government's policies. While these protests were often theatrical, they usually served a concrete purpose rather than just making a spectacle.

On the other hand, while the DK stuck closely to its theoretical principles, the DMK took a more pragmatic approach. It refined and modernised its ideology, making it not just more relevant but innovative for their time – its response to the Sixteenth Constitutional Amendment Act is a case in point. In fact, one could argue that the DMK's true strength wasn't just in its electoral campaigns or alliances, but in its consistent work in non-electoral politics. This allowed the party to embed politics into everyday life and make it inclusive, transforming Dravidian-Tamil society rather than treating politics as a one-off event.

Even in the early 1950s, when the DMK wasn't participating directly in elections, it was still active in politics, focusing on three essential pillars of its ideology: economic assertion to break the monopoly of North Indian traders and businessmen, geographic assertion and regional autonomy against Delhi's centralising rule, and opposing the subtle incursion of caste hegemony through the education policy of the Madras government. The DMK was so strongly committed to each of these causes that its leaders were ready to face jail time rather than back down on any of them. They understood that compromising on these principles would delegitimise their movement. For them, social justice wasn't just a goal—it was non-negotiable.

The impact of this kind of politicking is crucial to understanding both Tamil and Indian politics. It marked the beginning of the

Congress party becoming more regional, and the fact that it was a Nadar non-Brahmin leader who took the reins of this shift is significant. Over time, this would take on a life of its own, as the values of social justice, nurtured by the DMK's struggles, became fundamental to any political discourse in Tamil Nadu.

Periyar's continued support for Kamaraj, despite his opposition to the Congress-led Union government's imposition of Hindi, often puzzles political analysts. Many, especially those focused on ideological purity, view it as opportunism. However, what they overlook is that Periyar's approach was not about political expediency but the continual reinvention of horizontal solidarity. For him, social justice was not a rigid doctrine but a fluid and dynamic force—one that resisted absolute adherence to notions of purity and fixed principles.

The transition of the Dravidian movement into party politics was an astute move that recognised the nature of power and its potential for effecting change within India's federal framework. The DMK's broad and inclusive Dravidian-Tamil identity, revolving around the empowerment of the maginalised, allowed them to democratise power, recognise specific grievances, and redistribute resources. But after such a transformative shift, an important question arises: what happened after that? To answer this, an epilogue is needed.

EPILOGUE

THE DRAVIDIAN-TAMIL ETHOS TODAY

The transition left a long-lasting impact on Madras State for over half a century and, across caste, class, gender, and sexuality, and in the arenas of development and political culture. The Dravidian-Tamil identity continues to evolve, gaining new meanings with each passing decade. The rivalry between the DMK and the AIADMK has played a pivotal role in politicising multiple caste groups, broadening the reach of Dravidian-Tamil ideals. M.G. Ramachandran breaking away from the DMK in the 1970s and forming the AIADMK, for instance, extended the ethos to regions and communities that had previously leaned towards the Congress party. This expansion was also evident in the numerous commissions formed to evaluate and adjust reservation quotas for marginalised caste groups.

While the implementation of the Mandal Commission's Other Backward Classes reservation quota faced severe backlash from elites across the country, the people of Tamil Nadu lauded V.P. Singh, the then Prime Minister. Tamil Nadu's commitment to affirmative action intensified under the leadership of Karunanidhi, M.G.R., and Jayalalithaa. Between the 1970s and 1990s, reservation quotas in the State surpassed two-thirds. When it exceeded the 50% cap set by the Supreme Court in the 1992 Indra Sawhney judgment, the State ensured their continuance through negotiations with the

Union by placing reservations under the Ninth Schedule of the Constitution, shielding them from judicial review.

Notably, in 2019, the breach of the 50% reservation limit occurred at the national level with the implementation of a 10% quota for the Economically Weaker Sections (EWS) among non-reserved caste groups. By implementing the EWS reservation, the Supreme Court recognised economic backwardness as an additional criterion for quotas, alongside the constitutionally mandated focus on social and educational backwardness. The DMK was one of only five political parties across India that opposed the EWS reservation and it also criticised the Supreme Court for upholding it.[1]

Tamil Nadu's quota system is designed to address the most marginalised among the Dalits (particularly Arunthathiyars), women, and Muslims, through sub-categorisation.[2] The Other Backward Classes reservation quota (50%) is sub-categorised into two segments: Backward Classes (30%) and Most Backward Classes (20%). On 19 April 2023, the Tamil Nadu Legislative Assembly passed a resolution[3] calling on the Union government to extend the Scheduled Caste quota to Dalits who have converted to Christianity.[4]

The issue of Dalits from the Muslim and Christian communities not receiving reservation, while Buddhists, Sikhs, and Hindus do, has been in a subject of national debate. However, Tamil Nadu's approach to ascertaining backwardness remains sensitive to the persistence of discrimination despite religious conversion.

In the realm of non-binary genders, the DMK established a Transgender Persons Welfare Board[5] in 2008, and the then Chief Minister Karunanidhi replaced the prevalent derogatory references and introduced the term *thirunangai* (transwoman)—a civil term signalling respect. The welfare board was instrumental in providing essential services to transwomen, including settlements, ration cards, and voter identity cards. Furthering the cause, Tiruchi Siva,[6] a Member of Parliament from the DMK, introduced the Rights of Transgender Persons Bill in 2014. It was passed by the Rajya Sabha in April 2015, making it the first successful Private Member's Bill introduced by a parliamentarian outside of the Council of Ministers in over four decades.[7]

In 2014, the Chennai Rainbow Pride March was renamed *Vaanavil Suyamariyathai Perani* (Rainbow Pride / Self-Respect March). The pride flag of the LGBTQIA+ movement was also redesigned with streaks of blue, denoting Ambedkarite thought, and black, signifying Periyarist thought. This redesign acknowledged the intersectionality and multiplicity of identities. The new rainbow flag was unveiled on 7 July 2018[8] at the Queer LitFest in Chennai, unsurprisingly drawing criticism from a section of elites.[9]

In 2022, the Tamil Nadu government became the first in the country to issue a glossary of respectful terms for addressing persons belonging to the LGBTQIA+ community and urged media outlets to adopt these terms.[10] By early 2024, the DMK government had also drawn up a draft policy to protect the rights of the LGBTQIA+ community.

Thus, the Dravidian-Tamil identity, which initially grew to encompass non-Brahmin elite caste groups (as discussed in the first half of this book), and lower-caste groups (addressed in the second half), now continues to include the LGBTQIA+ community. This ongoing process reflects the politics of *becoming*, driven by inclusive policies and the transformative ideologies of the Dravidian movement.

Taking Stock of the Mobility of the Marginalised

One of the central pillars of the Dravidian movement has been the socioeconomic mobility of marginalised communities. Kalaiyarasan and Vijayabaskar (2021: 125) establish that the anti-caste movement led to the creation of a chain of equivalence across communities through the Dravidian-Tamil identity. This broad-based identity, which brought together various marginalised caste groups, has made the Dravidian-Tamil bloc more resilient. As a result, Tamil Nadu has outperformed states like Gujarat or Himachal Pradesh in terms of growth and development indicators,[11] whereas the latter two have excelled only in one of these areas.

Overall, Tamil Nadu ranks second only to Maharashtra in terms of Gross State Domestic Product (GSDP) and second to Kerala in several development indicators. By mobilising a range of datasets,

Kalaiyarasan and Vijaybaskar empirically demonstrate that this growth and development have been facilitated by democratisation. For instance, Tamil Nadu stands as the most urbanised among major Indian states, boasts the highest Gross Enrolment Ratio (higher education), and is home to the highest number of medical colleges. The poverty ratio in the State is the fourth lowest in the country[12] (Multi-dimensional Poverty Index), a considerably low percentage of households are dependent solely on agriculture for their income, and it has the highest number of women who work in factories.[13]

This impressive trajectory cannot be solely attributed to the DMK. The broader Dravidian movement, including the Justice Party, the AIADMK, and even the Congress party, also played a crucial role in shaping the State's socioeconomic landscape.

Drawing from Laclau (2005: 78), Kalaiyarasan and Vijayabaskar argue that the particularistic grievances of various communities were grouped together into universalistic grievances, forming an equivalence chain. However, the concern arises that such grouping might lead to differential outcomes and experiences concerning the particular grievances of different communities. This critique of differential developmental outcomes was earlier raised by scholars like Narendra Subramanian (1999: 72–73). In response, Kalaiyarasan and Vijayabaskar highlight significant socioeconomic mobility, citing the high Gross Enrolment Ratio among Dalit students, Tamil Nadu's status as home to the highest number of Dalit-owned enterprises in India, and notable convergence between Dalits and lower Other Backward Classes across indicators such as education, employment, and wealth.

One Group A officer working in the Tamil Nadu Secretariat for more than thirty years shared that the Dravidian parties are particularly focused on expediting cases filed under the Scheduled Castes and Scheduled Tribes (Prevention of Atrocities) Act.[14] She also said that the Tamil Nadu government has reached a historical milestone with the highest number of Dalit Secretary-level positions in its administrative history (Kundavai,[15] 2021: 5 October 2021).

Tamil Nadu also boasts a successful government-led cohabitation project called Periyar Ninaivu Samathuvapuram (Periyar Memorial Equality Village Scheme), launched in 1997 by the DMK government under Karunanidhi's leadership. The scheme aimed to construct hundred-home villages, with forty houses earmarked for Dalits, twenty-five for the Most Backward Classes, twenty-five for Backward Classes, and ten for other communities. As of June 2022, 235 such villages had been inaugurated across Tamil Nadu.[16]

While the concept of equality was spatially realised through Samathuvapuram, Karunanidhi linked this vision to the State's growing Information Technology (IT) sector. In 2000, during the inauguration of Chennai's Information Technology Park, he remarked that the technological advancement of the twenty-first century should not coexist with the outdated mindsets of the seventeenth century, particularly when it came to how people treat each other. He emphasised that Tamil Nadu should unite as a Samathuvapuram to fully benefit from the IT boom, and that technological progress without fraternity was meaningless (Karunanidhi, 2000 in Panneerselvan, 2021: 346).

This multi-dimensional understanding of social justice—combining spatial equality with technological progress—poses a radical challenge to discursive hegemonies. For instance, the democratisation of capital in the software industry allowed entrepreneurs and professionals, not from traditional business families but financially modest and lower-caste backgrounds (Kalaiyarasan & Vijayabaskar, 2021: 336–39 & 438–39), to enter and thrive. However, tensions remain, particularly in the realm of public political activity. As observed by scholars like Hugo Gorringe (2005: 196–203), and in my own fieldwork in Western Tamil Nadu in 2021, concerns persist about the ability of the marginalized to stage rallies or engage freely in political activities.

The Promise of Representation: Achievements and Fissures

Tamil Nadu boasts of the most caste-representative legislative assembly in the country. The broader spread of the Dravidian-Tamil ethos through both the DMK and the AIADMK has meant that, over time, more caste groups have found representation in the legislature. The DMK enjoys strong support from aspirational middle communities, while the AIADMK has built a 'sandwich alliance'—a coalition that spans both the powerful and marginalised communities.

Geographically, the AIADMK has largely consolidated its base among numerically dominant caste groups in western and southern Tamil Nadu, while the DMK has secured a foothold in the northern and Delta regions.

Together, the two parties command around two-thirds of the vote share in the State, with their alliances pushing this number up to around 80-85% of votes. During the 1970s and 1980s, the DMK and the AIADMK alternated in securing higher vote percentages, but the 1990s and 2000s were marked by AIADMK's dominance.

Several factors contributed to the DMK's downturn in the 1990s. These included reputational damage following the assassination of Rajiv Gandhi,[17] the formation of Pattali Makkal Katchi[18] (Toilers' Party) from the Vanniyar Sangam (Vanniyar Caste Association)—which brought back the caste-based parties that emerged and declined in the late 1950s and early 1960s—and the defection of DMK's firebrand leader, Vaiko. He formed the Marumalarchi Dravida Munnetra Kazhagam (MDMK) citing alleged nepotism, stripping the DMK of a few of its district secretaries, weakening its internal structure in the process.

The 1990s also saw some tactical missteps and a lack of long-term strategic vision within the Dravidian parties, which affected the DMK more than the AIADMK.[19] However, despite these setbacks, the DMK managed to form governments in 1996 and 2006. The party's resurgence began in earnest during the 2016 elections when M.K. Stalin's '*Namakku Naamey*' march (loosely translates to 'we for ourselves') across Tamil Nadu re-energised its base.

Overall, it can be argued that Tamil Nadu's legislature reflects a near proportional representation of caste categories.[20] For example, the Other Backward Classes continue to hold over 70% of seats (76.1% population)[21] and the Scheduled Castes (through constitutional reservation) hold 18% of seats (20.01%

of the population). When disaggregated further, we see the over-representation of three caste groups: the Vanniyar, Mukkulathor, and Kongu Vellala Gounder, who together constitute around 29% of the population of Tamil Nadu.[22]

Between 1971 and 1991 (six election cycles), the representation of upper castes fluctuated, ranging from 8.12% in 1971 to 4.70% in 1991, with an average of 6.04%. The representation of intermediate castes ranged from 12.82% in 1977 to 5.13% in 1989, averaging at 9.6%. The representation of Other Backward Classes[23] averaged at 59.53% between 1971 and 1991.

In the twenty-five years between 1996 and 2021 (six election cycles), upper caste representation ranged between 7.73% in 2016 and 3.39% in 1996, averaging 5.18%, while that of the intermediate castes ranged between 13.22% in 2001 and 8.05% in 1996, an average of 10.76%. The OBCs' representation[24] ranged between 61.44% (1996) and 56.25% in 2011, averaging at 59.07%.

The AIADMK caters to dominant communities more than the DMK, and therefore, DMK-led legislatures tend to consist of greater caste diversity than those of the AIADMK. While the numerically significant caste groups enjoy continued representation, smaller caste groups find representation on a rotational basis. The dependence on multiple communities and the limitation of accommodating them in the first-past-the-post electoral system when there are three numerically-dominant politicised communities is another reason why the DMK advocates a bicameral legislature, which would allow it to nominate members from multiple communities in each electoral cycle.

The Dalits

The representation of Dalits has stayed around 18.5% on average, which matches the seat quota set for Dalits across twelve elections from 1971 to 2021. The AIADMK fares better than the DMK when it comes to fielding Dalit candidates. On the other hand, the DMK often brings in Dalit candidates in through its coalition partners like Vidhuthalai Chiruthaigal Katchi (VCK), Aathi Tamilar

Peravai (ATP), Makkal Viduthalai Kazhagam (MVK), and Puthiya Tamizhagam Party (PTP). Dalits themselves can be disaggregated into Paraiyars, Devandra Kula Vellalars or DKV, formerly called Pallars, and Arunthathiyars.

M.C. Rajah introduced the idea of a supra-local identity, i.e., Adi-Dravidars (influenced by Iyothee Thass' framing of Dravidian) in the late nineteenth century, which Periyar and other leaders later promoted. However, over the past fifty years, this identity has mostly become tied to Paraiyars. Socioeconomically, Paraiyars are the most mobile and occupy a higher position ritually, followed by DKVs and Arunthathiyars. The VCK, PTP, and ATP came together to address their specific grievances, as they felt that the broader Dalit or Dravidian-Tamil identities didn't quite fit them and so were unacceptable to them. During the 1980s and 1990s, under AIADMK (thirteen years in power) and DMK (seven years), there was a resurgence of caste pride among backward classes, exacerbated by government decisions like renaming public transportation companies after prominent caste leaders.

In the late 1990s and early 2000s, the Dalit parties began working with the DMK and the AIADMK to build a composite political identity and vision. They drew inspiration from Ambedkar, Periyar, and other thinkers who sought to advance socioeconomic mobility. As they did this, the Dalits also recalibrated how they voiced their specific concerns, aiming to join the mainstream.[25]

In a video interview from 27 January 2023,[26] Thirumavalavan, the President of the VCK, warned his supporters against breaking away from the composite Dravidian-Tamil ethos when the idea of contesting elections separately was brought up. He acknowledged the electoral dominance of the Dravidian parties, pointing out that while the VCK had not built up a vote bank like some regional parties, it was still a major player in Tamil Nadu's secular political space, carved out by the DMK. He also noted that if VCK were went solo, they may win a seat or two and get some positive feedback from their own circle, but that would not really push forward the empowerment of marginalised communities.

Amit Ahuja[27] suggests that, unlike Uttar Pradesh and Bihar—where strong Dalit parties focus exclusively on Dalit grievances—

states like Maharashtra and Tamil Nadu show a different trend. There, Dalit parties are less about separate power and more about joining broader, inclusive movements. There is, therefore, a wider understanding of grievances of the Dalits among other communities. This raises an interesting question: if the Dravidian-Tamil identity has been a progressive force but also hegemonic, how comfortably can it coexist with the assertion of the Dalits?

Around two-thirds of Dalit candidates[28] fielded across political parties come from the Paryaiyar community, while the DKVs and Arunthathiyars make up just over a quarter and about 5%, respectively. Between 1951 and 2021, fewer than forty legislators were from the Arunthathiyar community. This shows that even within the Scheduled Caste category, the dominant caste group still holds a disproportionate amount of power.[29] To make up for the reduced representation, the Dravidian parties try to compensate by offering other positions, like appointing people from these categories as Speaker of the Legislative Assembly or giving them seats in the Rajya Sabha.

Activists and a section of scholars raise two main questions about fielding Dalit candidates—one of which comes up frequently, and the other less so. The more common question is: why not field Dalit candidates from general seats? It seems radical and progressive at first, but when you consider the demands from lower caste groups that aren't proportionally represented, along with the constitutionally guaranteed proportional representation for Dalits, it doesn't seem very logical because fielding Dalit candidates from general seats would unsettle the idea of near-proportional representation. Take the 2021 State Assembly elections, for example: the DMK-led alliance allotted six seats to VCK (four reserved and two general), and VCK, in turn, fielded non-Dalit candidates on those general seats.

The less frequently asked question, however, is more crucial—how well are Dalits represented in party positions, especially when it comes to roles like District Secretary? And what kind of portfolios do Dalits get when they're included in the Council of Ministers? Over the years, both DMK and AIADMK cabinets have been dominated by upper and intermediate castes, with Dalit representation falling short considerably of what is proportional. At times, Dalits have had barely one or two ministerial positions, and sometimes even zero, unless the Scheduled Castes' Welfare portfolio is considered.

But the 2024 reshuffling of the Council of Ministers has brought some hope. While Udhayanidhi Stalin's rise to Deputy Chief Minister grabbed plenty of attention (and sometimes criticism), the promotion of two Dalit leaders marks a significant shift. Dr Govi Chezhiaan has been appointed Minister for Higher Education, and N. Kayalvizhi Selvaraj, previously the Minister for Adi Dravidar Welfare, is now the Minister for Human Resources Management. Now, there are four Dalits in the Council of Ministers, including C.V. Ganesan (Minister for Labour Welfare and Skill Development) and Dr M. Mathiventhan (Minister for Adi Dravidar Welfare), and they all hold key portfolios. This shift is encouraging, but if reversed or not continued, it could reveal a gap in the Dravidian-Tamil ethos, which is something worth looking into through further research.

The Muslims

Muslims make up about 6% of Tamil Nadu's population, and their role in the State's regional identity, politics, and culture has evolved significantly since the 1920s. Over time, they have contributed to the formation of a distinct Dravidian-Tamil version of Islam, integrating with other communities and asserting themselves politically, all without much tension.

When it comes to electoral representation, Muslims have typically been co-opted by the Dravidian parties, who have worked closely with Muslim groups since the early twentieth century. Between 1971 and 2021, in twelve Legislative Assembly elections, Muslim representation averaged at 3.07%. Under DMK-led governments, that average is slightly higher at 3.81%, while in the AIADMK-led governments, it's a bit lower at 2.5%. In both parties, Muslims typically held one or two ministerial positions.

Notably, Tamil Nadu ranks first and second in terms of educational and economic mobility for Muslims compared to all states.[30] But there is a need for future research to explore the role of caste within the Muslim community—especially whether the higher, more affluent Muslims castes dominate key positions, while lower-caste, less affluent Muslims remain underrepresented.

Women

Women's representation in Tamil Nadu has been one of the weakest aspects of Dravidian mobilisation. In a State where female voters actually outnumber male voters, the DMK has fielded, on average, just nine women candidates per election between 1971 and 2021. Of those, three became elected legislators on average. The number of women candidates has varied from just three to 18, and the number of women candidates who won has ranged from zero[31] to eight.

In contrast, the AIADMK, under the leadership of J. Jayalalithaa from 1988 to 2016, fielded an average of fourteen women per election between 1977 and 2021, with around eight winning on average. The number of women AIADMK candidates varied widely from two to thirty, and the number of elected legislators ranged from zero[32] to twenty-five during this period.

As the 2021 elections approached, A. Raja, Deputy General Secretary of the DMK said in a video interview[33] on 18 March 2021 that while the DMK aimed to allocate 30–40 seats for women, most of these seats ended up going to their alliance partners. This explanation does not seem very convincing. As of 1 June 2024, the DMK has just one woman District Secretary, and just two women are part of the government formed by Chief Minister M.K. Stalin in May 2021.

That said, the DMK is an outspoken supporter of the Women's Reservation Bill. Kanimozhi Karunanidhi, the party's former Women's Wing Secretary and now Deputy General Secretary and Member of Parliament, has also taken steps to introduce quotas in party positions at the sub-district level. In addition, after the 2021 elections, a significant number of tickets were given to women in the local body elections. The DMK's support for the Women's Reservation Bill and their efforts to introduce quotas at the grassroots levels of the party show the tension between pushing for social transformation and managing representative politics.

The party has also recently appointed women to a newly created position of associate District Secretaries across the State. Given the DMK's rigid organisational structure and the indifference of the district-level leadership, some kind of external or constitutional push may be needed to truly change the gender composition in the legislative assemblies. But for now, the steps being taken to cultivate leaders at the sub-district and district levels are a positive move. Even though there's a high female workforce participation rate, the rapidly rising costs of elections and the oligarchising tendencies emerging in Indian democracy (Berenschot, Bagchi, & Karthik, 2024) make it much harder to improve women's representation in Tamil Nadu. This challenge is similar across the country, whether it's in Kerala, Haryana, or Madhya Pradesh. That said, the quest for social justice isn't complete if the gender question is left unaddressed.

The Anti-Dravidian-Tamil Discourse: A Tale of Two Sanctimonies

While many have written off the Dravidian Movement and Dravidian parties, two political forces aiming to challenge the Dravidian-Tamil ethos have gained momentum. The first is the Hindu nationalist push led by the BJP, backed by an alliance of traditional elites and upwardly mobile subaltern groups. The second is a nativist form of Tamil nationalism, represented by Naam Tamilar Katchi (NTK, 'We are Tamils Party'), which is mainly supported by lower classes within the backward caste groups.

The rise of the Hindu nationalist movement has been fuelled by the BJP's political aggression and the weakening of the AIADMK after Jayalalithaa's death. Historically, the BJP had a reputation as a Brahmin-led party, but recent years have seen an influx of leaders from lower-caste and Dalit backgrounds, which has expanded its support base, especially since it has given or offered them key political roles and appointments. As noted by Karthik, Jumle, and Karunanithi (2020: 21), the Hindu nationalist push aims to undermine the Dravidian-Tamil identity by promoting a Hindu-Tamil ethos.

This populist ideology criticises the diverse, aspirational coalition that has emerged from various castes and religions, framing them as polluters of the land of the "pure". It often deploys tropes like calling them "slaves of the colonisers", accusing them of anti-national politics, minority appeasement, and promoting casteist, communal, and corrupt politics. In this narrative, the terms Hindi and Hindu are used loosely to represent anyone who supports the BJP or opposes its adversaries. The primary aim is to delegitimise the Dravidian-Tamil vision and its achievements.

A section of the upwardly mobile lower-caste groups like Nadars and Gounders—who once benefited from the Dravidian movement—along with traditional elites like Brahmins and Chettiyars, have lent their support to the BJP. This appeal is especially strong among lower sections of backward class groups that didn't gain as much from the Dravidian-Tamil framework. The current economic shifts, such as fewer public sector jobs and a shrinking job market for educated youth, also contribute to this appeal. Additionally, the history of communal clashes and extremism in western Tamil Nadu during the 1990s, and the presence of socioeconomically mobile Christians in the southern part of the State, make these regions ripe for the BJP's anti-minority rhetoric. The BJP has accused the DMK and, to a lesser extent, the AIADMK of fostering the growth of these communities at the expense of Hindu-Tamils.[34]

The DMK-led Tamil Nadu government has faced backlash for its efforts to allow people from all castes to become temple priests, provided they undergo necessary training, and for promoting the use of Tamil in rituals as against Sanskrit. These moves have been criticised by Hindutva nationalists and elites. However, there was some relief for the government when the Madras High Court upheld the decision, and the Supreme Court refused[35] to stay the order.[36] Even though the pushback against using Tamil exclusively continues, there have been some positive steps in this direction.

The core ideas of the Dravidian-Tamil ethos, like the two-language policy (Tamil and English) in government-run schools, are being challenged either through Union government pressures or by reopening old, settled debates without bringing in any fresh arguments. In a recent instance (September 2024), Tamil Nadu's education funding was placed on hold as it did not adopt the three-language policy in schools as spelt out by the Centre's New Education Policy 2020.[37]

Other instances of unsettling the ethos include portraits of secular icons like Thiruvalluvar being shown in saffron attire, and statues of Periyar being vandalised. While the BJP remains a minor player in elections, its access to abundant resources and state power at the Centre are helping it make strides. Additionally, the weakening of the AIADMK after Jayalalithaa's untimely death, coupled with a long intra-party battle over stable succession, has allowed the BJP to gain more ground in the State.[38]

On the other hand, the Tamil nationalist movement offers a nativist form of politics rooted in Tamil pride, often linked to a romanticised vision of a glorious past. This vision projects society as stratified and gives native Tamil clans fabled and mythical histories. The movement calls for a return to agriculture and agriculture-based industries. Seeman, the current leader of the NTK, broke away from the Dravidian groups, including the DK, after the Sri Lankan Civil War ended in 2009. The NTK was revived[39] in 2010 and its agenda is built around a claim of a global conspiracy against Tamils, and a harsh critique of the DMK, which it accuses of betraying Tamil interests by allying with the Congress party during the civil war.[40] NTK also takes an aggressively anti-migrant labour stance and demands Muslims and Christians to turn to native Tamil religions.

Seeman's connections to the Tamil diaspora, particularly with his supposed ties to the LTTE leader, late Velupillai Prabhakaran, have helped the party gain some international support. In Tamil Nadu, the NTK has found a foothold among the lower echelons of the backward class groups that did not benefit from the Dravidian-Tamil agenda, and are frustrated by the rise of Dalit mobility in rural Tamil Nadu. The party's nativist Tamil nationalism often serves as a dog whistle to attack migrant labourers from other States. NTK also frames caste as *kudi* (clan) rather than *saadhi* (*jati*), emphasising the supposed uniqueness of Tamil society[41] and distancing it from the broader Indian caste system.

The NTK has introduced a policy of 50% reservation for women candidates in elections. Despite contesting alone, the party's vote share rose from 1.1% in 2016 to 6.6% in the 2021 Assembly elections, making it the third largest party in Tamil Nadu by vote share. In over 150 constituencies, the NTK secured more than 5% of votes, and in fourteen constituencies, it crossed the 10% mark. This is a remarkable achievement, especially considering that in thirty-nine constituencies, the victory margin between the DMK- and AIADMK-led alliances was under 5,000 votes, and in another thirty constituencies, it was between 5,000 and 10,000 votes. If the NTK continues to grow, it could start winning seats, making the competition in Tamil Nadu elections more open and the DMK- and the AIADMK-led alliances may come to dominate it less.

A common thread linking the BJP and NTK's nationalist agendas is the impression they give of having a 'messiah complex'. Both parties project a holier-than-thou tone, and it seems to be gaining some support. In January 2025,[42] Seeman criticised Periyar for not truly having supported women's freedom in Tamil Nadu, and accused him of promoting inappropriate relationships and making offensive remarks. While Seeman's attack sparked debates about whether his statements were accurate or motivated by political aims, they weren't a new phenomenon. They had deeper roots. In October 2021, the NTK organised a conference titled 'Tamil or Dravidian?' in which speakers criticised the Dravidian movement for having 'mislead' Tamil castes and causing demographic changes.

Seeman's hard-line stand directly supports the BJP's larger goal to weaken Dravidian politics. By targeting Periyar, he is helping his own Tamil nationalist agenda and the Hindu nationalist movement's goal to crush Tamil Nadu's social justice-focused politics and replace it with a pride-based and hierarchical identity politics.

Such developments should alert the DMK and the AIADMK. They'll need to push back against these efforts to undermine diversity and, in the process, revive outdated cate-based hierarchies under the guise of culture, nationalism, and Tamil pride. The Dravidian-Tamil ethos is anything but "pure". In fact, it is anti-purity—it challenges the idea of purity and works toward democratising power and public life. The Dravidian-Tamil identity is an inclusive, rebellious movement that used political opportunities to assert itself against the dominant forces that upheld hegemonic purity.

The DMK's Response to Anti-Dravidian-Tamil Discourse

There have been some efforts to re-politicise Tamil Nadu in recent years. In the past, public talks for students and youth were occasionally organised, but now there's a more structured approach.[43] One part of this is the government-sponsored 'Maaperum Tamil Kanavu' (Grand Tamil Dream) talks, run by the Tamil Virtual Academy, which is a distance education institution established by the Government of Tamil Nadu. The other is 'TN Talks', organised by the Department of School Education, Government of Tamil Nadu. These talks are held periodically in colleges, libraries, and public halls across the State, with domain experts, professionals, and academics leading the discussions.

Second, on the party front, the youth wing of the DMK, led by Udhayanidhi Stalin, has set up the Dravidian Model Workshops. These are a series of talks held in each constituency of Tamil Nadu, focusing on the contributions of the Dravidian Movement, the future direction of the State, and the impact of Tamil nationalist and Hindutva politics. The workshops feature a mix of young speakers and experienced figures, with one or two speakers addressing the gathering on the topic of the day.

The state government is also considering the revival of the reading room culture and libraries. Back in 1972, to curb the growing popularity of M.G.R., the Karunanidhi-led DMK passed a resolution requiring all reading rooms and public halls run by DMK sympathisers to register with the party and get permissions from local units before holding events or activities (Barnett, 1976: 296). This decision ended up weakening the independent nature of these spaces, which had been crucial for discursive political engagement. After M.G.R.'s defection, M.G.R. halls and fan associations started replacing the old reading rooms. Some reading rooms were later taken over by the Directorate of Public Libraries, Government of Tamil Nadu, under M.G.R.'s administration, effectively enfeebling them. Now, Tamil Nadu has around 4,640 functional public libraries, including 312 full-time branch libraries, 1,612 branch libraries, 1,915 village libraries and 751 part-time libraries. These libraries could be revived as spaces for active dialogue and debate, much like the reading rooms of the 1950s and 1960s, providing a platform for intellectual engagement or even regular community activity.

Third, the women's wing of the DMK has launched a state-wide quiz competition for school students as part of the centenary celebrations of Karunanidhi, featuring questions on the Dravidian movement, its contributions, and its leaders.

The grand arts and culture festival of Tamil Nadu, Chennai Sangamam, which was first launched by Karunanidhi and later run by Kanimozhi as a Civil Society Organisation event, was revived and transformed into a government initiative in 2023 to ensure continuity. Held during the Tamil harvest festival of Pongal, the event was overseen by the State's Minister of Tamil Official Language, Tamil Culture, and Archaeology. The 2023 edition featured performances from over 600 artists, showcasing a mix of Carnatic, folk, and modern art forms from Tamil Nadu and beyond. What made this event stand out was the inclusion of both Carnatic and folk artists performing in the same spaces and receiving equal pay for their performances. People gathered in beaches, parks, and grounds to enjoy these vibrant celebrations, creating a unique cultural experience.

Chennai Sangamam, also called '*Namma Ooru Thiruvizha*' was partly a response to the Kashi Tamil Sangamam—a month-long event held in Varanasi, Uttar Pradesh, aimed at reviving historical and civilisational ties between the North and South. The Kashi Tamil Sangamam was organised by the Government of India, the Uttar Pradesh government, and institutions like IIT Madras and Banaras Hindu University. As I had said elsewhere (Karthik and Vasanthakumar, 2023), "While the Hindu-Tamil ethos is forged with a flamboyant Kashi-Tamil Sangamam that is a quest for a glorious past, the Chennai Sangamam is eager to be seen as a common person's counter-hegemonic alliance that foregrounds the present and is keen on the sustenance of an equitable future."

A similar event called Neythal[44] has also been established as an annual festival in the southern district of Thoothukudi by Kanimozhi Karunanidhi, who represents the region in Parliament. Neythal is a celebration of local music, arts, and food designed to honour the subregional culture of the area. This secular event has been conceived as a bulwark against the divisive efforts of the BJP in the region, where there's a significant Christian population. It is seen as a way of celebrating Tamil culture and practices that unites people and resists attempts to polarise people.

The Challenges Confronting Dravidian-Tamil Ethos

The differences in levels of mobility achieved by caste groups and classes within these groups, especially among the lower levels of the Other Backward Classes, has been increasing their insecurity. This is especially true in the context of the mobility achieved by Dalits (Kalaiyarasan & Vijayabaskar, 2021: 550–51). The nature of caste-based violence is, therefore, changing—it's no longer about the status-based arrogance of the middle and intermediate caste groups but about their growing sense of desperation and insecurity. Lately, the violence against Dalits often involves acts like looting and destroying symbols of progress, such as degree certificates[45] (Pandian, 2013: 14).

Another issue at hand is the quality of education in both government and private institutions. The learning outcomes in Tamil Nadu are poor and, as a result, many educated youths struggle to find good jobs. This has forced a lot of them into low-wage, precarious work in the gig or platform economy, subsets of the large informal economy. Although the State government has tried to intervene with welfare boards to offset some of the neoliberal pressures and relaxed labour laws, the quality of jobs available to youth remains subpar. The promise of socioeconomic mobility feels fragile, and how the political system responds to the situation will shape its future.

Additionally, focusing on manufacturing and industry poses the risk of environmental degradation, which is something a section of people have become increasingly sensitive to in recent decades. In some cases, those who supported Dravidian modernity are now starting to have different aspirations related to their communities' traditional occupations. For example, there have been movements pushing for government procurement of palmyra[46] and coconut[47] toddy in Tamil Nadu hinting at the return to caste-based occupations. Such shifts need to be problematised through further research to understand the motivations and future trajectories.

I have previously discussed the rise of a broad-based entrepreneurial class in Tamil Nadu and the criticism that's been directed at the increasing influence of businessmen within the Dravidian parties. In this context, I spoke to a revenue service officer (Arulmozhi,[48] Personal Communication, 14 October 2021) who has worked in the State. He pointed out that as regional capitalists who were very involved with the Dravidian parties are now increasingly aligning with national parties—of late, the BJP—to fulfil their pan-Indian business aspirations, the Dravidian parties have started looking inward in two ways. First, there's a tendency among politicians to tap into rent-thick avenues within the system, such as securing government contracts or even benefiting from kickbacks. Second, there's a rising trend of politicians becoming businessmen themselves. He divided such people into two categories. One is politician-businessmen who are more politicians than businessmen—they are rooted in a region and their businesses are means to sustain their political careers and aspirations. The second category is businessmen-politicians who are more businessmen than politicians—they are keen to expand their enterprises and politics is a means to achieve this goal. He said that the first category of people is prevalent in Tamil Nadu and the second category of people has been prevalent in Andhra Pradesh and Maharashtra in recent decades. The politician-businessmen are more directly involved in party affairs and the local political scene. These politicians typically run monopolistic government-related businesses or engage in regular business activities with state support after entering politics. Defections among such people are lower. A shift has also been seen in the types of investments being made. In the past, investments were mostly in educational institutions, but now, the focus has shifted to real estate, hospitality, dealerships, and service sector firms. When I asked about the implications of this, he said there were a couple of important points to consider. First, he noted that presence of such politician-businessmen allows the political class to maintain a distance from big capitalists, which is crucial to prevent a constricting effect on Dravidian politics. However, he also pointed out, '…fighting a party like the BJP becomes viable [with the help of big capitalists as they are also rooted in local politics].' Second, he maintained that this system would likely lead to a blend of moderated cronyism and extensive welfare. The limitation of such a system is that it is unsustainable in the long term. As cronyism grows with the dominance of a few families within a party, the entry barriers get stronger for new candidates from humble backgrounds—like the Seenivasans or Thangappans discussed in the previous chapter—to break through. More importantly, while cronyism might help secure some immediate gains, it conflicts with the core values of the Dravidian-Tamil ethos of equity and social justice. Any mismanagement could tarnish the party's reputation, regardless of its progressive credentials. However, he also said such politician-businessmen in Tamil Nadu are very cautious individuals.

There have been frequent attempts to impose Hindi, especially when it is made the only non-English language for entrance exams to higher education institutions or government jobs. On top of that, there has been a push for a three-language formula under the National Education Policy, 2020, with the ruse of developing (Hindi as) a link language. Another ongoing issue is the failure to implement reservation quotas for backward classes in the national pool of seats for State higher education institutions.

In 2023, Tamil Nadu Governor R.N. Ravi sparked more debate by suggesting that the state be renamed Tamizhagam (Abode of Tamils). Along with this, there were delays in giving assent to bills passed by the legislature, and the Governor even chose to omit the names of social justice icons like Ambedkar, Periyar, and leaders like Kamaraj, Annadurai, and Karunanidhi during his address to the State Legislative Assembly. His words and actions have often stood in opposition to the Dravidian-Tamil ethos.

The proposed delimitation of constituencies in 2026 could significantly reduce the percentage of seats held by Tamil Nadu and other southern states in Parliament. This is mainly because of lower fertility rates in these states, leading to smaller populations compared to other parts of India, especially the geographically extensive Hindi belt. Right now, all five southern states together hold only 24% of the seats (130/543) in Parliament, which could fall as a proportion—even if the total strength of Parliament is increased through delimitation.

What's also concerning is that the current system itself is marred by inconsistencies. For example, Tamil Nadu, with a population of 7.2 crore and Bihar with 13 crore have the same number of seats in the Lok Sabha (39 and 40 each, respectively). Similarly, Kerala, with 3.5 crore people, gets 20 seats, while Jharkhand, with 4 crore people, only has 14 seats. It's clear that population cannot be the sole factor in determining seat allocation, and this complicates the debate. If the proposed delimitation happens, even if the proportion of seats remains the same, it could lead to smaller constituencies, with fewer voters in each. This could benefit both Tamil nationalists and the Hindu nationalists, who will gain an opportunity to convert their votes into seats more easily and enter the legislature. As we have seen, in previous elections, many constituencies are already decided by smaller margins, so this could make a significant difference. On a larger scale, though, such changes could further undermine a key principle of India's democracy: one person, one vote, one value.

Essentially, a vote from someone in South India could end up being 'worth' more than one from North India. Also, delimitation would not only skew representation but also penalise states (like Tamil Nadu) that have a good track record in public policy. The chief ministers of both Tamil Nadu and Andhra Pradesh, M.K. Stalin and N. Chandrababu Naidu, have raised concerns about smaller population sizes of constituencies. Stalin fears reduced representation in Parliament, while Naidu is worried about the challenges of an aging population. Naidu has even said that the Andhra government is considering legislation to encourage larger families with more children.[49]

The autonomy of states to generate their own revenue is also steadily diminishing, with the Goods and Services Tax (GST) framework enabling this at a structural level. On 17 March 2018, a day after the Telugu Desam Party (TDP) quit the BJP-led National Democratic Alliance (NDA) over the latter's denial of special status to the State following its bifurcation in 2014, a reporter asked M.K. Stalin if some southern states could come together and push for the demand of Dravida Nadu. Stalin responded that if such a proposal arose, he would welcome it, and that he had faith that it would arise.[50]

The DMK's unambiguous opposition to the abrogation of Article 370 of the Constitution, stripping Jammu and Kashmir of its Statehood overnight, drew criticism from M.K. Stalin on grounds of legislative high-handedness, and an attack on both the spirit and procedures of federalism. While some academics and critics, especially those with anti-Dravidian-Tamil or BJP-leaning views, dismiss the centralising tendencies stemming from the imposition of Hindi, and the Brahminisation of public life as exaggerated or non-issues, the Dravidian-Tamil ethos continues to stand strong against majoritarian politics.

Indrajit Roy, in his research (2021: 68) on the politics of Bihar and Lalu Prasad Yadav's role, urges scholars to embrace plurality when analysing the democratic rise of subaltern groups, and to steer clear from stereotypical portrayals and reductive or negative tropes. In this spirit, on 3 April 2023, M.K. Stalin took a significant step by founding the All-India Federation for Social Justice. This federation aims to unite opposition parties across India, drawing up a common minimum programme across states that focuses on the interests of the marginalised communities—going far beyond just reservations.[51] In the light of the rising demand for a caste census and increasing Union interference in State matters, the federation promises to be a means to unite like-minded parties on socio-political and electoral fronts.

Postscript

Annadurai's emphasis on patience and method reflects a timeless truth about Dravidian politics: patience, preparation, perseverance, and politicking have never been mere strategies but intrinsic to its core tenets. One could reduce Dravidian politics to a simplistic label—such as 'caste politics', as the media often does today. However, engaging with and understanding its foundational meaning requires resisting such misleading characterisations, which risk distorting its true significance and historical impact.

Drawing from his research in the United States and the United Kingdom, Professor Andrew Chadwick argues that the traditional and modern media platforms have developed mutually competitive and interdependent interests, as a result of how these platforms have been used—or deployed—by political actors and influencers to develop their own constituencies. In this context, I have argued elsewhere (Karthik, Jumle & Vasagam, 2023), that media platforms as well as a section of journalists are not offering the news to their audiences, but 'content'.

By design, outlets must continuously generate content to remain in business. Detailed, in-depth reporting is declining because media houses are struggling financially, and this crisis is worsened by the content-production-oriented model of journalism. At the same time, personality-driven journalism, in which opinions are presented as news, is on the rise in Tamil Nadu, as in the rest of the country and world. Social media and television 'personalities'—non-experts who participate in television debates—can now powerfully influence and shape opinions. Karthik, Jumle, and Karunanithi (2020: 20) have also recorded instances wherein award-winning journalists have been dismissed due to disinformation (usually in the form of allegations) propagated by such influencers. In such a situation, anecdotes, hearsay, and outright fictions—in the form of catchy sound bites—occupy the centre stage across online platforms in particular.

Such content is circulated by the sympathisers of political parties that stand to benefit from making unsubstantiated allegations. This propaganda is also covered by the legacy television channels that further disseminate the misinformation and disinformation. Non-engagement with such content gets construed as 'weakness'—if not as admission of guilt—giving the accusations a semblance of credibility. In a clear sense, the media is validating allegations in the guise of providing 'news' coverage of such allegations.

The parties in Tamil Nadu, be it the DMK, the AIADMK, or the VCK seem unable to convincingly counter the stir created by these media influencers. At times, they have moved the courts with charges of libel or slander against the sources of disinformation/ allegations. However, this is proving counterproductive. On other occasions, the knee-jerk reactions by supporters and office-bearers of the parties or the state government's high-handedness in dealing with influencers have also been ineffective.

* * *

The history of Dravidian politics goes beyond the tropes of 'consummation': it never advocated a conclusive end point; instead, it has always been in a process of consciously responding to, and tailoring, the cultural, material, ideological and, to an extent, conventional wisdom of Tamil society. Hence, the term 'caste politics' must be analysed from the point of view of what Dravidian politics intended to achieve, what it has already achieved, and how it has dynamically accommodated aspirations, ways of association, a sense of the past, collective experiences, and expectations and patterns of socialisation and mobilisation.

A frequently overlooked but crucial aspect of the Dravidian movement is its careful approach to the written word, speeches, slogans, and labels, as well as the sincerity and gravitas with which its leaders communicate them. This caution stems from a keen awareness that spoken and written words evolve into stories and anecdotes, shaping everyday experiences and conversations. Over time, they become embedded in the political vocabulary, fostering a shared sense of participation and community among people.

Essentially, the messages are meant to transform politics into action, and so the glossary of Dravidian politics is by no means an accident—it grew out of a deeply percipient repertoire in which the social, cultural, and political spheres converged to continually make the political the personal.

Annadurai (n.d. in Manoharan, 2013: 4) said at a public meeting that he was raised in a family of weavers, which taught him the importance of patience, for he observed how weavers restring threads and untie knots as they weave them into cloth. What Annadurai was aiming for is a far deeper engagement, and it is relevant to this book, for it establishes a fundamental aspect of Dravidian-Tamil identity and politics: it is a product of conscious and persistent labour—emotional, intellectual, social, economic, and, above all, political labour.

This labour is the flesh and blood of the movement as well as of the electorally agile parties that it grew into. It is an assiduously crafted and cultivated identity and politics. Does the movement still have what it takes to accommodate the dynamic aspirations of people? Do the political parties espousing the Dravidian-Tamil vision retain the ability to sustain their electoral viability while aligning with fulfilling those aspirations? These are questions for the times ahead.

APPENDICES

Appendix A: Tables[1] Showing the Spread of Reading Rooms in 1957 and 1967

District	Reading Rooms [1957]
Madras City	375
Kanniyakumari	471
Tirunelveli	834
North Arcot	825
Ramanathapuram	511
Madurai	714
The Nilgiris	259
Coimbatore	385
Chengalpet	622
South Arcot	831
Salem	797
Tiruchirappalli	1239
Thanjavur	1376
Total	9239

District	Reading Rooms [1967]
Madras City	800
Kanniyakumari	1000
Dharmapuri	675
Tirunelveli	1800
North Arcot	1800
Ramanathapuram	1050
Madurai	1501
Salem	1275
The Nilgiris	590
Coimbatore	809
Chengalpet	1350
South Arcot	1800
Tiruchirappalli	2663
Thanjavur	2875
Total	19988

(Data based on fieldwork estimates.)

Appendix B: Ratio of Reading Rooms run by DMK Sympathisers, DK Office and Sympathisers, Justice Party, and Caste associations in relation to the DMK Branches

Districts	DMK Branches	DMK Sympathisers	DK Office + Sympathisers	Justice Party	Caste Associations
Madras City	1	3	2	0	2
Kanniyakumari	1	1	0.5	1	1.5
Tirunelveli	1	1	0.5	0.5	1.5
North Arcot	1	1	0.5	0	1.5
Ramanathapuram	1	0.5	0.3	0	0.33
Madurai	1	1	0.375	0.25	0.375
The Nilgiris	1	0.5	0.5	0	0.33
Coimbatore	1	0.5	0.5	0	0.33
Chengalpet	1	0.5	0.25	0	0.5
South Arcot	1	0.67	0.33	0	1
Salem	1	0.5	0.33	0	0.5
Tiruchirappalli	1	1	1	0	0.33
Thanjavur	1	0.75	1	0	0.25

NOTES

INTRODUCTION

1. Madras State was renamed Tamil Nadu on 14 January 1969.
2. In the context of the book, Tamil language as a constituent of the Dravidian Movement is regarded in its oral and textual form. While there is a considerable degree of symbolism attached to the language (Ramaswamy, 1997), the book would argue that the Dravidian movement's use of Tamil language is predominantly in its written and read form, as a means to achieve socio-economic mobility of lower castes.
3. The DMK emerged in 1949 as a result of a series of political and socio-cultural developments chiefly around the questions of caste, social justice, and socio-economic mobility of lower castes and the Tamil language, which in turn are the key vectors of the DMK's politics. Though while writing in English, we use 'Dravidian' commonly, it is a homonym in the context of its usage. For instance, Dravida in DMK denoted land as against 'Dravidar' in Periyar's Dravidar Kazhagam (DK), which denoted a people.
4. The Dravidian Movement is loosely regarded as the movement of the subalterns against the Brahminical elite. Brahminical elite in this context does not denote people belonging to a particular caste but anybody from any caste who exhibited oppressive traits. For instance, a non-Brahmin subscribing to the caste-hierarchical practices was called *mukkaal paarpaan* [Transliteration: 3/4th Brahmin] or *onnarai paarpaan* [Transliteration: one and a half Brahmin] See Pandian (2007: 209–34), Jaffrelot (2003: 166–72) and Raja (2019).
5. E.V. Ramasamy was an anti-caste, women's empowerment activist and politician. He is also called *Periyar* [the Elder or the Great Man] and regarded as one of the central ideologues of the Dravidian movement. Khilnani (2016) regards the title *Periyar* as a "self-conscious dig at (Mahatma) Gandhi, the Great Soul".

6. C.N. Annadurai (1909–1969) was a former Chief Minister of Tamil Nadu and the founder of DMK. He was popularly called *Anna* (elder brother). A writer, playwright and an economist by training, he started working with Periyar in the 1930s. He played an active role in the Self-Respect Movement and was instrumental in propagating the ideas of Periyar through writings, plays, and speeches. By the mid-1940s, he was regarded as Periyar's most trusted lieutenant and probable successor.
7. Mylapore in this context refers to an upper caste enclave in the southern part of Madras city—primarily inhabited by a section of Brahmins who fused Brahminical orthodoxy with English education, and achieved dominance in the bureaucratic and professional spheres.
8. See Caldwell R. (1849): 4–5, in Muthuraman, P. (2004), *Agrarian Change and Identity Formation: Caste Mobilizations Among the Nadars of Tamil Nadu*. Ph.D. Thesis, University of Hyderabad, Hyderabad: India.
9. M. Karunanidhi (1924–2018) is the successor of Annadurai, and a former chief minister of Tamil Nadu. He is popularly called *Kalaignar* (Artist).
10. Positing Tamil as an 'empty signifier' overlooks the specific meanings it holds for people and the dynamic ways in which it conveys certain meanings while excluding others. For example, the leaders of the Congress party that belonged to the non-Brahmin communities and identified themselves as Tamils did not secure the mandate of the people. On another note, while my work appears to have subject overlaps with the work of Krishnan, Sriramachandran et al. (2022), conceptually, there is a significant disjuncture. While they are invested in discussing political and cultural theory by situating the Dravidian movement in a post-Marxist framework, my work is empirical in nature and theoretically rooted in the ethnic nationalism framework, as I trace the movement's transition into party politics.
11. "...DMK is not just about securing jobs for the poor and the marginalised, it is about empowering them. A poor Brahmin continues to be treated with respect; we bow to him. However, a rich Paḷḷar [Devendra Kula Vellalar] or a rich Nadar does not command such respect from the society. The DMK's struggle is to achieve dignity and equality... This is what Anna [Annadurai] told my father when my father was in the party...." (Dhanabalan, Personal Communication, 6 February 2020). A possible interpretation could be located in Weber's model of social stratification (Pyakuryal, 2001: 14). He argues that power supersedes class based on economic order and by power he means the chance of a person or a community to exercise his or her/their own will. Moreover, power is seen as a means to secure social honor, which in turn was one of the prime grievances of people owing to the prevalence of caste hierarchy. For instance, the practice of draping shawls (*ponnadai*) around people's shoulders has been a habit inculcated by the DMK leaders in 1950s. While it might look frivolous, situating it in the context of the social history of the State where wearing upper-body clothes were prohibited for a large

group of people is worth considering. Moreover, the act of publicly engaging in draping of shawls by a leader, in itself, denotes a socio-cultural and political move signifying emancipation.

12. Bate (2009: 65) suggests that the architects of Dravidian-Tamil identity primarily Annadurai had engaged in "invention of tradition" (Hobsbawm, 1983: 14). For instance, the body of work of Annadurai takes Tamils back to the Sangam Age, which is to a time more than two thousand years ago, to talk about equality and social justice. Armstrong (1982: 5–9) notes that such mythomoteurs are key in establishing solidarity within a community vis-à-vis the *other*, and differences between identities/communities. Such a message was communicated in a Tamil language that is formal but not classical or caste-laden. A.K. Ramanujam (1968) has recorded his observation of the arrival of what he calls a "middle caste, non-colloquial Tamil across the State, instead of the 'Brahmin Tamil', which also helped eliminate the regional and caste dialects. Moreover, the message of social justice and equality was communicated with the aim of ushering a future where biases and prejudices around social divisions had to be given up. Such a future would facilitate the growth of Tamils in a tangible sense, that is, better quality of life and access to resources. Moreover, journalistic activity, movies, and plays are all centered on such a conception wherein modernity is entangled with tradition. For instance, the use of festival celebration stages to promote the ideas of social justice and equality. (Subagunarajan, 2019: 322).
13. Gellner's preoccupation with urban classes or as Anthony Smith called aristocratic ethnic groups, was challenged by the latter, who argued that the rural world also had its share of demotic ethnic groups that could be mobilised by leaders of local repute on the basis of cultural homogeneity (Smith, 1986: 77–83). Chapters 1 and 2 have examples of the role played by caste associations and subregional religious leaders in furthering the Dravidian-Tamil ethos.
14. In this personal interview, Thamizhachi Thangapandian, currently a Member of Parliament, narrated the aforementioned incident as told to her by her father, the late V. Thangapandian [1933–1997], who was also a politician and former MLA belonging to the DMK.
15. When asked about the Dravidian movement's achievements, in a personal interview, the DMK's Virudhunagar town secretary told me that his father's name was Sangaiya Nadar, his name is S.R.S. Dhanabalan, son of Sangaiya Nadar and his son's name is D. Muthupandian, son of S.R.S. Dhanabalan. "Amid many caste surnames like *Sharma* and *Yadav* in the rest of India, we have achieved this," he said. (Dhanabalan, Personal Communication, 6 February 2020). While this is just one response, I have personally heard many such accounts in the course of my interaction with people across the society. Also see https://www.thejuggernaut.com/tamil-names-self-respect-movement-periyar

1. PERIYAR AND THE DMK

1. See https://youtu.be/Tw2ya9VGRcg The truncated version of the song is the highest viewed campaign song so far, which can be accessed here https://youtu.be/ta-xjvR0HiA
2. See https://scroll.in/article/994446/tamil-nadus-new-assembly-in-33-charts-lowest-women-representation-in-25-years-obcs-dominate
3. The Dravidian-Tamil bloc of non-Brahmin lower caste groups are also differentiated in terms of caste hierarchies. The first set of leaders that led the Justice Party were wealthy merchants and landlords within the *ryotwari* system. A section of them is considered upper and intermediate castes like the Vellalars, Vellala Mudaliars, Naidus, Reddys, Chettiyars, Pillais, Kongu Vellala Gounders, Agamudaiya Mudaliars, etc. The coming of Periyar, the Self-Respect Movement in the 1920s, and the massification of the Congress Party under Mahatma Gandhi led to another round of democratisation and entry of people belonging to lower castes like Mukkulathors, Nadars, Vanniyars, Konars, Isai Vellalars, and considerable number of leaders from depressed castes such as Paraiyars and Pallars. The caste hierarchies extant between these groups in secular matters of social relations in a region and representation in power was mediated through the Dravidian-Tamil identity in a significant way. In inter-personal relations and private affairs, the success of the Dravidian-Tamil ethos is chequered.
4. Government of India (2018), *Handbook on Social Welfare Statistics*, Ministry of Social Justice & Empowerment, New Delhi, 238.
5. *Tholkappiyam* is among the most holistic extant foundational Tamil texts on grammar, phonetics, and poetics.
6. Burton Stein referred to a nexus between Brahmins and the landed elite, the Vellalars. Based on his study of the Kondaikatti Thondaimandala Vellalars, Steve Barnett argues that the socio-economic status of the Vellalars enabled them to occupy a higher societal position as compared to the Kshatriyas (Pillay, 1977: 23–24).
7. *Dubashee* loosely translates into 'speaker of two languages'. In this context, it denoted a class of people predominantly belonging to upwardly mobile non-Brahmin *jatis* and, in some cases, Brahmin *jatis* who served as "interpreters and men of affairs for the Europeans both in their official and private capacities". Additionally, the *dubashee* engaged in trade in their personal capacities. (See Mukund, 2001: 20 and Mantena, 2012: 87–88).
8. The Madras region has always been a territory marked by the confluence of speakers of Tamil, Telugu, Malayalam, and Kannada, until formal borders were drawn time and again, culminating in The States Reorganisation Act, 1956.
9. The Nadars also emerged as an agile class of traders and merchants towards the end of the nineteenth century owing to two reasons. One, Chettiyars, the powerful community almost akin to Vaishyas of the North, were engaged

in moneylending more than trading. Two, and more importantly, from the 1830s onwards, Chettiyars moved away from Madras to Ceylon and Southeast Asia, as those regions were more profitable for the moneylending business. Though there is a considerable Chettiyar presence in the business world of Madras, they are not the only players, and are joined by other communities like Nadars, Gounders, Mudaliars and Naidus. Harish Damodaran (2008: 139 & 182) refers to this as the Vaishya vacuum.

10. See https://thewire.in/history/iyodhee-thass-pandithar-a-pioneer-in-dalit-history-and-literature
See https://indianexpress.com/article/opinion/columns/iyothee-thass-indias-first-subaltern-historian-6413504/
11. The Theosophical Society had a considerable number of Tamil-speaking non-Brahmin *jatis* in the 1880s, which is not the case in the 1890s, when the Brahmins begin to dominate the Theosophical Society (See Vaitheespara, 2009: 71 in Bergunder et al. eds.).
12. It is worth mentioning that as observed by Pandian (2007: 76–87) the temporal and spatial markers are ill-defined and ambiguous.
13. See https://www.roundtableindia.co.in/pandit-iyothee-thass-and-the-revival-of-tamil-buddhism/
14. Vellalar is a generic term used to denote a set of landowning castes or caste groups lower to the Brahmins who were engaged in agricultural activities. The Vellalars mostly followed the Saivite tradition; they were worshippers of Lord Shiva, 'the Destroyer', among the Hindu male Gods' trinity.
15. The early Dravidianists were responsible for carving out a divide between Brahmins and non-Brahmins through the constructs of Aryan and Dravidian. The distinctiveness was then proven by moving to the sphere of scriptures. *Periya Purana*m (Great Epic) and *Thiruvilayadal Puranam* (Miracles of Shiva), both composed by Saivite Bhakti saints, were foregrounded as native Tamil texts as against Vaishnavite texts (worshippers of Lord Vishnu, the Protector among the Hindu male Gods' trinity) that were seen as being influenced by Sanskrit, and non-native. However, a few Vaishnavite texts like the *Ramayan* were revered, albeit this was the *Ramayan* written by the Dravidian poet Kamban, and not the *Ramayan* of Valmiki (See Srinivasan, 1987: 5).
16. The Thani Tamil Iyakkam was started by Maraimalai Adigal in 1916 and aimed to get rid of loanwords and foreign language influences on the Tamil language, chiefly the influence of Sanskrit.
17. Meikandar here could possibly be a pseudonym deployed by the editorial board of *Kudi Arasu*. Meikandar otherwise is believed to be the figurehead of Saivite-Vellalar identity construction and such a line from him would be improbable.
18. Ramalinga Adigal or Vallalar was a saint with Saivite roots but went on to establish *Society of the True Path*. He envisioned a society based on voluntary association as against caste or birth. The Vallalar sect is seen as an example of a

synthesis of Western ideas of individual choice and personal transformation on one hand, and Saivite principles on the other. (Weiss, 2018: 19–21)

19. The Dravidian identity was sufficiently capacious to include Telugu speakers as well. Even today, many popular leaders in Tamil Nadu are not native Tamil speakers. The coming together of such communities indicates the pre-eminence of social conflicts as over the Tamil language, and Dravidian rendition of Tamil being a subscriptive identity rather than an ascriptive one.
20. See https://theperiyarproject.com/2021/06/30/gandhi-periyar-dialogue/
21. See Chokkalingam T.S. (1932) Rival Dogs (Justice Party) fight for the crumbs dropping from Governor's table. Suthanthira Sangu. 13 October in Venkatachalapathy, A.R. (2006). *In those Days there was No Coffee: Writings in Cultural History*. New Delhi: Yoda Press. Many such cartoons were published at the time against the Justice Party.
22. Kudi Arasu, 15 March 1936
23. See https://timesofindia.indiatimes.com/city/lucknow/BSP-haathi-turns-into-Ganesh/articleshow/1050578.cms
24. See https://indianexpress.com/article/opinion/columns/quotas-reservation-jobs-patidar-maratha-jat-agitation-4456247/
25. The Self-Respect Movement was a socio-political movement started by S. Ramanathan, a Congress Party member and a follower of Gandhi in the year 1925. He invited Periyar, another Congress Party member, to take over as the leader of the movement, while Ramanathan remained its secretary. The movement was founded owing to a falling out between the Brahmins in the Congress Party and the Non-Brahmins led by Periyar and Ramanathan when the latters' demand for passing a resolution supporting proportional representation in government jobs was rejected. In the following years, the Self-Respect Movement became popular and attracted a section of people who disagreed with elitist attitude of Justice Party's leadership. The movement actively worked with the caste associations in Madras State to spread awareness about the importance of education and employment along with spreading the ideas of social justice, anti-Brahminism, atheism, reason, and so on. The movement actively engaged with people of all lower caste groups irrespective of their numerical dominance, and ensured their representation in the movement. The support from Justice Party leaders and Periyar's own financial position helped the movement grow steadily through the decade of 1930s. Periyar's supporters followed him to Dravidar Kazhagam, a section of who chose to side with Annadurai when he formed the DMK (See Self-Respect Movement Annual Meeting Report 1929, Dravidar Kazhagam, Chennai and Venkatachalapathy (1990)).
26. Adi Dravidar (First/Native/Aboriginal Dravidar) was a term coined by one of the most revered anti-caste icons of the twentieth century—M.C. Rajah. He was nominated to the Madras Legislative Council in 1920 and in 1922. Through a resolution he sought the deletion of the words Panchama (fifth

caste people) and Pariah to refer to Depressed Classes and suggested the use of Adi-Dravida and Adi-Andhra to refer to Depressed Classes. Rajah was the secretary of the Adi Dravida Mahajana Sabha in 1916, and became the President of the All-India Depressed Classes Association in 1928. (See Gupta, 1985: in Jaffrelot, 2003: 169). Periyar popularised the usage of Adi Dravidar across Madras State.

27. Kudi Arasu, 4 December 1932.
28. See https://www.forwardpress.in/2019/06/tracing-periyars-thinking-and-struggles/
29. See https://www.thenewsminute.com/article/periyar-and-anna-conflict-over-electoral-politics-88609
30. The Justice Party lost the elections inter alia due to two reasons, one a series of factional fights within the party and to a lesser degree, party members and workers moving out of the party to join Periyar's Self-Respect Movement. Further, the prevalence of the freedom movement and the popularity of the Congress party worked against the Justice Party's prospects in the 1937 elections.
31. Non Brahmin Manifesto published in *The Hindu*, 20 December 1916.
32. Kudi Arasu, 6 June 1926.
33. Kudi Arasu, 22 November 1925.
34. The Sangam era is said to span nine hundred years between sixth century BCE and third century CE, based on recently found archeological evidence. The period is characterised by three major kingdoms, i.e., the Cholas, the Cheras, and the Pandiyas who ruled Tamizhagam (Tamil Country). At times there is a mention of a smaller fourth kingdom, the Satyaputras, in Asokan inscriptions. The era is known for and through its literary works viz., *Tholkappiyam*, *Ettuthogai*, *Pathuppattu*, *Pathinenkilkanakku*, *Silappathigaram* and *Manimegalai* to name a few. *Tholkappiyam* provides insights into Tamil civil society and polity. See https://www.newindianexpress.com/states/tamil-nadu/2019/sep/19/sangam-civilisation-older-than-thought-says-new-report-2036042.html
35. *Dravida Nadu*, 9 October 1955.
36. Periyar said he is not opposed to any omnipotent or omnipresent God, but is against a God that perpetuates the caste system (Periyar, 2011: 240). Manoharan (2022: 53) argued that Periyar perceived God to be a construct of an irrational past wielded by the Brahmins to uphold their dominance over the society and, instead, proffered rationalism as the solution.
37. Lamenting the ability of a small group of Brahminical elites to subjugate the majority subalterns, Annadurai (2010: 274) averred, "…if I am not a Hindu, why am I humiliated, and regarded as belonging to a lower caste?" He said that the aim of the Dravidians is not to rid the society of Aryans (read Brahmins) but Aryanism (read Brahminism).

38. The setting up of the Backward Classes (Sattanathan) Commission in 1969, efforts to expand Backward Classes lists, enactment of legislation related to sub-categorisation into Most Backward Classes (MBCs), creation of the category of Backward Class Muslims, laws related to SC-A sub-categorisation and quotas for women can be understood as a natural extension of Periyar's idea of category-wise rights.
39. This can be seen in multiple reforms that were brought in by Annadurai, Karunanidhi, M.G.R. and Jayalalitha during their respective regimes. For instance, Tamil Nadu exceeded the 50% ceiling on reservation quota, which was a combined effort of all these leaders, which continues to be in force against the Supreme Court of India-defined limit of 50%.

2. DISSEMINATING THE DRAVIDIAN-TAMIL ETHOS THROUGH READING ROOMS

1. Mandrams can also mean physical spaces, which then translates to halls or community centres.
2. The term subaltern originally coined by Antonio Gramsci is borrowed from Gayatri Spivak's presentation in 'Can the Subaltern Speak?' in *Marxism and the Interpretation of Culture*, ed. Cary Nelson and Larry Grossberg (Chicago: University of Illinois Press, 1988): 271–313. The term counterpublic is borrowed from Rita Felski, *Beyond Feminist Aesthetics* (Cambridge MA: Harvard University Press, 1989). The paper does not discuss the participation of women in the making of the counterpublic sphere owing to its focus on the role DMK. The participation of women in the DMK-run reading rooms has been minimal, and women participated mostly in the activities undertaken by the E.V. Ramasamy Periyar-led DK (Nadar, S., Personal Communication, 8 February 2020).
3. *Suyamariyathai* (Self-Respect) or *Seerthirutha* (Reform) marriages were proposed by Periyar as a counter to conventional Hindu marriages presided over by priests. He believed that the Hindu marriages enslaved women. (Periyar, 2012: 32). There are many variants of self-respect marriages, of which a few common practices include the absence of a priest, and reading out vows that emphasise on the equality of the partners. A translated version of the key vow is: *"Through the joys and troubles in our life ahead, we swear to share equal responsibility and rights, living as thick companions. Whatever expectations you have of me in our relationship, I have the right to expect the same of you."* The person conducting the marriage and the people seated on the stage talk on topics like women's empowerment, social justice, contributions of the leaders of the Dravidian movement, and then go on to wish the couple. These marriages were given legal sanction by the DMK-led government of Tamil Nadu through The Hindu Marriage (Tamil Nadu) (Amendment) Act, 1967. See http://lawsofindia.org/pdf/tamil_nadu/1967/1967TN21.pdf

4. A couple of examples include the Scheduled Castes Federation which transformed into the Republican Party of India in 1957 and the Dalit Shoshit Samaj Sangharsh Samiti that was absorbed by the Bahujan Samaj Party in 1984. The social movements discussed above took to politics after broadening their support base through their work. However, in spite of widening the support base, Periyar decided against contesting elections.
5. On 24 August 1947, Annadurai wrote an open letter to Jawaharlal Nehru through his periodical, Dravida Nadu rebuking the handing over of the *Sengol* [Saivite Sceptre] by the Thiruvaduthurai Aadheenam [Head Priest of the Thiruvaduthurai Saivite Monastery]. Annadurai remarked that the sceptre symbolised the sanction of social discrimination by hegemonic forces, who were seeking legitimacy and tacit from the newly formed Indian government. See Dravida Nadu 24 August 1947.
6. See Dravidar Kazhagam. Annual Report 1950, Madras: 21.
7. Maniammai was a member of the Dravidar Kazhagam and the caretaker of Periyar. In a sudden turn of events, Periyar married her in July 1949 in spite of repeated attempts by the members of the DK to have him reconsider the idea.
8. The leaders of the faction were commonly referred to as *Aimperum Thalaivargal* or the five great leaders namely, C.N. Annadurai, E.V.K. Sampath, V.R. Nedunchezhiyan, K.A. Mathiazhagan and N.V. Natarajan. Muthuvel Karunanidhi was also a part of the faction that defected from DK.
9. K. Rajendran also known as "Viduthalai" Rajendran is the current General Secretary of the Dravidar Viduthalai Kazhagam [Dravidian (People) Freedom Association], who was previously associated with Dravidar Kazhagam and *Vidhuthalai* the magazine run by Periyar.
10. See Dravidar Kazhagam, Annual Report 1947, Madras: 162 and Barnett, 1976: 69.
11. Joining the party as a member, inter alia, entailed two conditions i.e., signing a declaration accepting the party's principles and a payment of eight annas (fifty paise or threepence as of 1949 exchange rate) as joining fees.
12. H.V. Hande was first elected to the Madras Legislative Council as an independent member in 1964 from the graduates' constituency and later joined the Swatantra Party in 1965. He was elected as an MLA in the 1967 elections. After the demise of Rajaji, he joined the Anna-DMK and, in 2006, he contested the elections representing the Bharatiya Janata Party (BJP).
13. Suba Veerapandian is a Tamil scholar who founded the Dravida Iyakka Tamilar Peravai (Conference of Tamils of the Dravidian Movement) in 2007. He is the Chairperson of Social Justice Monitoring Committee of Tamil Nadu (since 22 October 2021) and Member of the Advisory Committee for Tamil Nadu Text Book and Educational Services Corporation (since 27 July 2021). He lived in Karaikudi, a town in southern Tamil Nadu, between 1952 and 1971.
14. Thirunavakkarasu is a regional historian and a chronicler closely affiliated with the DMK and the Dravidian movement. He is currently working on

an eight-part book series documenting the evolution of the DMK from its inception.

15. Sources for the maps include annual reports of the DK and DMK, Barnett (1976), interviews with senior leaders and the chronicler of the DMK, Thirunavakkarasu (Personal Communication, 27 February 2020). The maps depict the geographical spread of the reading rooms run by the DMK and its allied associations. See Appendix A.
16. Viduthalai Virumbi is a former Member of Parliament and completed two terms in the Rajya Sabha. He was born in 1939 and has been in charge of reading rooms run by the DMK in the 1950s and 1960s in and around Coimbatore district. It is worth noting that his name literally translates to 'Freedom Lover' and belongs to the group of Dravidian / Tamil names that were in use since the early Dravidian movement days.
17. The relationship between the cadres of the DK and DMK was not cordial all the time. Though DMK exhibited reverence towards Periyar and both the organisations were fighting for similar causes, often supporting each other, at the ground level they were functioning separately.
18. See https://youtu.be/3oEAYummfsk?si=xYseh-2gqNz1f4vH
19. Umapathy or *Pollachi* Umapathy is the State Secretary of the Art, Literature, Culture and Rational Thought Wing of the DMK.
20. Periyar's engagement with caste association and the role of caste associations, predominantly the Nadars and Vanniyars will be discussed in Chapter 1.
21. Periyar supported Kamaraj in the 1957 elections because he was a subaltern Tamilian, and the farmers' wing of the DK campaigned extensively for Kamaraj, which helped the Congress party increase its vote share across Madras State. Members of the DMK on the other hand, contested as independent candidates and the party did not have a common symbol (DMK was a registered party in 1962), which hampered the party's prospects. A detailed analysis will be presented in Chapters 3 and 4.
22. The sources of the maps include annual reports of DK and DMK, Barnett (1976), interviews with senior leaders and chronicler of the DMK, Thirunavakkarasu (Personal Communication, 27 February 2020). The maps depict the regions where the reading rooms run by DMK and its allied associations were present. The maps showing the electoral performance of DMK were drawn using data from the Election Commission of India, annual reports of DMK and *Thiruvarur Ara Thriuvidam* (2018: 430–37). While the TN district map has the borders, the constituency map used is a later version (2009). However, the regions shaded pertain to the older borders. In this context, in the electoral map of Figure 3, the regions shaded in black denote the regions encompassing constituencies won both by the DMK and Congress in the context of redrawing of constituency borders.
23. Kanyakumari is an exception as it is a bastion of the Congress party till date.
24. Census of India 1971, Tamil Nadu, Part IX, Census Atlas: 235.

25. In the 1920s the library was a site of conflicts within the Nadar community between the Justice Party leaders, a few Self-Respecters and Congress Party supporters. The section of Nadars that supported the Congress Party was influenced by Mahatma Gandhi and used the library to spread the message of the nationalist movement. Pamphlets about the nationalist movement were printed and circulated among the common public. On the other hand, the Justice Party leaders established a separate library for themselves. (Kandasamy, MSP, Personal Communication, 6 February, 2020).
26. As one of the better endowed reading rooms, its catalogue of books was considerably rich, with over 250 books. There were four full cabinets with multiple shelves filled with books which Selvaraj claimed were from since the reading room was instituted. I found books on enlightenment luminaries like Immanuel Kant, Voltaire, Montesquieu, and Jean-Jacques Rousseau; revolutionaries like Giuseppe Garibaldi, Giuseppe Mazzini, and Vladimir Lenin; scholars like Karl Marx, B.R. Ambedkar, Mahatma Gandhi; compilations by Periyar; books on history of Nadars, Sangam literature, Indian Independence Movement, multiple editions of Tamil dictionaries, memoirs and biographies of a few priests. Selvarajan (Personal Communication, 6 February 2020) told me that the reading room used to house periodicals published by the DMK leadership in the 1950s and 1960s, but they were disposed as a part of a renovation in the late 1990s. He said that a similarly rich, if not better, catalogue of books would be available in the Rathinasamy Nadar Memorial Library, especially on the freedom movement, and then he quickly asserted that the Ariviyal Mandram is a lot more accessible compared to the former. He said that in the past, the smaller reading rooms would generally feature two or three newspapers or periodicals, whose contents would be discussed among the visitors.
27. The electoral symbol of the Indian National Congress is the image of a right hand with palm facing outwards and the fingers held together.
28. *Sudar* translates to flame and *Manaadu* means public meeting. A series of *Sudar Manaadus* were held by the DMK in the 1950s and 1960s across Madras State to highlight the injustices done to Tamils.
29. Most of the DMK branch offices (*kilai*) were functioning in work premises or at the homes of party members or office bearers. The party had to run its affairs in such a manner, initially owing to the shortage of funds, and over the years, it became common practice. Designated party offices are also prevalent in quite a few places. (Veerapandian, Personal Communication, 5 February 2020).
30. Mariamman is a Tamil folklore goddess, usually dark-skinned, and is believed to be a manifestation of Goddess Kali. The practices followed to worship Mariamman are mostly non-Vedic. Parasakthi is a prefix used to signify eternal might. The origin stories of Mariamman are varied and, at times, region-specific. However, the stories are woven

around harvests, fertility, and the general well-being of the people. The deity is regarded as fierce, who must be worshipped for timely rains. The priest is a non-Brahmin, and members of all castes can establish Mariamman temples and worship her. The offerings to the deity include cow, buffalo, or goat meat. The harvest festival offerings to Mariamman are sourced from people of all castes and shared by devotees. The offerings to the male counterpart of Mariamman include toddy, tobacco, and meat, which are consumed by the worshippers.

Mariamman temples do not have entry barriers for menstruating women. Many Mariamman temples accorded first honours to the Dalits of the village. (Sivasubramanian, Personal Communication, 28 February 2020) In other words, Hindu folklore deities were subalternised to the lives of the worshippers and made accessible. Consequently, such temples and their followers helped foster a conflict-free civil society. In its criticism of religious practices, the DMK was soft on such communities and deities. The DMK government sought to promote practices around folk deities in the name of promoting Tamil folk culture. Statewide cultural events called 'Chennai Sangamam' were held in 2007 and 2008 during Pongal, the harvest festival (Arivazhagan, Personal Communication, 3 March 2020). Similar folklore practices around Draupadi from the epic *Mahabharatam* are popular in parts of northern Tamil Nadu.

31. Ayyavazhi is a sect within the Hindu fold started by Muthukutty, also known as Ayya Vaikundar. It is a seemingly Vaishnava sect, but claims to be a sect drawing from the triumvirate of Lord Brahma [the Creator], Lord Vishnu [the Protector] and Lord Shiva [the Destroyer]. The sect gained popularity in parts of Travancore and Tirunelveli, mainly among the Nadars and other community people.

    Inter-caste harmony, widow remarriage and inter-dining were promoted by the followers of the sect. It is also observed that the sect adopted and fused numerous principles from Christianity, and subsequently emerged as a competitor to missionary activities in the region. (See Selvanayagam (2015) *Counter-Liberation and Cult-Formation: The Case of a Socio-Religious Movement in Southern India, Black Theology*, 13:3, 247–57, DOI: 10.1179/1476994815Z.00000000061). A similar sect around a saint called Vallalar is popular in parts of Northern Tamil Nadu.

32. Sankaralinganar was a renowned Gandhian who advocated for prohibition of alcohol and urged politicians to give up lavish spending. He went on an indefinite fast on 27 July 1956 with twelve demands, of which renaming Madras State to Tamil Nadu was popular. (Thirunavakkarasu, 2015: 1065–72)

33. The affluent Nadars of Virudhunagar belonged to the Justice Party. M.S. Periasamy Nadar, V.V. Ramasamy Nadar, and A.V.P. Asaithambi played a key role in the spread of the principles of social justice and self-respect. Establishing reading rooms, helping other reading rooms with financial aid, and

publishing newspapers and journals, were undertaken by these prominent figures. V.V. Ramasamy even owned a printing press. *Marumalarchi* (Renaissance) and *Tamil Thendral* (Tamil Breeze) were periodicals run by Asaithambi and Ramasamy respectively. While Ramasamy was commonly known as *Virudhai Periyar* (Periyar of Virudhunagar), Asaithambi was called *Vaalibha Periyar* (Young Periyar) (Jagannathan, 2007: 179–80).

34. V.V.R. refers to V.V. Ramasamy Nadar. 'Ayya' in this context denotes respect or reverence. In a few cases it could also have a hierarchical connotation.
35. *Theruvu* translates to street. At times, in colloquial terms, it could also mean a couple of streets together.
36. *Udhaya Suriyan* or Rising Sun is the election symbol of the DMK.
37. In the 1937 elections in the Madras Presidency, the Congress party was allotted a yellow box and the Justice Party a green box for people to drop their ballots. He told me that the Congress gave the rhyming slogan, "*Mangalaramaana Manjal Petti*" (auspicious yellow box).
38. Erecting *kodimarams* or flag posts is popular in parts of Tamil Nadu, and is done to acknowledge an achievement by the person in whose name the flag post is erected.
39. The Thevars are a middle caste group (also called Mukkulathors) consisting of three castes—Kallars, Maravars, and Agamudiyars—who account for eight per cent of the population and are spread across the southern parts of the erstwhile Madras State. In the late nineteenth century, the Nadars and Maravars had hostile relations, which found expression in the Sivakasi Riots of 1899. See Hardgrave (1969: 118).
40. He was named Sankaralinga Nadar but he gave up the caste reference in his name, and chose to go by Sankaralingam.
41. A section of Nadars moved towards the Congress in the 1930s. Rudolph & Rudolph (1967: 49) note that the entry of Nadars into temples through the Temple Entry Authorisation and Indemnity Act, 1939 engendered the change in political orientation of a section of Nadars away from the Justice Party towards the Congress Party.

    As the popularity of the Justice Party waned, and the Government of India Act, 1935 led to Indians forming governments, the Nadars saw an opportunity to secure political power through the Congress Party. An important development in this context is the election of Kamaraj Nadar as the Congress Party's provincial president in 1940. In other words, while the DMK enjoyed support from the majority of Nadars, a section of them continued to support the Congress.

3. THE DMK'S MANOEUVRES IN MADRAS STATE

1. Despite a rich history of anti-caste mobilisations, as early as the 1930s, a dominant section of Marathas allied with the Brahmins to subvert the cause

of separate electorates for Dalits. In other words, the political movement espoused Hindu-ness as an important element of Indian nation. (Godsmark, 2018: 169)

2. Arivarasu's birth name was Madasamy. However, after joining the Self-Respect Movement, he changed his name in a public meeting held by Periyar in Madras city. Such meetings were held in the 1940s, 1950s, and 1960s, and, in them, the names of people belonging to marginalised communities and names that had Sanskrit undertones were changed to Tamil names. Inspired by Annadurai, Arivarasu joined the DMK and he was a member till 1996, the year in which he passed away.
3. The Princely State of Travancore had agitations opposing the recruitment of non-native individuals, mostly Tamil Brahmins, in government jobs and Shahu Maharaj of the Princely state of Kolhapur passed an order to reserve 50% seats in government jobs. See https://frontline.thehindu.com/social-issues/article30224191.ece and https://thesatyashodhak.com/what-was-shahu-maharajs-historic-1902-reservation-order/
4. See https://www.thehindu.com/opinion/op-ed/from-a-manifesto-to-a-movement/article25674237.ece
5. Omanthur Ramasamy Reddiar, an Indian freedom fighter and politician, served as the Premier or Chief Minister of the Madras Presidency from March 23, 1947, to April 6, 1949. He passed the Madras Temple Entry Authorisation Act 1947, which granted Dalits and other Hindus full access to Hindu temples, and the Devadasi Dedication Abolition Act of 1947.
6. *The Times of India*, 6 August 1950.
7. The fact that Champakam Dorairajan did not have any locus standi was very useful for mobilisation, on the streets. The DMK argued that the move to strike down the reservation was not to secure a seat to study but to prevent non-Brahmins from studying [Thirumaran 2020: 8 February Personal Communication].
8. *Dravida Nadu*, 3 February 1952.
9. The decision to support Communist Party candidates was based on how able the candidates were to win against the Congress. In places where the DK thought that Communist candidates did not stand a chance, they supported a candidate from any party other than the Congress (Dravidar Kazhagam Executive Committee Resolution, Trichy, 15 November 1951).
10. *Viduthalai*, 27 November 1951.
11. See https://timesofindia.indiatimes.com/city/chennai/kongu-vellalar-goundars-seek-mbc-status/articleshow/3429697.cms
12. Full forms are the following. CPI: Communist Party of India; CWP: Commonweal Party; FBL-MG: All India Forward Bloc – Marxist Group; INC: Indian National Congress; IND: Independent; JUSP: Justice Party; KMPP: Kisan Mazdoor Praja Party; SCF: Scheduled Castes Federation; SP: Socialist Party; TTP: Tamil Nadu Toiler's Party.

13. See https://frontline.thehindu.com/books/article31389297.ece
14. E.V.K. Sampath was a senior leader in the DK and belonged to the faction (aimperum thalaivargal or five great leaders) that broke out to form the DMK. He was the nephew of Periyar. Aimperum Thalavargal plus Karunanidhi formed the DMK's top brass till Sampath's defection in 1962.
15. On 26 September 1952, Nehru spoke at the Central Scientific Research Institute at Hyderabad on the occasion of the opening of the Tuberculosis ward at the Yarragadda Hospital. He welcomed the criticism of the Dravidian leaders regarding their claims of five-year plans' discrimination against the South. However, he opined that for logical reasons Hindi ought to be the common language across the country and at the same time a south Indian language should be taught in the North for harmonious exchange of ideas (Nehru, 1984, 19: 67).
16. In his famed book *Panathottam*, published in 1949, Annadurai exposits his concerns about the increasing dominance of North Indian businessmen in South India, which he argued was contributing to the accumulation of wealth in the hands of a few at the cost of rendering the South Indian States as merely a big market filled with consumers. The slogan *vadakku vaazhkirathu, therku thaeikirathu* (The North is thriving and the South is eroding) became popular in the 1950s. While Dalmia's cement manufacturing unit was functioning in Kallakudy town and caused the emergence of settlements, the issue came up over a decision to rename the town after Dalmia, as it was perceived as an act of economic imposition by the North on the native Dravidian-Tamil (Hardgrave, 1965: 43). The name Dalmiapuram continued despite a massive protest that popularised Karunanidhi as a firebrand leader and was re-renamed Kallakudi-Palanganatham in 1969. See https://www.newindianexpress.com/states/tamil-nadu/2018/aug/08/political-career-of-karunanidhi-gained-momentum-after-the-agitation-on-july-15-1953-at-kallakudi-1854854.html & https://www.thenewsminute.com/article/how-kallakudi-agitation-became-turning-point-karunanidhi-s-political-life-145744
17. In a correspondence with his friend Navaratna Rama Rao, a reputed figure in Mysore, about intra-party opposition, an astute Rajaji expressed his awareness of the situation and conveyed that he would stay until he enjoyed a majority, or until he wished to. However, Rama Rao's response, in the form of a cricket analogy, was compelling. He said, "It would be a pity for a Bradman (Rajaji) to be bowled over by a long hop sent down by a village-green trundler (Kamaraj)." Gandhi (1984: 249). It is worth noting that Rama Rao's response came off as brusque and far removed from reality, at best in the way events unfolded.
18. The S.K. Dhar Commission Report revolved around national integrity, financial feasibility, and homogeneity, both cultural and economic, while considering the request to redraw boundaries of states. The report stated that the clashes between group-conscious minorities had hampered the quality of

government and governance in Madras State. See https://indianculture.gov.in/reports-proceedings/report-linguistic-provinces-commission-1948

19. See https://frontline.thehindu.com/books/the-birth-of-a-state/article9449149.ece
20. The linguistic reorganisation of states was a moment of relief for Periyar, and he welcomed it. He contended that the leaders representing the Telugus, Kannadigas, and Malayalis were neither proud nor committed to the self-respect of their own identities and did not possess rationalist values. He cited their failure to oppose *varnashrama dharma*, their acceptance of discrimination perpetuated by the caste system, adherence to superstitious practices of Hinduism, and willingness to be subjugated by the dominant Union Government of the North as reasons for his remarks. In the context of the reorganisation, he observed that while the word 'Dravidian' could be replaced by 'Tamil', such a substitution would make Tamil, without Dravidian, vulnerable to appropriation by Aryans/Brahmins. He cautioned that the Brahminical ethos would then subvert the egalitarian political ideals forged through the capacious Dravidian-Tamil identity. See *Viduthalai*, 12 December 1955.
21. Rajaji, as early as 1952, vehemently opposed the idea of Madras city becoming a part of Andhra State or making it a Union Territory or even making Madras city the temporary capital of Andhra Pradesh, despite attempts by Andhra leaders to garner support in New Delhi. See Gandhi (1984: 237–38). Similarly, a section of Andhra leaders reached out to Ma Po Si in 1956, seeking his support to make Madras city the temporary capital of Andhra Pradesh. However, Ma Po Si refused. See *Dinamalar*, 7 April 2014.
22. The DMK and its leadership made multiple attempts in this regard. On 7 May 1957, a resolution introduced by the DMK in the State Legislative Assembly was defeated. On 10 March 1961, Bhupesh Gupta, Member of Parliament (Rajya Sabha) of the Communist Party introduced a Constitution Amendment Bill to change the name of Madras State to Tamil Nadu. In May 1963, Annadurai made a long and impassioned speech in support of the Bill, citing ancient Tamil literature in support of his claim. In July 1963, a resolution was introduced by Arangannal of the DMK which was again defeated in the State Legislative Assembly. On 18 July 1967, Annadurai as the Chief Minister of Madras State introduced a resolution to rename the State as Tamil Nadu. He recalled the sacrifices and contributions of leaders like Sankaralinganar and Ma Po Si. On 14 January 1969, the State was officially renamed as Tamil Nadu. See Ramachandran (1975: 51–59) and Madras Musings Vol. XXVIII No. 9, August 2018: 16–31.
23. Please note that the individual numbers have been rounded off.
24. Brahminical majoritarianism refers to a socio-political dominance in India where Brahmins, despite being a minority, have a disproportionate influence on various sectors due to historical privileges and vital position in social

hierarchies. The prevalence highlights how a minority group can maintain systemic advantages over others and this majoritarianism is based on social capital and institutional control, rather than numerical strength.

25. Periyar moved on to the slogan, 'Tamil Nadu Tamizharkalukke' (Tamil Nadu for Tamils), which became popular in the anti-Hindi agitations of 1965.
26. The excerpt appeared in *Homeland,* an English publication run by Annadurai. It was accessed from a narrative account written by Eelaventhan M.K., a former Member of Parliament of Sri Lanka and Member of Transnational Government of Tamil Eelam (TGTE), representing Canada. The account can be accessed here: https://sangam.org/annadurai-champion-eelam-tamil-liberation/
27. Eelaventhan notes that Annadurai sharply retorted to Krishna Menon's insistence on non-intervention in Sri Lanka's internal affairs on the question of equal rights for Tamils. Citing the metaphor of a domestic relationship between a husband and wife, Annadurai said that the neighbour did not have any business as long as they are living harmoniously. However, when the husband threatens to kill the wife and she shouts out of anguish, [the] neighbour should intervene and such an intervention is imperative. See https://sangam.org/annadurai-champion-eelam-tamil-liberation/
28. V.P. Raman had drafted the constitution of the DMK. Raman had been extremely vocal about the non-viability of Dravida Nadu on two counts. As a federation of South Indian States, it was not viable owing to the linguistic reorganisation and the lack of support for the idea from the other States. As an independent Tamil country, it was not viable due to economic and military constraints (See Barnett, 1976: 109).
29. *Link* 3 July 1960 in Hardgrave, 1965: 65.
30. Notably, Karunanidhi's vision for building the party organisation and its communication framework was considerably influenced by Kamaraj's approach towards building the Congress Party in Madras State. (Thirumaran, 8 February 2020, Personal Communication)
31. Barnett (1976: 107) noted that Karunanidhi built a network of supporters that backed him while he was expanding the party's presence in Madras State. She argued that by forging a mutually beneficial relationship between his supporters and himself, he was able to influence candidate selection, both for party positions and for elections. Akin to the supporters' network, Karunanidhi also shared a symbiotic relationship with film industry artistes, who propagated Dravidian-Tamil ethos and, in turn, attained fame and popularity.
32. Kannan (2017: 267–74) mobilised evidence to argue that Karunanidhi's faction was responsible for the scuffle in the General Council meeting. In the November 1960 General Council meeting that was to elect the General Secretary of the DMK, Karunanidhi's faction backed C.P. Chitrarasu and Sampath's faction backed Mathiazhagan. However, Annadurai intervened, contested for the position, and won unanimously. Kannan also argued that Annadurai was not

unaware of Karunanidhi's moves. Sampath and his associate Kannadhasan, leader of the DMK, veteran poet and sought-after lyricist in the Tamil film industry were attacked again in Trichy, for which they held the leadership responsible. Sampath went on a fast in retaliation, which Annadurai talked him out of.

33. Ironically, Sampath was a part of the meeting in 1960 that sought to convince Annadurai to give up on the Dravida Nadu claim. It is also one of the very few instances in which Karunanidhi and Sampath agreed on an issue.
34. Annadurai and other DMK leaders regarded absence on the ground to be the reason for the former's defeat. The DMK's use of resources and vicarious campaign methods, as against, personal touch, did not sit well with the voters (Aranganal, 1988: 192).
35. Kamaraj made these remarks in the Chief Ministers' Conference when the members were contemplating a broader conference on national integration (Kannan, 2017: 282).
36. Please note that the individual numbers have been rounded off.
37. The Committee on National Integration and Regionalism chaired by C.P. Ramaswamy Ayyar with multiple chief ministers including Kamaraj (Kannan, 2017: 291) as members, had submitted his recommendations in November 1962. Imposition of restrictions against any secessionist claims for electoral purposes was the purpose of the Bill. Such claims were equated to acts aiming at the disintegration of Indian Union. Notably, the committee acknowledged and appreciated the embargos on agitations put in place by the All-Party Hill Leaders Conference (APHLC) of Assam, Akali Dal of Punjab, and the DMK of Madras State, and their support for the Indian Union. The Law Minister Ashoke Kumar Sen, however, was not pleased with the temporary moratoriums. He contended that the aforesaid forces "had sought to undermine our strength and sap the very vitality which sustains the nation as a unit" [Lok Sabha Debates (1963) Vol. XII, Col. 5815 in Rao 1963: 155]. The committee was constituted by the National Integration Council. See https://www.mha.gov.in/sites/default/files/2022-10/NATIONALINTEGRATIONCOUNCIL_26082022_1%5B1%5D.pdf
38. See https://www.india.gov.in/my-government/constitution-india/amendments/constitution-india-sixteenth-amendment-act-1963
39. Annadurai started by saying that C.P. Ramaswamy Ayyar heading the committee on national integration was ironical as he sought to split away from India and ally with Pakistan when he was the Dewan ofTravancore (Annadurai, 1963 in Rajya Sabha: 4892).
40. He also said that the move and the Bill was non-Nehruvian and subverted Nehruvian ways which relied more on engaging with different communities and people to foster the spirit of unity as against enacting laws to force unity (ibid., 4895).
41. See https://eparlib.nic.in/bitstream/123456789/58623/1/jcb_03_1963_constitution_16th_amendment.pdf

42. See https://youtu.be/Znbo6zEgS0o
43. Narayana Rao (1963: 156–58), an eminent lawyer who worked in the Indian Law Institute and the Law Commission of India argued that the amendments to the oath proposed by the Bill did not need a constitutional amendment. Either mechanisms were in place, or an ordinary amendment of the Constitution, would have been sufficient. He also argued that the Bill made it impossible to cede a territory of the country if the Union wished to, even by a constitutional amendment, which would, in turn, have a bearing on the execution of international treaties and border disputes. Drawing from the argument, it is safe to contend that the leaders in charge in Delhi at the time wanted to make a spectacle out of the Sixteenth Constitutional Amendment Act to infuse the 'putting-together' spirit within the 'holding-together' federal structure that was in place. The ramification, however, was that the tendencies to breakaway were not engaged with or assimilated but covered up and sidelined.
44. The policy saw the coming together of the Self-Respect Movement led by Periyar, Tamil Purist Movement with Maraimalai Adigal, caste association leaders like W.P.A. Soundarapandian, Justice Party, and Muslim League leaders to stage a massive protest thereby damaging Rajaji's popularity and the subsequent recalling of the policy.
45. A few exceptions include leaders like Qazi Syed Karimuddin [Urdu script] and Subbarayan [Roman script] who advocated for Hindustani. Subbarayan wanted English to be retained as well. Leaders like T.A. Ramalingam Chettiar pressed for the 15-year preparation time and opposed the use of the phrase 'national language'. See https://loksabha.nic.in/writereaddata/cadebatefiles/vol9.html (12–14 September 1949).
46. The adoption of Hindi by the Indian Constitution led to the DMK observing 10 January as Anti-Hindi Day and the party workers waved black flags against Union Ministers in opposition to the policy on official language. The official language policy also led to the overhaul of signages in the Madras State, especially at railway stations. The boards had Hindi names first, followed by English and then Tamil, which motivated the Periyar-led DK and the Annadurai-led DMK to stage protests with thousands of volunteers in the Trichy and Erode railway stations, respectively. The protesters blackened the Hindi letters with tar. While this continued and expanded to post offices over the next couple of years Kamaraj assuaged the protesters in July 1955, by issuing a statement and railway authorities, too, reordered the boards which then had Tamil first, followed by Hindi, and then English (Ramasamy, 2020: 16).
47. Sampath was tasked with the protest of waving black flags against the President of India on August 6.
48. *Sunday Times*, 7 August 1960, in Hardgrave, 1965: 68.

49. As discussed in the previous section, by now, the Anti-Secession Bill (part of the sixteenth constitutional amendment), had been passed in Lok Sabha and tabled in Rajya Sabha, where Annadurai appealed to the house to give up the amendment.
50. It is worth noting that a large section of school teachers were politically active, which drew the ire of Kamaraj in the aftermath of the 1967 elections, which I discuss in Chapter 4.
51. 23.7% and 3.1% of respondents voted for Hindi imposition and improvement of Tamil, respectively.
52. India was struck by floods, drought, and locust attack, in 1961. However, S.K. Patil, the then Union Minister of Food and Agriculture, claimed that food production was still on the rise (Ramachandran, 1975: 109). Further, in 1960, he had signed an agreement with the United States whereby the latter would export surplus food to India against payment in Indian rupees, which was in turn lent to India for development projects. S.K. Patil assured the Rajya Sabha in 1961 that he would stop imports in three years. However, the government could not control the rising prices of essential commodities. See https://www.nytimes.com/1964/07/28/archives/patil-scores-hoarders.html
53. Grains include rice, wheat, maise and soybean. Coarse grains are included for Korea, and cereals and pulses for Taiwan (FAOSTAT data).
54. Grain Self Sufficiency Ratio (Grain SSR): The territorial capacity of a specific territory to meet its own grain requirements from domestic production without considering the shares of exports of the same product. The SSR calculates the percentage of food consumed and produced domestically.
55. The data collected by the author Keijiro Otsuka was at a later stage and therefore his paper mentions the region as Bangladesh. However, in 1961, the region was known as East Pakistan.
56. The Public Accounts Committee report on fertilisers discussed in 1962 stated that the prices of the fertilisers were intentionally kept high with a motive to make profits, thereby defeating the purpose of the fertiliser scheme. (Ramachandran, 1975: 114).
57. The food shortage in the run up the 1967 elections was attributed to the dominance of private players in the trading space who moved goods out of Madras State primarily to Kerala (Ramanujam, 1967: 278).
58. The DK, in some ways, resembled a family with an ageing patriarch (Periyar) at its helm, who, for all his best intentions, could not completely yield trust and control to his lieutenants, including Annadurai. It is one thing to treat land and material assets as property, but to treat an organisation as property is where the DK imploded. To dismiss Periyar's reluctance as mere patriarchal insecurity would be reductive. Yet, ignoring it altogether would risk erasing the human contingencies that shaped the DK's internal tensions.

4. A METICULOUS UNDERDOG AND A SEEMINGLY LAX STALWART

1. While this chapter engages with Kamaraj extensively, it is not within its scope to provide a full biographical sketch. Narasimhan (1967), Forrester (1970), Gopanna (2008), and Jeyaraman (2013) have produced excellent biographies of Kamaraj.
2. See https://thecommunemag.com/dheerar-satyamurti-the-fervid-fervent-fiery-freedom-fighter/
3. See https://www.inc.in/our-inspiration/shri-k-kamaraj
4. The Indian National Congress was the single largest party and, therefore, inviting the Congress to form the government despite not having the majority was a conventional solution. Before Sri Prakasa did so, his predecessor, Governor Krishna Kumarsinhji Bhavsinhji, had referred the matter to the President of India (See Gandhi, 1984: 226).
5. See https://web.archive.org/web/20081105171101/http://www.hindu.com/thehindu/2001/05/31/stories/0231000q.htm
6. The Commonweal Party (CWP) led by Manickavelu Naicker and the Tamil Nadu Toilers Party (TTP) led by S.S. Ramasamy Padayatchi were parties that stemmed from the Vanniyar caste associations and their subsequent politicisation. They were approached by Rajaji while he was forging the post-poll alliance in 1952. While CWP took up Rajaji's offer and supported the Congress, which landed Manickavelu Naicker a Cabinet berth, the TTP did not support the alliance. Rajaji's bid to convince both the parties to merge with the Congress, however, was unsuccessful. In 1954, however, the TTP supported Kamaraj and Ramasamy Padayatchi landed a berth in Kamaraj's cabinet. More importantly, both the parties merged with the Congress party (Hardgrave, 1965: 44–45).
7. The Congress offered to field a Vanniyar candidate as Chairperson of North Arcot and South Arcot District Boards in response to CWP's and TTP's offer to merge themselves into the Congress party. However, when local leaders of the Congress elected a Reddiar candidate, Congress suspended the members who did not toe the party line (Hardgrave, 1965: 45).
8. Thirumaran K. is a retired Professor of Tamil in Virudhunagar Hindu Nadars' Senthikumara Nadar College, Virudhunagar. He is the brother of DMK's former General Secretary K. Anbazhagan and studied at Annamalai University.
9. Although the number of members of the DK went down significantly (from ~75,000 to 25,000) with the formation of the DMK in 1949, as discussed in Chapter 2, the DK's membership stayed intact and saw some growth as well. Therefore, the DK was influential in terms of its leader Periyar and its cadres on the ground across the Madras State.
10. *Viduthalai*, 22 September 1962.
11. Vaikom Satyagraha was a two-year-long agitation (March 1924 to November 1925) seeking access to public roads around the Vaikom Temple in the Kingdom of Travancore to members belonging to the lower and untouchable castes, led

by notable Congress leaders of the region, Sree Narayana Dharma Paripalana Yogam, and other activists. Mahatma Gandhi, Rajaji, and Periyar were other notable leaders in the agitation. The settlement arrived at by Gandhi involved opening of roads in three directions, except the eastern direction, which was criticised by Periyar. The eastern side was opened in 1936 (Diehl, 1977: 24).

12. *Navasakthi*, 11 April 1961.
13. Kamaraj was aware of Periyar's previous remarks against him. He maintained that Periyar had called him a 'poisonous snake' in 1952. He contended that Periyar and the DK's support to the Congress in the 1957 election was due to the welfare measures instituted by the government for non-Brahmin communities, and the conflict between the DK and the DMK (See *The Hindu*, 14 February 1957).
14. On Kamaraj's advice, Lal Bahadur Shastri was reinstated as a minister without portfolio. Gopalkrishna Gandhi noted that Shastri was seen as the Deputy Prime Minister and Nehru's successor. Read: https://www.thehindu.com/opinion/lead/A-Kamaraj-Plan-for-our-times/article12715025.ece
15. Read https://www.thehindu.com/opinion/lead/A-Kamaraj-Plan-for-our-times/article12715025.ece
16. See https://www.thehindu.com/news/national/tamil-nadu/battle-of-ballots-is-nothing-new-in-the-congress/article65955114.ece
17. *The Hindu*, 25 September 1963.
18. *The Hindustan Times*, 14 July 1966.
19. Devaluation of currency involves reduction of the value of currency in the prevalent exchange rate system. While such a move would make exports cheaper, imports would become costlier. Nadars were primarily engaged in trading rather than investing their capital in big industries. However, the emergence of policies to cut out middlemen, and the institution of bodies like the Food Corporation of India, prompted the apex Nadar caste association to motivate Nadars to set up industries in the years 1965 and 1965 (Hardgrave 1969: 151).
20. *The Hindustan Times*, 14 July 1966.
21. *The Mail* (Madras), 16 June 1966.
22. The publications run by the DMK leaders and supporters chided Kamaraj occasionally, and such articles would be unsigned. See 'Kamarasare! Unmaidhaana?' in Murasoli, 8 August 1956, where an unsigned article called Kamaraj a 'timid' person.
23. The Jana Sangh was the only exception that was in favour of Hindi (Nathan, 1967: 2135).
24. Rajaji's support for the DMK helped assuage the concerns of the Brahmin community over the apparent dominance of non-Brahmins, which they feared would affect the opportunities available to Brahmins. (Hardgrave, 1965: 74). However, Murphy Gardener (1953: 104–06 in Ross, 1961: 194) argues that while the accounts of and sentiments towards displacement seem believable,

the Brahmins continued to occupy a higher proportion of sought-after positions in comparison to other caste groups, despite a quota system being in place. He interprets this not as a case of forced or imminent parity among all caste groups, but rather as one of relative displacement of Brahmins.

25. *The Hindustan Times*, 14 July 1966.
26. The Swatantra leaders backed the DMK in 1962 elections as well. See Hardgrave, 1965: 75.
27. *The Hindustan Times*, 24 February 1967.
28. *The Hindustan Times*, 2 January 1967.
29. The evaluation of two caste groups is in relation to one another in the region. Naidus, in today's classification of caste groups, fall into the category of intermediate castes, and Nadars fall into the category of backward classes.
30. *The Hindustan Times*, 24 February 1967.
31. *The Hindustan Times*, 4 March 1967.
32. T.K.S. Elangovan is the national spokesperson of the DMK and was a Member of Parliament [Rajya Sabha] representing the State of Tamil Nadu until June 2022.
33. *The Hindustan Times*, 4 March 1967.
34. *The Hindustan Times*, 4 March 1967.
35. *The Hindustan Times*, 4 March 1967.
36. Read more: https://www.thenewsminute.com/article/rm-veerappan-turns-95-driving-force-tamil-cinema-and-politics-155067
37. Read more: https://www.thehindu.com/news/cities/chennai/the-day-mr-radha-shot-mgr/article12059018.ece
38. See https://www.madrasmusings.com/vol-28-no-20/the-shootout-with-political-recoil/
39. *The Hindustan Times*, 24 February 1967.
40. The Justice Party had initiated the meals scheme, and hostel facilities for non-Brahmin students, and encouraged education of non-Brahmin students on a limited scale in the 1920s. However, Kamaraj's interventions were methodical and were instituted across Madras State.
41. Mentioned as just 'Postgraduates' in 1967.

CONCLUSION

1. The introduction of the MSEE scheme by Rajaji in a society seeking to move away from hereditary occupations and towards socioeconomic mobility presented an opportune moment for the DK and the DMK to further their politics. Rajaji's obduracy damaged the Congress party's reputation and paved way for the elevation of Kamaraj as the non-Brahmin Chief Minister of Madras State, thereby marking the start of the subalternisation of the legislature.

2. The only exception is the State of Goa, whose first Chief Minister, Dayanand Bandodkar, rose to the position as a result of an anti-caste movement. See Parobo, 2015.

EPILOGUE

1. See https://twitter.com/mkstalin/status/1589568394290139139?s=20
2. Tamil Nadu had earmarked 3.5% quota each for Christians and Muslims on 15 September 2007 within the BC quota. See https://mumbaimirror.indiatimes.com/news/india/karuna-orders-3-5-quota-for-muslims-christians-in-govt-jobs/articleshow/15741290.cms However, a year later following a representation made by the community citing shrinking of benefits, the quota for Christians was recalled. See https://www.hindustantimes.com/india/tn-accepts-christians-plea-to-scrap-exclusive-quota/story-A1waWDRuCtC6UkkkTJRANP.html
3. The DMK led by Karunanidhi had also appealed to former prime ministers to include Dalit Christians in the Scheduled Caste reservation quota on three occasions—1996, 2006 and 2011.
4. M.K. Stalin argued that unlike religion, caste is not horizontal but a vertical framework that engenders discrimination. See https://www.thehindu.com/news/national/tamil-nadu/tamil-nadu-assembly-adopts-resolution-urging-centre-to-extend-reservations-to-christian-adi-dravidars/article66754950.ece
5. See https://www.newindianexpress.com/states/tamil-nadu/2018/aug/09/m-karunanidhi-transwomen-recall-man-who-gave-them-identity-1855245.html
6. See https://scroll.in/article/723205/why-tiruchi-siva-moved-a-private-members-bill-to-ensure-rights-for-transgender-people
7. It is worth noting that Siva's bill had a rocky journey. After passage in Rajya Sabha, it remained pending in the Lok Sabha, which ultimately passed different versions of the bill in 2018 and 2019. The 2019 version was passed by the Rajya Sabha as well in that year, and has been in effect since January 2020. Siva has protested repeatedly that this Bill was not the same as his Bill, and had been diluted significantly.
8. See https://www.thequint.com/news/india/social-justice-pride-flag-at-chennai-queer-lit-fest
9. The co-founder of Queer Chennai Chronicles, C. Moulee remarked that social justice in India could not be discussed by ignoring Ambedkar and Periyar. He also noted that a placard in the 2018 Pride March mentioned that gender could not be discussed without talking about caste. See https://bumpahead.net/not-about-the-ambedkar-periyar-rainbow-flag-902da38a5b46
10. The glossary was notified on the direction of the Madras High Court in a judgment delivered in 2021 on a case filed by a lesbian couple seeking the

court's intervention to protect them. The case was taken up by Manuraj Shanmugasundaram, a spokesperson of the DMK, who appealed to the judge of the High Court presiding over the case to issue orders to sensitise people regarding LGBTQIA+ community. See https://scroll.in/latest/1031176/tamil-nadu-government-releases-glossary-of-terms-to-address-lgbtqia-community

11. Growth indicators include per capita income, size of the state's GDP, rates at which different sectors of the economy are growing. On the other hand, development indicators include the maternal mortality rate, stunting in children, infant mortality rate and other such indicators that talk about qualitative changes in people's lives.
12. See https://www.niti.gov.in/sites/default/files/2021-11/National_MPI_India-11242021.pdf (p. 34)
13. See https://theprint.in/india/43-of-1-6-million-women-factory-workers-in-india-work-in-tamil-nadu-alone-finds-study/1358869/
14. A quick quinquennial analysis (2017–2021) reveals that Tamil Nadu fares well on the indicators pertaining to atrocities against Dalits in comparison to other South Indian States and all-India averages, be it in disposal rates (police station and courts), pendency rates, and number of atrocities. The average state share of Dalit population to all-India level is higher in TN at 7.2% in comparison to AP 4.2%, KA 5.2%, KL 1.5% and TS 2.7%. The share of Dalits *vis-à-vis* the population of the state is also higher in TN at 20.01% in comparison to AP 17.04%, KA 17.1%, KL 9.1%, and TS 15.5%. However, the average state share of crimes against Dalits to all India level in TN lower only to KL at 2.8% in comparison to AP 4.2%, KA 3.4%, KL 1.9%, and TS 3.6%. The average rate of total crime against SCs is also significantly lower in TN at 9.1% in comparison to AP 23.3%, KA 14.8%, KL 29.3%, TS 30.9% and the all-India average stands at 23.18%. In charge-sheeting rate, which is a useful metric of police performance, TN's 5-year average is higher at 84.6% in comparison to AP 66.2%, KA 81.1%, KL 78.4%, TS 76.2% and the all-India average 80.6%. Average pendency percentage (police station) in TN is 33.5% which is lower than AP 50.3%, KA 33%, KL 45.4%, and TS 49.5% but higher than all-India average 27.84%. In the courts, the average conviction rate in TN is 16.1% which is higher than AP 6.7%, KA 4.2%, KL 7.7%, and TS 8%, but lower than the all-India average 34.86%. The average pendency rate of cases is lower in TN at 87.6% in comparison to KA 93.3%, KL 92.8%, TS 89.2%, and all-India average 94.36% but higher than AP 86.8%. Charge-sheeting rate signifies the percentage of cases charge sheeted out of total true cases (cases in which charge sheet is not laid but final report submitted as true + cases charge sheeted) under IPC. See https://ncrb.gov.in/sites/default/files/crime_in_india_table_additional_table_chapter_reports/Chapter%204-15.11.16_2015.pdf (p. 69)
15. I have pseudonymised the name of the respondent on request.

16. See https://indianexpress.com/article/cities/chennai/tamil-nadu-cm-mk-stalin-inaugurates-equality-village-in-sivaganga-district-7958824/
17. After losing power to M.G.R.—who was pliant to Indira Gandhi's imposition of Emergency—in 1977, the DMK came back to power only after his death (1987) in the 1989 elections. The pressure from the AIADMK in exchange for support led to the dismissal of the DMK government on the grounds of law and order by the Union Government led by former Prime Minister Chandra Shekhar in 1991. The DMK's extensive support to the Sri Lankan Tamils' cause was the reason for its reputational damage after Rajiv Gandhi's assassination.
18. The DMK's strength in the northern Tamil Nadu region was challenged by the PMK in a conspicuous manner. Though the DMK was able to wrest the region back from PMK, the DMK and even the AIADMK lost their ability to field candidates from numerically non-dominant backward class groups, owing to the mobilisational efforts of the PMK on the lines of caste. Of late, one way to circumvent the Vanniyar preponderance has been to give party positions to the Vanniyars and field non-Vanniyar candidates, either by the Dravidian parties themselves or their alliance partners, or vice versa.
19. The 1990s and early 2000s saw the DMK and AIADMK engage with Hindu-nationalist organisations, form electoral alliances with the BJP and demonstrate their inability to contain the rise of Hindu-Muslim clashes in the State. While Karunanidhi entertained all sorts of self-styled political parties that were otherwise casteist outfits, which contributed to the DMK's rout in 2001 elections, Jayalalithaa attempted to introduce the anti-conversion Bill in 2002. The DMK, being a party dependent on smaller and numerically non-dominant caste groups, took a bigger hit in comparison to the AIADMK, whose vote base remained relatively resilient. The lax Dravidian-Tamil phase ended with the DMK breaking away from the alliance with the BJP in 2004 and the arrest of the head priest of the Sri Kanchi Kamakoti Peetham, ordered by the AIADMK-led government. In 2014, when Narendra Modi turned the election into a presidential contest, Jayalalithaa stepped up the contest and presented herself as the Dravidian-Tamil bulwark against BJP's majoritarian wave with her popular election cry—*Who is a better administrator* (*leader*): *Gujarat's Modi or Tamil Nadu's lady*?"

    See https://www.indiatoday.in/magazine/states/story/20010409-tamil-nadu-elections-parties-play-caste-card-dmk-frontrunner-775350-2001-04-08

    https://www.thehindu.com/news/national/tamil-nadu/this-lady-is-better-than-modi/article5934593.ece

    https://www.indiatoday.in/magazine/cover-story/story/20041129-kanchi-shankaracharya-jayendra-saraswati-arrested-for-murder-788845-2004-11-28
20. The data has been collected under the framework of the CNRS-supported research program associating Sciences Po and Ashoka University, on the Social

Profile of India's National and Provincial Elected Representatives (SPINPER). The repository can be accessed at https://lokdhaba.ashoka.edu.in

21. This includes a few intermediate caste groups like Pillais, Rajus, and Naidus.
22. *The Times of India*, Chennai edition, 13 March 2019, p. 10.
23. Of the OBCs' representation between 1971 and 1991, the representation of the share of the Kongu Vellala Gounder-Mukkulathor-Vanniyar combine ranged between 41.46% (1971) and 46.15% (1991) and averaged at 43.88%. The other OBCs' representation ranged between 17.52% (1977) and 13.62% (1980) and averaged at 15.64%.
24. Of the OBCs' representation between 1996 and 2021, the representation of the share of Kongu Vellala Gounder-Mukkulathor-Vanniyar combine ranged between 46.19 (1996) and 30.47% (2016) and averaged at 40.55%. The other OBCs' representation ranged between 27.9% (2016) and 12.08% (2011) and averaged at 18.52%.
25. A case in point is Anitha, a seventeen-year-old student belonging to the Dalit community who committed suicide in protest against the National Eligibility and Entrance Test (NEET) for medical admissions on 1 September 2017. The suicide sparked protests across Tamil Nadu and Anitha emerged as the daughter/sister/friend of every other person in Tamil Nadu. NEET was seen as everyone's issue, though it discriminated against the Dalit student. In contrast, a 19-year-old girl belonging to the Dalit community was brutally gang-raped in Hathras District, Uttar Pradesh. In less than a fortnight, she died in a hospital. The protest that ensued saw the participation of Dalit activists and some progressive groups. However, people across communities in Uttar Pradesh did not take up this issue. In other words, her plight was not seen as mainstream-worthy, despite the frequent occurrence of rapes and the presence of Dalit parties in Uttar Pradesh.
26. See https://youtu.be/Y8nddtbwTe0
27. See https://youtu.be/6NIOQl751YQ
28. Population breakdown among Dalits is as follows; Paraiyars 12%, Devendra Kula Vellalars 5%, and Arunthathiyars 3%. *The Times of India*, Chennai edition, 13 March 2019, p. 10.
29. The social and political fracturing of the solidarity between Dalit caste groups is a phenomenon that is prevalent in other states too, which is one of the reasons for the electoral ascendance of the Hindu nationalists, as pointed out in emerging research by scholars such as Sandeep Badole. However, the magnitude of such fracturing is contained, at least electorally, in Tamil Nadu so far.
30. See https://indianexpress.com/article/opinion/columns/muslim-community-youth-india-marginalisation-6096881/
31. The DMK did not have any woman MLA on 5 occasions—1977, 1980, 1984, 1991 and 2001.
32. The AIADMK did not have any woman MLA on 2 occasions—1989 and 1996.

33. See https://youtu.be/7PU223I0lbk
34. It is worth noting that such dog-whistling is encouraged by members in constitutional positions. For instance, G.R. Swaminathan, a judge of the Madras High Court, took part in a book launch event [April 2023] on management lessons from the Vaishnavite text Thiruppavai (authored by Aandal Nachiyar, the only woman of the 12 Alwars). He said that the Constitution of India will survive only if the demographic profile of the country is maintained as it was during the implementation of the Constitution. "The Constitution will survive only if people belonging to Bharatiya Dharma and Samprataya continue to be at the helm within its fold. I am a judge so I cannot say anything more. I hope you understand." He also made a jibe by saying many people who pride themselves as defenders or cognoscenti of Tamil possess very little knowledge of Tamil. The larger idea is to make Tamil, which is currently a vehicle of subaltern mobilisation, into a language belonging to the antique past, when the Brahminical elites were at the helm, and render all the subsequent Tamil aficionados—who are mostly subaltern—as not "pure" or scholarly but brokers of sorts who use language for 'political ends' and do not really work towards its conservation. In the name of constitutional morality, it is a mere dog-whistle against religious freedoms enshrined in the Constitution. See https://youtu.be/W2DJETnRLYE?si=KhdD9p-mMPZNzuX2
35. As of 1 June 2024, this matter is in the court. The High Court's August 2022 order was not a blanket endorsement of the State's position, and the Supreme Court has declined subsequent pleas by the State.
36. See https://www.livelaw.in/top-stories/supreme-court-declines-tamil-nadus-plea-to-allow-it-to-appoint-archakas-to-agamic-temples-status-quo-previously-ordered-to-continue-241947?infinitescroll=1
37. See https://www.thehindu.com/education/why-is-tamil-nadus-education-funding-on-hold-explained/article68648084.ece
38. The BJP is riding on the AIADMK's back forcibly, akin to its alliance with Janata Dal (United) in Bihar. The recent expulsion of former Chief Minister and Chief Coordinator of the AIADMK, O. Panneerselvam, belonging to the dominant Mukkulathor community, has opened up an avenue for the BJP to expand its base in South Tamil Nadu, as it is already courting the support of DKVs in the region. The AIADMK's strong cadre base has not been easily poachable for the BJP so far. Though the DMK made inroads into the South in the 2021 elections, the resilience of the AIADMK is key to contain the BJP and its political offering.
39. The Naam Tamilar Katchi (NTK) was founded by media baron and politician S.P. Adithanar in 1958. After an unsuccessful outing in the 1962 elections, NTK joined the DMK-led alliance in 1967 elections after which the party merged with the DMK. Adithanar was a minister in the Government of Tamil Nadu between 1968 and 1977.

40. Seeman holds the dubious record of supporting the AIADMK and hailing Jayalalithaa as the 'Mother of Tamil Eelam', whereas she demanded the dismissal of the DMK-led government on the grounds of DMK's vocal support to the LTTE. See 1) https://www.newindianexpress.com/states/tamil-nadu/2014/mar/30/NTK-Neutral-on-Vaiko-to-Back-Jaya-592409.html

 2) https://www.oneindia.com/2007/11/04/jaya-demands-dismissal-of-dmk-govt-for-hailing-ltte-member-1194163376.html?story=3
41. In this context, when I asked a field journalist who covers the NTK about their usage of the word *kudi*, she said that the word and its usage by the party is suffused with the notion of caste pride. Subsequently, when I asked her about the difference between the Dravidian-Tamil offering and the NTK's Tamil nationalist offering, she proffered caste fanaticism (Natarajan, 31 January 2020) as the distinguishing feature of the latter. In its 2021 Assembly election campaign, the NTK, ironically, was attacking the then opposition party, the DMK, that was not in power for a decade rather than attacking the AIADMK.
42. See https://thewire.in/politics/seemans-anti-periyar-stance-is-a-means-to-his-survival-at-the-cost-of-tamil-nadus-progressive-ethos
43. Owing to my research on the reading rooms and public-talks culture of the DMK, I had shared my findings in meetings with DMK's leadership and their core team members before the 2021 Legislative Assembly elections.
44. Neythal is a term used to refer to the coastal ecosystem in Sangam literature. See https://timesofindia.indiatimes.com/city/madurai/neythal-festival-logo-released/articleshow/92556833.cms
45. See https://frontline.thehindu.com/other/article30223229.ece/amp/
46. See https://www.news18.com/news/india/tamil-nadu-toddy-movement-holds-protest-urging-state-govt-to-revoke-ban-on-palm-wine-heres-why-4684178.html
47. See https://www.newindianexpress.com/states/tamil-nadu/2022/oct/04/low-prices-turn-coconut-farmers-into-toddy-sellers-in-tamil-nadu-2504729.html
48. I have used a pseudonym on request.
49. See https://www.thehindu.com/news/national/tamil-nadu/delimitation-making-us-rethink-small-families-remarks-tn-cm-stalin/article68778241.ece
50. See https://youtu.be/GcKdp_r6GrI
51. Pinarayi Vijayan, Chief Minister of Kerala and leader of the Communist Party of India (Marxist), invited M.K. Stalin to the centenary celebrations of Vaikom Satyagraha on 1 April 2023. The move was a way of recognising anti-caste struggles across communities and states as against containing them as sub-regional affairs. A Vaikom award is being set up by the Tamil Nadu government to celebrate people who had worked to empower marginalised communities outside Tamil Nadu. https://www.thehindu.com/news/national/kerala/pinarayi-stalin-jointly-inaugurate-vaikom-satyagraha-centenary-fete/article66688989.ece

APPENDICES

1. The tables have been extrapolated from the number of branches of the DMK as presented (Barnett, 1976) and the annual reports of the DMK, 1956–1957 and 1966–1967. A ratio (Appendix B) was built to estimate the number of reading rooms through personal interviews, viz., Virumbi (March 2 2020), Thirunavakkarasu (February 27 2020), Umapathy, P. (February 27 2020), Veerapandian, S. (February 5 2020), Rajendran, K. (January 30 2020), and Dhanabalan, S.R.S. (February 6 2020).

BIBLIOGRAPHY

1. Adigal, M. 1975. *Velalar Nagarigam*, 2nd Edition. Tirunelveli: The South India Saiva Siddhanta Publishing Society.
2. Aloysius, G. 1998. *Religion as Emancipatory Identity: Buddhist Movement Among the Tamils Under Colonialism*. Chennai: New Age International Pvt. Limited.
3. ———. 2019. *Periyar and Modernity*. New Delhi: Critical Quest.
4. ———. 2022. 'E.V. Ramasami Periyar on Caste-society and Category-wise Rights', in S. Somanaboina and A. Ramagoud (eds), *The Routledge Handbook of the Other Backward Classes in India: Thought, Movements and Development*, 1st edition. Oxon and New York: Routledge India. Retrieved from https://doi.org/10.4324/9781003152873
5. Ambedkar, B.R. 1916. 'Castes in India: Their Mechanism, Genesis and Development', Paper presented at the Anthropology Seminar, Columbia University, New York in V. Moon (ed.). 1979. *Dr Babasaheb Ambedkar Writings and Speeches*, (compilation) Vol. 1, 3–22, Bombay: Education Department, Government of Maharashtra.
6. ———. (n.d). *Untouchables, or the Children of India's Ghettos*. Retrieved from http://www.ambedkar.org/ambcd/22A.Untouchables%20or%20the%20children%20of%20India%27s%20Ghetto%20PART%20I.htm
7. Anandhi, S. 2018. 'Education and Dravidian Common Sense', *Seminar*, August. Retrieved from https://www.india-seminar.com/2018/708/708_a_anandhi.htm
8. Anderson, B. 1983. *Imagined Communities. Reflections on the Origin and Spread of Nationalism*. London: Verso.

9. Annadurai, C.N. 2010. *Perarignar Annaavin̲ Kaṭṭuraikaḷ*, Vol. 1, 3rd Edition. Chennai: Poompukar Pathippakam.
10. Anwar. S. 2018. 'Muslims and the Dravidian Movement', *Seminar*, August. Retrieved from https://www.india-seminar.com/2018/708/708_s_anwar.htm
11. Arangannal, R. 1988. *Ninaivugal*. Chennai: Nakkeeran Pathippagam.
12. Armstrong, J.A. 1982. *Nations Before Nationalism*. Chapel Hill: University of North Carolina Press.
13. Arooran, K.N. 1980. *Tamil Renaissance and Dravidian Nationalism, 1905–1944*. Madurai: Koodal.
14. Arunan. 2008. அண்ணா ஆட்சியைப் பிடித்த வரலாறு. Madurai: Vasantham.
15. Baker, C.J. 1976. *The Politics of South India, 1920–1937*. Cambridge: Cambridge University Press.
16. Balan, J. 2012. 'The Possibilities and Discourse for Dakshina Pradesh, A Union State of Madras and Travancore-Cochin', *Proceedings of the Indian History Congress*, 73: 1412–1423. Retrieved from http://www.jstor.org/stable/44156345
17. Barnett, M.R. 1976. *The Politics of Cultural Nationalism in South India*. NJ: Princeton University Press. Retrieved from http://www.jstor.org/stable/j.ctt13x0wjd
18. Barth, F. 1969. *Ethnic Groups and Boundaries: The Social Organization of Culture Difference*, Introduction, 9–38.
19. Bate, B. 2009. *Tamil Oratory and the Dravidian Aesthetic: Democratic Practice in South India*. New York: Columbia University Press.
20. Bayly, C. 1988. *Indian Society and the Making of the British Empire* (The New Cambridge History of India). Cambridge: Cambridge University Press. Retrieved from doi:10.1017/CHOL9780521250924
21. Berenschot, W., Bagchi, S., & Karthik K.R.V. 2024. *The Oligarchisation of India's Democracy*. *Economic and Political Weekly*, 59 (48). Retrieved from https://www.epw.in/journal/2024/48/general-elections-2024/oligarchisation-indias-democracy.html
22. Brass, P. 1981. 'Class, Ethnic Group, and Party in Indian Politics', *World Politics*, 33(3): 449–67. Retrieved from https://doi.org/10.2307/2010211.
23. Brimnes, N. 1999. *Constructing the Colonial Encounter: Right- and Left- hand Castes in Early Colonial South India*. New York: Routledge.

24. Caldwell, R. 1849. *The Tinnevelly Shanars: A Sketch of their Religion and their Moral Condition with Special Reference to the Facilities and Hindrances to the Progress of Christianity Amongst Them*. Madras: R. Twigg.

25. Connolly, W. 1996. 'Suffering, Justice and the Politics of Becoming', *Culture, Medicine and Psychiatry*, 20(3): 251–77.

26. Damodaran, H. 2008. *India's New Capitalists: Caste, Business and Industry in a Modern Nation*. New York: Palgrave Macmillan.

27. Deutsch, K.W. 1969. *Nationalism and Social Communication: An inquiry into the Foundations of Nationality*. Cambridge: MIT Press.

28. Devji, F. 2013. *Muslim Zion: Pakistan as a Political Idea*. Cambridge, MA: Harvard University Press.

29. Diehl, A. 1978. *Periyar E.V. Ramaswami: A Study of the Influence of a Personality in Contemporary South India*. New Delhi: B.I. Publications.

30. Dirks, N.B. 1992. 'Castes of Mind', *Representations*, 37: 56–78. Retrieved from https://doi.org/10.2307/2928654

31. Dumont, L. 1972. *Homo Hierarchicus: The Caste System and its Implications*. London: Paladin.

32. Elder, J.W. 1966. 'Religious Beliefs and Political Attitudes', in D.E. Smith (ed.), *South Asian Politics and Religion*, 249–76. NJ: Princeton University Press. Retrieved from http://www.jstor.org/stable/j.ctt183pvc8.15

33. Eldersveld, S.J. 1970. 'The 1967 Indian Election: Patterns of Party Regularity and Defection', *Asian Survey*, 10(11): 1015–30. Retrieved from https://doi.org/10.2307/2642821

34. Eriksen, T.H. 2002. *Ethnicity and Nationalism: Anthropological Perspectives.* London: Pluto Press.

35. Fakhri, S.M.A.K. 2008. *Dravidian Sahibs and Brahmin Maulanas: The Politics of the Muslims of Tamil Nadu*. New Delhi: Manohar Press.

36. Fallers, L.A. 1961. 'Ideology and Culture in Uganda Nationalism', *American Anthropologist*, 63(4): 677–86.

37. Forrester, D.B. 1970. 'Kamaraj: A Study in Percolation of Style', *Modern Asian Studies*, 4(1): 43–61. Retrieved from http://www.jstor.org/stable/311752

38. Fraser, N., Dahl, H.M., Stoltz, P. and Willig, R. 2004. 'Recognition, Redistribution and Representation in Capitalist Global Society: An Interview with Nancy Fraser', *Acta Sociologica*, 47(4): 374–82. Retrieved from http://www.jstor.org/stable/4195051

39. Gandhi, R. 1984. *The Rajaji Story, 1937–1972*. Bombay: Bharatiya Vidya Bhavan.

40. Ganeshwar. 2022. 'Periyar's Spatial Thought: Region as Non-Brahmin Discursive Space', *Caste: A Global Journal on Social Exclusion*, 3(1): 89–106. Retrieved from https://www.jstor.org/stable/48674174
41. Geertz, C. 1961. 'The Integrative Revolution: Primordial Sentiments and Civil Politics in the New States', in C. Geertz (ed.), *Old Societies and New States: The Quest for Modernity in Asia and Africa*. New York, 1963: The Free Press of Glencoe & London, 1963: Collier-Macmillan: 105–57.
42. Geetha, V. and Rajadurai, S.V. 1998. *Towards a Non-Brahmin Millennium: From Iyothee Thass to Periyar*. Calcutta: Samya.
43. Gellner, E. 1964. *Thought and Change*. London: Weidenfeld and Nicolson.
44. Glazer, N., Moynihan, D.P. and Schelling, C. S. (eds). 1975. *Ethnicity: Theory and Experience*. Cambridge, MA: Harvard University Press.
45. Gnanadason, J. 1969. 'The Nagercoil By-Election, January 1969: A Study of the Congress Campaign', *Economic and Political Weekly*, 4(33): 1337–40. Retrieved from www.jstor.org/stable/40739924
46. Godsmark, O. 2018. *Citizenship, Community and Democracy in India: From Bombay to Maharashtra, c. 1930–1960*. Oxon: Routledge.
47. Gopanna, A. 2008. காமராஜ் ஒரு சகாப்தம் [*Kamaraj Oru Sagaptham*]. Chennai: Nava Inthiya Pathippakam.
48. Gorringe, H. 2005. *Untouchable Citizens: Dalit Movements and Democratisation in Tamil Nadu*. New Delhi: Sage Publications.
49. Guha, S. 2003. 'Castes of Mind: Colonialism and the Making of Modern India' [Book Review], *Indian Economic and Social History Review*, 40(4): 459.
50. Gupta, D. 1981. 'Caste, Infrastructure and Superstructure: A Critique', *Economic and Political Weekly*, 16(51): 2093–04. Retrieved from http://www.jstor.org/stable/4370503
51. Gupta, D. 2000. *Interrogating Caste: Understanding Hierarchy and Difference in Indian Society*. New Delhi: Penguin Books.
52. Hardgrave R.L. 1965. *The Dravidian Movement*. Bombay: Popular Prakashan.
53. ———. 1969. *The Nadars of Tamilnad: The Political Culture of a Community in Change*. Berkeley: University of California Press.
54. ———. 1970. 'The Congress in India: Crisis and Split', *Asian Survey*, 10(3): 256–62. Retrieved from https://doi.org/10.2307/2642578

55. Harrison, S.S. 1960. *India: The Most Dangerous Decades*. NJ: Princeton University Press. Retrieved from http://www.jstor.org/stable/j.ctt183q2cm
56. Harriss, J. 2001. 'Populism, Tamil style: Is it Really a Success?' Development Studies Institute Working Paper Series: 1–15.
57. Hjejle, B. 1979. 'Recent research on South Asia by Swedish scholars', *Scandinavian Economic History Review*, 27(1): 68–76. Retrieved from https://doi.org/10.1080/03585522.1979.10415643
58. Hobsbawm, E.J. 1983. *The Invention of Tradition*. Cambridge, Cambridgeshire: Cambridge University Press.
59. Hodges, S. 2005. 'Revolutionary Family Life and the Self-Respect Movement in Tamil South India, 1926–49', *Contributions to Indian Sociology,* 39(2): 251–77. Retrieved from https://doi.org/10.1177/006996670503900203
60. Irschick, E.F. 1969. *Politics and Social Conflict in South India: The Non-Brahman Movement and Tamil Separatism, 1916–29*. Berkeley: University of California Press.
61. Jaffrelot, C. 2000. 'The Rise of the Other Backward Classes in the Hindi Belt', *The Journal of Asian Studies*, 59(1): 86–108. Retrieved from https://doi.org/10.2307/2658585
62. ———. 2003. *India's Silent Revolution: The Rise of the Lower Classes in North India*. London: Hurst.
63. ———. 2005. 'For a Theory of Nationalism', in C. Jaffrelot. and A. Dieckhoff (eds) *Revisiting Nationalisms: Theories and Processes*, 10–55. New York: Palgrave Macmillan.
64. ———. 2008. 'Hindu Nationalism and the (not so easy) Art of Being Outraged: The Ram Setu Controversy', *South Asia Multidisciplinary Academic Journal*, 2 (2). Retrieved from https://doi.org/10.4000/samaj.1372
65. Jagannathan N. 2007. *Virudhunagar Varalaaru (History of Virudhunagar)*, Part 1. Virudhunagar: Anbu Training Centre
66. Jeyaraman, B. 2013. *Kamaraj: The Life and Times of K. Kamaraj*. New Delhi: Rupa Publishers.
67. Kaali, S. 2018. 'Making of a New Public Sphere,' *Seminar*, August. Retrieved from https://www.india-seminar.com/2018/708/708_sundar_kaali.htm
68. Kalaiyarasan, A. and Vijayabaskar, M. 2021. *The Dravidian Model: Interpreting the Political Economy of Tamil Nadu*. Cambridge: Cambridge University Press.

69. Kandaswamy, P. 2001. *The Political Career of K Kamaraj: A Study of Politics of Tamil Nadu, 1920–75*. New Delhi: Concept Publishing Company.
70. Kannan, R. 2017. *Anna: The Life and Times of C.N. Annadurai*. New Delhi: Penguin Random House India.
71. Kapila, S. 2021. *Violent Fraternity: Indian Political Thought in the Global Age*. Princeton: Princeton University Press.
72. Karthik, K.R.V. and Wyatt, A. 2022. 'Dravidian Politics and Political Elites in Tamil Nadu', in C. Jaffrelot and G. Verniers (eds), *Resilient Elitism. The Changing Profile of India's Regional Assemblies*, London: Routledge [unpublished chapter].
73. Karthik, K.R.V. and Vasanthakumar, V. 2022. 'Caste, then Class: Redistribution and Representation in the Dravidian Model'. *Caste: A Global Journal on Social Exclusion*, 3(1), 107–22. Retrieved from https://www.jstor.org/stable/48674175
74. Karthik, K.R.V. and Baskar, P.M. 2021. 'Towards Equal Terms', *Caravan*, 30 June. Retrieved from https://caravanmagazine.in/politics/women-dmk-aiadmk-tamil-nadu-election
75. Karthik, K.R.V. and Vasanthakumar, V. 2023. 'A Tale of Two Sangamams,' *Wire*, 20 January. Retrieved from https://thewire.in/culture/a-tale-of-two-sangamams
76. Karthik, K.R.V. Jumle, V. and Karunanithi, J. 2020. 'BJP's Twitter Experiments and Tamil Resilience', *Economic and Political Weekly*, 55(44): 20–23.
77. Karunanidhi M. 2015. *Nenjukku Neethi*, Vol. 1. Chennai: Thirumagal Nilayam.
78. Khilnani, S. 2016. *Incarnations: India in 50 lives*. London: Allen Lane.
79. Kripalani, J.B. 1948. *Fateful Year: Being the Speeches and Writings during the Year of Presidentship of Congress* (1st edition). Bombay: Vora and Co. Publishers Limited.
80. Krishnan, R., Sriramachandran, R. and Subagunarajan, V. 2022. *Rule of the Commoner: DMK and Formations of the Political in Tamil Nadu, 1949–1967* (Metamorphoses of the Political: Multidisciplinary Approaches). Cambridge: Cambridge University Press. Retrieved from doi:10.1017/9781009197168
81. Kumar, Arvind. 2024. 'Candidate Selection and Voting Behaviour: The BJP's Mobilisation of Marginal Castes in Uttar Pradesh, India'. PhD Thesis, Royal Holloway, University of London, London.
82. Laclau, E. 2005. *On Populist Reason*. London and New York: Verso.

83. Leonard, D. 2021. 'Caste-Less Tamils and Early Print Public Sphere: Remembering Iyothee Thass (1845–914)', *South Asia Research*, 41(3): 349–68. Retrieved from https://doi.org/10.1177/02627280211034858
84. Manoharan, K.R. 2017. 'Anti-Casteist Casteism?', *Interventions*, 19:1,73–90. Retrieved from DOI: 10.1080/1369801X.2016.1142885.
85. Manoharan, K.R. 2020. 'In the Path of Ambedkar: Periyar and the Dalit Question', *South Asian History and Culture*, 11:2, 136–49. Reetrieved from DOI: 10.1080/19472498.2020.1755127
86. Manoharan, K.R. 2022. *Periyar: A Study in Political Atheism*. Hyderabad: Orient Blackswan.
87. Manoharan, K.R. and Karthik, K.R.V. 2021. 'A lengthening Shadow of Tamil nativism', *The Hindu*, 11 October. Retrieved from https://www.thehindu.com/opinion/op-ed/a-lengthening-shadow-of-tamil-nativism/article36933400.ece
88. Manoharan, P.K. 2013. 0பரறிஞர் அண்ணாவின்_சமூக, பொருளாதாரச் சிந்தனைகள் (*Perarignar Annavin Samuga Porulathara Sinthanaigal*). Chennai: International Institute of Tamil Studies.
89. Mantena, R.S. 2012. 'The Kavali Brothers: Native Intellectuals in Early Colonial Madras', in: *The Origins of Modern Historiography in India*, 87–121. New York: Palgrave Macmillan.
90. Mouffe, C. 2000. *Deliberative Democracy or Agonistic Pluralism*. Reihe Politikwissenschaft / Political Science Series, 72. Department of Political Science, Institute for Advanced Studies. Retrieved from https://www.ihs.ac.at/publications/pol/pw_72.pdf
91. Mukund, K. 2001. 'The Dynamics of Social Mobility in Pre-Colonial South India: Some Reflections', *Review of Development and Change*, 6(1): 17–27. Retrieved from https://doi.org/10.1177/0972266120010102
92. Muthuraman, P. 2004. *Agrarian Change and Identity Formation: Caste Mobilizations Among the Nadars of Tamil Nadu*. Unpublished Thesis. Hyderabad: University of Hyderabad. Retrieved from https://shodhganga.inflibnet.ac.in/handle/10603/26059
93. Narasimhan, V.K. 1967. *Kamaraj: A Study*. New Delhi: NBT.
94. Narayana Rao, K.V. 1973. *The Emergence of Andhra Pradesh*. Popular Prakashan.

95. Nathan, S.K.S. 1967. 'The DMK and the Politics of Tamilnad', *Economic and Political Weekly*, 2(48): 2133–40. Retrieved from http://www.jstor.org/stable/24478287
96. Nehru, J. 1984. *Selected works of Jawaharlal Nehru: Second Series* (Vol. 19). New Delhi: Oxford University Press.
97. Otsuka, K. 2013. 'Food Insecurity, Income Inequality, and the Changing Comparative Advantage in World Agriculture', *Agricultural Economics*, 44: 7–18. https://doi.org/10.1111/agec.12046
98. Pandian, J. 1998. 'Re-Ethnogenesis: The Quest for a Dravidian Identity among the Tamils of India', *Anthropos*, 93(4/6): 545–52. Retrieved from http://www.jstor.org/stable/40464849
99. Pandian, M.S.S. 1994. 'Notes on the Transformation of Dravidian Ideology: Tamilnadu, c. 1900–40', *Social Scientist,* 22(5/6): 84. Retrieved from doi: 10.2307/3517904
100. ———. 2007. *Brahmin and Non-Brahmin: Genealogies of the Tamil Political Present*. Ranikhet: Permanent Black & Ashoka University.
101. ———. 2009. 'Nation Impossible', *Economic and Political Weekly*, 44(10): 65–69. Retrieved from http://www.jstor.org/stable/40278782
102. ———. 2013. 'Caste in Tamil Nadu - II: Slipping Hegemony of Intermediate Castes', *Economic and Political Weekly*, 48(4): 13–15. Retrieved from http://www.jstor.org/stable/23391332
103. Panneerselvan, A.S. 2018. 'Indian federalism: An innovative response', *Seminar* 708, August. Retrieved from https://www.india-seminar.com/2018/708/708_as_panneerselvan.htm
104. ———. 2021. *Karunanidhi: A life*. Gurugram: Penguin Random House India Private Limited.
105. Parobo, P.D. 2015. *India's First Democratic Revolution: Dayanand Bandodkar and the Rise of Bahujan in Goa.* New Delhi: Orient BlackSwan.
106. ———. 2020. 'Histories, identities and the subaltern resistance in Goa', *Journal of Human Values*, 26(2): 177–85.
107. Pillay, K.K. 1977. *The Caste System in Tamil Nadu*. Chennai: University of Madras.
108. Pyakuryal, K.N. 2001. *Weberian Model of Social Stratification: A Viewpoint.* [Image]. Retrieved from http://www.dspace.cam.ac.uk/handle/1810/229129

109. Raja. A. 2019. Saadhi Enga Irukkiradhu? Where does Caste Exist? Speech. Hosur, Tamil Nadu, 2 January, 2019. Retrieved from https://www.youtube.com/watch?v=TeoRIJ5y9Vc
110. Rajadurai, P. 1983. *Nadars Uravinmurai*. Virudhunagar: Ilamaran Publication.
111. ———. 1991. *WPA Soundara Pandian's Tenure in Tamil Nadu Legislative Assembly*. Virudhunagar: Ilamaran Publication.
112. ———. 1992. *Suyamariyathai Iyakkathiruku Nadarkal Aattriya Tondu*, (*Contribution of the Nadars to the Self-Respect Movement*). Virudhunagar: Ilamaran Publication.
113. Ramachandran, S. 1975. *Anna Speaks: At the Rajya Sabha 1962–66*. New Delhi: Orient Longman.
114. Ramakrishna, V. 1990. 'Modern Language Reform Movement in Telugu', *Proceedings of the Indian History Congress*, 51: 566–72. Retrieved from www.jstor.org/stable/44148292
115. Ramanathan, K.V. (ed.) 2008. *The Satyamurti Letters: The Indian Freedom Struggle Through the Eyes of a Parliamentarian*, Vol. 1. New Delhi: Pearson Longman.
116. Ramanujam, A.K. 1968. 'The Structure of Variation: A Study in Caste Dialects' in M.B. Singer and B.S. Cohn. *Structure and Change in Indian Society*, 461–72. Chicago: Aldine Press.
117. Ramanujam, K.S. 1967. *The Big Change*. Madras: Sundara Prachuralayam.
118. Ramasamy, A. 2020. *Struggle Against Hindi Imperialism*. Chennai: Aazhi Publishers.
119. Ramaswamy, S. 1997. *Passions of the Tongue: Language Devotion in Tamil India, 1891–1970*. Berkeley: University of California Press.
120. ———. 1999. 'The Demoness, the Maid, the Whore and the Good Mother: Contesting the National Language in India', *International Journal of the Sociology of Language*, 140: 1–28. Retrieved from https://doi.org/10.1515/ijsl.1999.140.1
121. Ramaswamy, U. 1949. 'The Belief System of the Non-Brahmin Movement in India: The Andhra Case', *Far Eastern Survey,* 18(3): 290–300. Retrieved from https://doi.org/10.2307/2643221
122. Rao, K.N. 1963. 'The Constitution (Sixteenth Amendment) Bill, 1963-Anti-Secession Measures', *Journal of the Indian Law Institute*, 5(1): 153–58. Retrieved from http://www.jstor.org/stable/43950337

123. Ross, A.D. 1961. *The Hindu Family in its Urban Setting*. Toronto: University of Toronto Press. Retrieved from http://www.jstor.org/stable/10.3138/j.ctvfrxm5q
124. Roy, I. 2021. 'Dignified Development: Democratic Deepening in an Indian State', *Commonwealth and Comparative Politics*, 59(1): 47–73. Retrieved from https://doi.org/10.1080/14662043.2020.1823677
125. Rudolph, L. I. and Rudolph, S. H. 1960. 'The Political Role of India's Caste Associations. Pacific Affairs', 33(1): 5. Retrieved from https://doi.org/10.2307/2753645.
126. ———. 1967. *The Modernity of Tradition: Political Development in India*. Chicago: University of Chicago Press.
127. ———. 1969. *The Modernity of Tradition: Political Development in India*. Chicago: University of Chicago Press.
128. Ryerson, C.A. 1988. *Regionalism and Religion: The Tamil Renaisance and Popular Hinduism*. Madras: Christian Literature Society.
129. Saraswathi, S. 1974. *Minorities in Madras State: Group Interests in Modern Politics*. New Delhi: Impex India.
130. Sitapati, V. 2016. 'Reservations', in S. Choudhry, M. Khosla, and P.B. Mehta, (eds) *The Oxford Handbook of the Indian Constitution*, 720–41. New Delhi: Oxford University Press.
131. Smith, A.D. 1986. *The Ethnic Origins of Nations*. Oxford: Blackwell.
132. Srinivas, M.N. 1952. *Religion and Society among the Coorgs of South India*. Oxford: Clarendon Press.
133. Srinivasan R. 1987, 'The Ideological Genesis of the Dravidian Movement' *Indo-British Review*, 13: January–June.
134. Stepan, A. 2005. 'Federalism and Democracy: Beyond the US Model' in D. Karmis and W. Norman, (eds), *Theories of Federalism: A Reader*, 255–68. New York: Palgrave Macmillan.
135. Subagunarajan, V.M. 2019. 'Thangal Niruvana Balathai Engirundhu Peruginrana Dravida Katchigal?' (Where are the Dravidian Parties Getting their Organisational Strength from?) in K. Asokan (ed), *Maperum Tamil Kanavu* (The Great Tamil Dream), 319–26. Chennai: KSL Media Limited.
136. Subagunarajan, V.M. (ed). 2018. *Namakku Yen Intha Izhinilai: Jaathi Maanaadukalilum Jaathi Ozhippu Maanaadukalilum Periyar*. Chennai: Kayal Kavin.
137. Subramanian, A. 2019. *The Caste of Merit: Engineering Education in India*. Cambridge, MA: Harvard University Press.

138. Subramanian, N. 1999. *Ethnicity and Populist Mobilization: Political Parties, Citizens, and Democracy in South India*. New Delhi: Oxford University Press.

139. ———. 2002. 'Identity Politics and Social Pluralism: Political Sociology and Political Change in Tamil Nadu', *Commonwealth & Comparative Politics*, 40(3): 125–39. Retrieved from https://doi.org10.1080/713999599

140. Suri, K.C. 2000. 'Non-Brahman Movement in Andhra: A Study of The Nature of Protest Against Brahmanical Order in Andhra During Colonial Times. Dr Garigipati Rudraya Chowdary Endowment Lecture, 25 February, East Godavari District, Andhra Pradesh.

141. Swamy, A.R. 1996. *The Nation, the People and the Poor: Sandwich Tactics in Party Competition and Policy Formation, India, 1931–1996*. (Unpublished Dissertation) Berkley: University of California.

142. Thapar, R. 1971. 'The Image of the Barbarian in Early India', *Comparative Studies in Society and History*, 13(4): 408–36. Retrieved from https://doi.org/10.1017/S0010417500006393

143. Thirumavelan, P. 2016. பெரியோர்களே தாய்மார்களே (Periyorgalae Thaimargalae), Vikatan.com Private Limited.

144. Thirunavakkarasu, K. 2015. *Thi. Mu. Ka. Varalaaru* (History of DMK). Chennai: Nakkheeran Press.

145. Tillin, L. 2012. 'Caste, Territory and Federalism', in *Caste Matters*. Seminar, 633: May. Retrieved from https://www.india-seminar.com/2012/633/633_louise_tillin.htm

146. Tillin, L. 2021. 'Building a National Economy: Origins of Centralized Federalism in [Authors/ editors?] India', *Publius: The Journal of Federalism*, 51(2): 161–85. Retrieved from https://doi.org/10.1093/publius/pjaa039

147. Vaithees, V. 2015. 'Maraimalai Adigal and the Naveenar (Modernist) Saivite Revival in Tamil Nadu', *Religion, Caste, and Nation in South India: Maraimalai Adigal, the Neo-Saivite Movement, and Tamil Nationalism, 1876–1950*, 61–164. Oxford: Oxford University Press. Retrieved from https://doi.org/10.1093/acprof:oso/9780199451814.003.0003.

148. Vaitheespara, R. 2009. 'Forging a Tamil Caste: Maraimalai Adigal (1876–1950) and the Discourse on Caste and Ritual in Colonial Tamil Nadu,' in M. Bergunder, H. Frese and U. Schroeder (eds), *Ritual, Caste, and Colonial Discourse in South India*, Neue Hallesche Berichte, vol. 8, Halle: Verlag der Franckeschen Stiftungen.

149. Vedaratnam, S. 1951. *A Plea for Understanding*. Conjeevaram: Vanguard Publishing House.
150. Venkatachalapathy, A.R. 1990. 'Suyamariyathai Iyakkamum Saivarum, 1927–44', *Economic and PoliticalWeekly*, 30 (14): pp 761–68. Retrieved from https://www.jstor.org/stable/4402599
151. ——— . 1994. 'Reading Practices and Modes of Reading in Colonial Tamil Nadu', *Studies in History*, 10(2): 273–90. Retrieved from https://doi.org/10.1177/025764309401000207
152. ———. 1995. 'Dravidian Movement and Saivites: 1927–1944', *Economic and Political Weekly*, 30(14): 761–68. Retrieved from http://www.jstor.org/stable/4402599
153. ———. 2018. 'DK and DMK: The Double-barrelled Gun', *Seminar*, 708: August 2018. Retrieved from https://www.india-seminar.com/2018/708/708_ar_venkatachalapathy.htm
154. Visswanathan, E. Sa. 1983. *The Political Career of E.V. Ramasamy Naicker: A Study in the Politics of Tamil Nadu, 1920–49*. Madras: Ravi & Vasanth.
155. Walch, J. 1976. *Faction and Front: Party Systems in South India*. New Delhi: Young Asia Publications
156. Washbrook, D.A. 1976. *The Emergence of Provincial Politics: The Madras Presidency, 1870–1920*. Cambridge: Cambridge University Press.
157. Weiss, R.S. 2018. 'Voluntary Associations and Religious Change in Colonial India: Ramalinga Adigal's "Society of the True Path"', *South Asia: Journal of South Asian Studies*, 41:1: 18–32. Retrieved from https://doi.org/10.1080/00856401.2018.1388205
158. Wyatt, A. 2014. 'Caste and Vernacular Politics in Tamil Nadu, South India', in T. Neyazi, A. Tanabe, and S. Ishizaka (eds), *Democratic Transformation and the Vernacular Public Arena in India* (1st ed.), 153–71. London: Routledge. Retrieved from https://doi.org/10.4324/9781315777627

INDEX

Note: Page numbers followed by "*n*" refer to notes, "*t*" refer to tables and "*f* " refer to figures.

Aariyam Irukkum Idam (Annadurai), 58
Aathi Tamilar Peravai (ATP), 197–8
Abdul Rahman, *Kaviko*, 61
Adi Dravidars, 48, 49, 104, 198
Adigal, Maraimalai, 5, 37, 38, 185, 225*n*16, 239*n*44
agraharams, 48–9
Ahuja, Amit, 198–9
Aikya Kerala, 118
Akira Kurosawa, 115
Ali, Fazal, 116
All-India Anna Dravida Munnetra Kazhagam (AIADMK), 6, 8, 16, 65, 96, 194, 205, 246*n*17, 246*n*18, 246*n*19, 248*n*38
  caste diversity, 195–7
  Jayalalithaa's death impacts on, 202, 204
  rivalry between the DMK and, 191
  troubled by media influencers, 214
  women representation in elections, 201
All-India Congress Committee
  Guwahati, 136
  Patna, 41
All-India Students' Anti-Hindi Agitation Council, 164
Aloysius, G., 29, 33–4, 52
Amarams, 34
Ambedkar, B. R., 47, 54, 198
  graded inequality, 58
  support to Dalits, 99–100, 123
Amudhan, 93, 164
Anbazhagan, K., 169
Anderson, Benedict, 22
Andhra Pradesh, 11–12, 13, 33, 140, 162–3, 209, 236*n*21
  dominant caste groups moved to, 187
  political landscape, 100
Andhra State, creation of, 11, 114, 116–17, 151, 162–3, 187
Anglo Indians, 103, 104
Annadurai, C.N., 2, 17, 20, 23, 24, 31, 63, 86, 173, 213, 237–8*n*32, 238*n*34, 238*n*39, 240*n*49

Ceylon and Indian Tamils, approach towards, 123–4
DK and Congress, views on, 120–1
Dravida Nadu, backed, 127–8
Dravidian-Tamil identity, conception of, 56–61
gender question in Tamil politics, 61
Indian independence, views on, 59, 72
padippakams (reading rooms), emergence of, 75–86
protests against imposition of Hindi, 136–7
Rajaji support to, 161
Salem Conference (1944), 71–2, 74, 177–81
shock over Kamaraj's defeat, 25, 168–9
speech at public meeting, 215
speech in Rajya Sabha, 130, 131–2, 141, 143
support to Communal GO, 105
support to India's independence, 100

anti-Hindi agitations (1937), 2
anti-Hindi protests (1965), 102, 141, 167
anti-Hindi public conference (1963), 138, 139
anti-Tamil pogrom (1956), 123, 139
Ariviyal Mandram (Virudhunagar), 87–9
Arivoli Iyakkam, 66–7
Ariya Mayai (Annadurai), 56, 57
Arooran, Nambi, 4
Article (15), 104
Article (370), 212
Article (46), 104
Article 29(2), 104
Arunthathiyars, 46, 198, 199, 247*n*28
Aryanism, 58, 59
Aryans, 37, 112, 113
Assam, 140
Assembly elections (1957), 119, 122*t*
assertive populism, 6
Asuras (Demons), 113
ATP. *See* Aathi Tamilar Peravai (ATP)

Bahujan Samaj Party, 44–5
Baker, Christopher, 3, 4
Banaras Hindu University, 207
Bandodkar, Dayanand, 100, 147
Bangalore, 140
Baniya, 119
Barnett, Marguerite Ross, 9–10, 16, 20, 57, 237*n*31
survey on Congress leaders, 143–4
survey on DMK, 142
Barth, Frederik, 22
'Base–Superstructure' framework, 46
Bate, Bernard, 10–11
Bayly, C.A., 35
'Bazaar Nadars', 93, 95
Besant, Annie, 4, 36, 40, 135
Bhaktavatsalam, 139, 141, 155, 157, 166, 170
Bharat Ka Raj Patra, 140
Bharatiya Janata Party (BJP), 202–6, 208, 209, 210, 229*n*12, 246*n*19, 248*n*38
Bhopal, 100
Bihar, 188, 198–9, 211, 212, 248*n*38
Bolshevik Revolution, 178
Bombay, 107, 140
Brahmin & Non-Brahmin: Genealogies of the Tamil Political Present (Pandian), 7
Brahminical value system, 2

Brahminism, 4, 29, 30, 49, 56, 57–8, 59, 95, 117, 189
Brahmins, 113, 203, 233–4*n*1, 236–7*n*24
  colonial government's special treatment to, 42
  dominance, 4, 7–8, 34, 35
  MSS's opposition to, 39
  non-Brahmin communities and, competition between, 40
  political preferences, 108–9
  resistance to Communal GO, 102–6
  Saivite-Vellalar criticism of, 38
  varnashrama system, 32
Brass, Paul, 10
Brimnes, Niels, 33
Brown, Charles Philip, 12
Buddhism, 36, 37, 39
Buddhists, 192

cabinets
  caste composition of, 173–7, 174*t*, 176*t*, 177*t*
  women candidates, 181–2, 182*t*
Caldwell, Robert, 9, 35
caste associations, 13–17, 46, 51–2, 82
caste system, 44
  'Base–Superstructure' framework, 46
  in the Dravidian region, 31–4
Centamil, 11
Ceylon Tamils Freedom Day, 123
Ceylon, 123–4, 139
Chadwick, Andrew, 213
Chengalpattu, 121
Chennai Rainbow Pride March (2014), 193
Chetty, P.T., 4
Chezhiaan, Govi, 200
Chidambaram, C.T., 78, 80
China, 143, 155
Chinnasamy, A., 139–40
Chittoor, 117
Civil Disobedience Movement (1930), 150
Cody, Francis, 66–7
Coimbatore, 123, 139, 140, 230*n*16
Collective Action and Community (Freitag), 67
Commonweal Party, 83, 107, 151, 241*n*6
communalism, 67
Communist Party of India, 18, 24
Comparative Grammar of the Dravidian or South Indian Family of Languages, A (Caldwell), 35
Congress party, 3, 4, 18, 24, 25, 42, 68, 83, 94, 105, 145, 155, 237*n*30
  anti-Congress *padippakam*, 93
  anti-Congress sentiments, 95, 96
  assembly elections (1952), 150, 187
  controversies in, 186
  criticised by DMK, 160
  criticised by Periyar, 152
  declined in Madras State, 166
  election victory (1962), 128, 129*t*
  Hindi compulsory, push for making, 51
  Kanchipuram Provincial Congress Session, 41
  nationalism, 51, 52, 53
  questions raised against, 158
  setbacks faced by, 141, 154–6
  shift during Kamaraj's leadership, 115–16
  State Assembly elections (1967), 1, 3, 17, 20, 21, 25, 68, 86, 148, 167, 172
  TNP merged with, 127

violence unleashed by, 139–40
Congress Reform Committee, 120
"Congress-Dravidians", 112
Connolly, William, 55
Constitution (First Amendment) Act (1951), 24, 102, 105–6, 186
Constitution (Sixteenth Amendment) Act (1963), 24, 102, 125, 130–1, 133, 187, 189, 239*n*43
Council of Ministers, 192, 200
Cudappa, 140
cultural nationalism, 10

Dakshina Pradesh, 117, 118–19
Dalits, 29, 47
as Adi-Dravidars, 41
Ambedkar's support to, 99–100, 123, 231–2*n*30, 233–4*n*1, 234*n*5, 245*n*14, 247*n*28
convergence between OBC and, 194–5
electoral representation, 197–200
quota system, 192
reading rooms, 66, 78
violence against, 208
Yatharththa Brahmana, 37
Dalmia, Ramakrishna, 113
Dalmiapuram, 113, 235*n16*
Darul Islam (magazine), 45
Das, B.N., 137
Defence of India Rules, 140, 164
Delhi, 114, 127, 149, 189
Kamaraj moved to, 168
Kamaraj's focus on, 150, 157
support for Hindi in, 135
Department of School Education, 206
Depressed Castes, 42–3, 48
Desai, Morarji, 155
Deutsch, K.W., 21–2
Devendra Kula Vellalars, 33, 46, 48, 198, 199
Devji, Faisal, 99
Dhanabalan, S.R.S., 89, 90, 91
Dhar Commission, 116
Dhinasari (newspaper), 106
Diehl, Anita, 29
Dinakaran (newspaper), 88, 92
Directorate of Public Libraries, 207
Dirks, Nicholas, 53
Diwali, 113
DKV. *See* Devandra Kula Vellalars
Dorairajan, Champakam, 104, 234*n*7
Dravida Mahajana Sabhai, 36
Dravida Munnetra Kazhagam (DMK), 236*n*22, 246*n*17, 246*n*18, 246*n*19
alliance, 83
altering of Dravidian ideology, 10
caste diversity, 195–7
district conferences, 74
Dravida Nadu, demand for, 123–9, 134, 135
elections (1962) success, 127
elections (1967), 1, 3, 17, 20, 21, 86, 148, 167, 172
electoral success, 83, 84*f*, 85*f*
emerged from DK, 145–6
formation of, 1, 72
goals, 23
ideology, spreading, 20–1
influence growth, 121
journalistic activity in, 22, 77–8, 82–3, 88
journalistic work of leaders, 24
Legislative Assembly elections (2021), campaign song, 27
Nadar community support, 82, 89
organisational structure, 69
padippakams (reading rooms), emergence of, 75–86
as a party of writers and orators, 77

protests against Official Languages Act, 137–9
protests led by, 112
public meetings, 74, 75
raised issue of rising commodity prices, 142–3
Rajaji support to, 160
respect for Kamaraj, 169
rise of, 178
rivalry between AIADMK and, 191
Sampath left from, 125–6
support to Kamaraj, 152
support to non-Brahmin caste parties, 107
supported merger of Chittoor with Madras State, 117
supported MLAs, 172–3
Tamil-folklore deities and, 89–90
town office, 89–91
Transgender Persons Welfare Board, established, 192
troubled by media influencers, 214
women representation in elections, 201–2

Dravida Nadu (Tamil weekly), 58, 81, 94, 105, 106
- Annadurai's argument in, 113, 118

Dravida Nadu, 130–4, 212
- DMK's demand for, 123–9, 142, 129*t*

Dravida Pandian, 36

Dravidar Kazhagam (DK), 105, 189, 234*n*9, 240*n*58, 241*n*9
- anti- Brahmin sentiments, 112
- challenged Indian Union, 100–1
- DMK emerged from, 145
- influence growth, 106, 115
- membership, 73, 73*f*, 74
- rebranded, 50, 71–2
- Salem Conference (1944), 71–2, 74, 177–81
- split, 72
- support for Congress, 119, 242*n*13
- support to communists, 107

Dravidar Ponmozhigal, 70

Dravidian Model Workshops, 206

Dravidian movement
- criticised by NTK, 205
- 'horizontal solidarities', 26, 28, 54–5
- party politics, transition to, 1, 2, 3
- pillars of, 193–5

Dravidian Progressive Federation. *See* Dravida Munnetra Kazhagam (DMK)

Dravidians, 99, 117
- conflict between Aryans and, 112, 113, 227*n*37
- term, 2

Dravidian-Tamil ethos, spread of, 50, 56, 77, 81, 94–6

Dravidian-Tamil identity
- creation of, 2–3
- as an ethno-nationalist platform, 23
- identity-building, 3, 20, 23
- redefining identity and social relations, 34–42
- works on, 9–11

dubashee entrepreneurs, 34, 40

Dumont, L., 23, 44, 45

Dusshera, 113

East Pakistan, 143, 240*n*55

Economically Weaker Sections (EWS), 192

Elder, Joseph, 101

Eldersveld, Samuel J., 147

Election Commission of India, 18

empowerment populism, 5–6
Eriksen, Thomas, 22
Ethnicity and Populist Mobilization (Subramanian), 7
Europeans, 103, 224*n*7
EWS. *See* Economically Weaker Sections (EWS)

farmer protests (2020–2021), 45
Federation of Depressed Classes, 112
Federation of Madras State Panchayat Union, 112
Forrester, Duncan B., 163
Forward Bloc, 159
Fraser, Nancy, 43

Gandhi, Mahatma, 42, 111, 135
Gandhi, Rajiv, 196, 246*n*17
Gandhi, Rajmohan, 111
Ganesan, C.V., 200
Geetha, V., 28, 29
Gellner, E., 21
Gnanadason, Jonathan N., 163
Goa, 100, 147
Godsmark, Oliver, 100
Goods and Services Tax (GST), 212
Gorringe, Hugo, 195
Goud Saraswat Brahmins, 100
Gounders, 108, 128, 203
Gross Enrolment Ratio, 194
Gross State Domestic Product (GSDP), 193
GSDP. *See* Gross State Domestic Product (GSDP)
GST. *See* Goods and Services Tax (GST)
Gujarat, 188, 193
Gupta, Bhupesh, 132, 236*n*22
Gupta, Dipankar, 35, 46

Hande, H.V., 75, 77
Hardgrave, Robert L., 15
Harichandra Puranam, 36
Harrison, Selig, 107
Haryana, 202
Himachal Pradesh, 193
Hindi, imposition of, 50
Hindu Free Thought Union (MFTU/MSS), 39
Hindu Tribes and Castes (Sherring), 53
Hindustan Times, The (newspaper), 156
Hjejle, B., 30
Home Rule League, 40
Husain, Zakir, 112
Hyderabad, 100, 116

IIT Madras, 207
Imagined Communities (Anderson), 22
Ina Mulakkam (newspaper), 82
Indian Christians, 103, 104
Indian National Congress. *See* Congress party
Indian Union Muslim League, 159, 161
Indo-Chinese war (1962), 125, 126, 159
Indonesia, 143
Information Technology (IT), 195
Information Technology Park (Chennai), 195
Irschick, Eugene, 3, 4, 102
Islam, 45
Ismail, Mohammad, 161
IT. *See* Information Technology (IT)
Iyengar, C.V. Venkataramana, 41
Iyer, Swaminatha, 9
Iyothee Thass, 2, 7, 20, 29, 36, 37, 38, 185

Jaffrelot, Christophe, 14, 17, 20, 21, 22
Jai Andhra Movement (1972), 11

Jai Telangana Movement (1969), 11
Jammu and Kashmir, 212
Jana Sangh, 101, 242*n*23
Japan, 143
Jayalalithaa, J., 156, 191, 201, 202, 204, 246*n*19
    See also All-India Anna Dravida Munnetra Kazhagam (AIADMK)
Jharkhand, 211
Jinnah, Muhammad Ali, 123
Joint Parliamentary Committee, 132
Jumle, V., 202–3, 213
Justice Party, 4, 5, 7–8, 20, 27, 46, 50, 68, 73, 86, 91, 95, 150, 194, 219*t*, 243*n*40
    achievements, 40–1
    establishment of, 40
    Nadars, 95–6
    non-Brahmin elites support to, 151
    passed Communal GO, 103–6
    provincial elections (1937) defeat, 50
    reading rooms, 68
    Salem Conference (1944), 71–2, 74, 177–81
    woman member in Legislative Council, 181

Kakkan, 105, 175
Kalaiyarasan, A, 193–4
Kalimuthu, 93, 164
Kallakudi (town), 113
Kamaraj, Kumaraswami, 3, 16, 20, 24, 68
    cabinet formation, 175
    caste identity, 14
    challenge to DMK, 139
    change in public perception about, 156–9
    as Chief Minister of Madras State, 151
    comments on Congress party's defeat, 144–5
    Congress success, role in, 147–8
    death of, 169
    DK support to, 120
    downfall of, 188
    K-Plan, 155–6, 173
    Seenivasan's campaign against, 162–6
    State Assembly elections (1967), 1, 3, 17, 20, 21, 25, 68, 86, 148, 167, 172
    supported by Periyar, 152–4, 182, 190
Kammas, 12
Kandeepan (newspaper), 106
Kannagi, 61
Kannan, R, 125, 127, 237–8*n*32
Kapila, Shruti, 54
Karnataka, 187
Karthik, K.R.V., 202–3, 213
Karunanidhi, Kanimozhi, 201, 207, 208
Karunanidhi, M., 17, 31, 69, 77, 90, 113, 160, 169, 192
    Chennai Sangamam, launched, 207–8
    Periyar Ninaivu Samathuvapuram, launched, 195
    as president of DMK's Agitation Committee, 137
    Sampath conflict with, 125
Kashi Tamil Sangamam, 207–8
Kashmir, 100
Kennedy, John F., 163
Kerala, 140, 165, 187, 202, 211
Khan, Rahman, 164
Kongu Vellala Gounders, 108–9, 121, 128, 172

cabinet berths, 175, 176*t*
Korea, 143, 240*n*53
Kothandaraman, 151
Kovilpatti, 140
Kripalani, Acharya J.B., 133, 134, 155
Krishnamachari, T.T., 151
kudi (clan), 204–5
Kudi Arasu (Republic) (newspaper), 23, 38
Kula Kalvi Thittam, 96, 151, 153
kuladharmam, 114
Kunzru, H.N., 116
Kurnool, 116

Lahore Resolution (1940), 99
Left Communist Party, 159
LGBTQIA+, 193, 244–5*n*10
Linguistic Provinces Commission, 116
Lohia Socialists, 101
Lohia, Ram Manohar, 155
Lok Sabha, 130–1, 211, 240*n*49

'Maaperum Tamil Kanavu', 206
Madanapalli, 140
Madhya Pradesh, 202
Madras High Court, 203, 244–5*n*10
Madras Presidency
  identity, redefining, 35
  imposition of Hindi, 50
  Sanskrit-Brahmin supremacy, 35–6
  Telugu-speaking regions of, 12
Madras Secular Society (MSS), 39
Madras State
  anti-hindi agitations, 135–42
  bifurcation of, 173, 175
  DMK influence growth in, 121
  Dravidian movement, growth of, 1
  elections (1952), 107, 109*t*, 110*t*
  food shortages and rising prices of essential commodities, 142–5
  literacy rate in, 77, 77*t*
  Marwari dominance in, 119
  political culture, 101
  population, 73, 74*f*
  student protests (1950), 105
  three-cornered protests, 113
Mahajana Sangam, 15
Maharashtra, 100, 193, 199, 209
Maharashtrawadi Gomantak Party, 100, 147
mahimai (tax), 15
Makkal Viduthalai Kazhagam (MVK), 198
Mandram (newspaper), 82
Manoharan, Karthick Ram, 29, 30, 43
Marakkairs, 34
Maran, Murasoli, 154
Marumalarchi Dravida Munnetra Kazhagam (MDMK), 196
Marwari, 119
Marxists, 46
Masani, Minoo, 155
Mathiazhagan, K.A., 124
Mathiventhan, M., 200
MDMK. *See* Marumalarchi Dravida Munnetra Kazhagam (MDMK)
media influencers, 214
Ministry of Home Affairs, 136
MLA (Members of the Legislative Assembly), 177*t*
  caste references, 177–81, 179*t*, 180*t*, 181*t*
Modified Scheme of Elementary Education (1953), 24, 96, 102, 151
  introduction and failure, 111–16
Mohammedans, 103, 104
Mouffe, Chantal, 54

MSEE. *See* Modified Scheme of Elementary Education (1953)
Mudaliar, Natesa, 41
Mukkulathors, 91, 108, 121, 172
  cabinet berths, 175, 176*t*
Mummunai Porattam, 112–13
Murasoli (newspaper), 81, 82, 88, 89, 92, 94
Muslim League, 99–100, 239*n*44
Muslims, 45, 61, 192
  electoral representation, 200–1
  political aspirations, 99–100
  political representation, 175
Mustafa, Manavai, 61
Muthiah Mudaliar, 103, 105
Muthu, Sathyavani, 175, 182
MVK. *See* Makkal Viduthalai Kazhagam (MVK)
'Mylapore Brahmins', 4
Mysore, 117, 136, 140, 164

Naam Tamilar Katchi (NTK), 159, 202–6, 248*n*39, 249*n*41
Nadar Christians, 109
Nadar, Seeni, 91–2
Nadar, V.V. Ramasamy, 15, 16
Nadars, 14–16, 39, 95, 108, 121, 203
  Kshatriya status, claiming, 36
  reading rooms, 68, 82, 86, 89
  Self-Respect Movement's impact on, 16
  Shanan (Nadar) protest (1858), 13–15
  uravinmurai, 15
Nagercoil, 25
Naidu, K.V., 41
Naidu, Krishnasamy, 163
Naidu, N. Chandrababu, 211–12
Naidu, Varadarajulu, 114
Naidus, 108, 243*n*29
Nair, T.M., 4
Nam Naadu (newspaper), 94
'Namakku Naamey' march, 196
Nanda, Gulzarilal, 138–9
Naragasooran, 113
Natarajan, N.V., 131
National Democratic Alliance (NDA), 212
National Education Policy (2020), 210
Nayakar, Ayyakannu, 36
NDA. *See* National Democratic Alliance (NDA)
Nedunchezhian, V.R., 124
Nehru, Jawaharlal, 114, 130, 136, 235*n*15
  amended Article (15) and Article (29), 105
  correspondence between Rajaji and, 148
  death of, 148, 159
  formed SRC, 116
Neythal, 208, 249*n*44
Non-Brahmin Manifesto (1916), 40, 51, 95, 103
non-Brahmin movement (1900 to 1930), 12

Official Languages Act (1963), 135, 137
Olcott, Henry, 36
Omanthur P. Ramaswamy Reddiar, 104, 114–15, 135, 234*n*5
organisational pluralism, 6, 68–9, 94
Orissa (Odisha), 137
Oswald, Harvey, 163
Other Backward Classes, 108–9, 208
  reservation quota, 191, 192
  seat allocation, 106, 121, 128, 172–3, 175, 196

padippakams. See reading rooms (*padippakams*)

Pakistan, 99–100, 123, 238*n*39
Pallars, 198, 224*n*3
Pallava dynasty/Pallavas, 32, 36
Palyamkottai, 140
Pandian, M.S.S., 2, 4, 7, 8, 16, 19, 28, 29, 31, 38
Panikkar, K.M., 116
Pant, G.B., 136
Paraiyars, 37, 46, 198, 224*n*3
Parliament, 105, 135, 211
  Official Languages Bill, 136–8, 141
Patel, Sardar Vallabhbhai, 116, 150
paternalist populism, 6
Patil, S.K., 155, 240*n*52
Patnaik, Biju, 155
Pattali Makkal Katchi, 196
PDS. *See* Public Distribution System (PDS)
Periya Puranam, 36, 38
Periyar and Modernity (Aloysius), 29
Periyar Memorial Equality Village Scheme. *See* Periyar Ninaivu Samathuvapuram
Periyar Ninaivu Samathuvapuram, 195
Periyar, E.V. Ramasamy, 2, 3, 9, 16–17, 23, 41, 189
  anti-caste activism, views on, 30
  anti-caste ideas and activism, 28
  on Buddhism, 45
  caste association meetings, 13, 23, 46–7
  caste associations, 46, 52, 82
  on caste, 23
  category rights, idea of, 54
  criticized Indian communists, 107–8
  disagreement with Annadurai, 123
  Dravidian-Tamil identity, conception of, 56–61
  Dravidian-Tamil identity, ideas of, 31
  electoral politics stance, 49–50
  engagement with Rajaji, 30, 57
  horizontal Dravidian-Tamil solidarity, 54–5
  Indian independence, views on, 59, 72
  literature on, 28–30
  Madras State creation, involvement in, 117
  and Maniammai's marriage, 72
  MSEE scheme, views on, 112–13
  Nationalism, vision of, 51–3
  organised conference on Communal GO, 105
  proportional representation, 41–2
  rise of, 20, 30
  Saivite-Vellalar criticism of Brahmins, 38
  segregating social infrastructure practice, criticised, 48–9
  self-respect, idea of, 29, 42–50
  speech to the Adi Dravidar (Erode, 1932), 48, 74
  support for Islam, 45
  support for Kamaraj, 25
Philippines, 143
Pillais, 108
Pillay, K.K., 32
Pongal, 207, 231–2*n*30
'populism'
  term, 5
  variants of, 5–6
Por Vaal (newspaper), 82
Poraiyar Rao Bahadur Rathinasamy Nadar Memorial Library (Virudhunagar), 86–7
Prabhakaran, Velupillai, 204
Praja Socialist Party, 159, 172
Praja Socialists, 101

Prakasa, Sri, 151
Prakasam, Tanguturi, 147, 150–1
Prasad, Rajendra, 136
print capitalism, 22
print culture, 76
protection populism, 6
Provincial Congress Committee, 149, 150
PTP. *See* Puthiya Tamizhagam Party (PTP)
Public Distribution System (PDS), 159
Puthiya Tamizhagam Party (PTP), 198

Queer LitFest (Chennai), 193

Raavana, 113
Radha, M.R., 166
Raja, A., 201
Rajadurai, P., 15–16
Rajadurai, S.V., 28, 29
Rajagopalachari, C. (Rajaji), 9, 50, 57, 58, 160, 187, 235*n*17
  alliance with Annadurai, 126, 128
  conflict between Satyamurti and, 149–50
  MSEE scheme, introduced, 111–16
  push for Dakshina Pradesh, 117–18
  Seenivasan and, 163
  support to Annadurai, 161
Rajah, M.C., 198, 226–7*n*26
Rajarathnam, 170
Rajendran, K, 73, 117, 229*n*9
Rajus, 108
Rajya Sabha, 130–4
  Transgender Persons Bill, 192
Ram, Jagjivan, 155
Ramachandran, M.G. (M.G.R.), 78, 156, 160, 166, 191, 206–7
  protection populism, 6
  See also All-India Anna Dravida Munnetra Kazhagam (AIADMK)
Ramakrishna V., 11–12
Ramamoorthy, Kota P., 163
Ramamurthy, Gidugu, 12
Raman, V.P., 121, 124, 237*n*28
Ramanujam, A.K., 142, 156–7, 223*n*12
Ramaswamy, Sumathi, 9, 28, 29
Ramaswamy, Uma, 12
Ramiah, 170
Ranga, N.G., 168
Ranganathan, 140
Rao, K.V. Narayana, 12
Rathinam, John, 36
Ravi, R.N., 210–11
reading rooms (*padippakams*), 3, 24, 30, 60, 66–71, 75–94
  density of, 79*f*, 84*f*, 85*f*
  DMK's approach, 68
  DMK's organisational structure, 69
  Dravidian-Tamil ethos, spread of, 94–6
  emergence of, 75–86
  journalistic activity, 22, 77–8, 82–3, 88
  literacy rate in, 77, 77*t*
  Nadars and, 68, 82, 86, 89
  organisational pluralism, 68–9
  private reading rooms, 91
  self-respect marriages, 69–71
  setting up, 80–1
  silent and oral reading, 76
  social pluralism, 68
  spread of, 81
  in Virudhunagar, 86–9
Reddiars, 108
Reddis, 12
Reddy, Muthulakshmi, 181

Religion and Society Among the Coorgs of South India (Srinivas), 44
Revolt (newspaper), 23
Rights of Transgender Persons Bill (2014), 192
Roy, Indrajit, 212
ryotwari system, 34

saadhi (jati), 204–5
Saivite-Vellalar, 37–8
Sakkiliyar (now called Arunthathiyar), 33
Salem, 121, 138
Samaneedhi (journal), 78
Sampath, E.V.K., 113, 124, 125–7, 235*n*14, 238*n*33
Samyukta Karnataka, 118
Samyukta Maharashtra Movement, 100
Sangam era, 32, 56, 57, 178, 227*n*34
Sanjivayya, 175
Sankaralingam, 92–4, 153, 167
Sankaralinganar, 90, 118, 154, 232*n*32, 236*n*22
Sanskrit, 2, 35–6, 37, 39, 203, 225*n*15
Sanskrit-Brahmin supremacy, 35–6
Sanskritisation, 44
Santhanam, K., 161
Satavahana period, 32
Sattur, 163
Satyamurti, Sundara Sastra, 148–50
Scheduled Castes, 32, 48–9, 108
  quotas allocation, 105, 106, 173, 175, 196–7
Scheduled Tribes, 32, 105, 108
Seeman, 204–5, 249*n*40
Seenivasan, P, 25, 162–6, 168
Self-Respect Movement, 5, 16, 42–50, 59, 82, 150, 178, 226*n*25, 239*n*44
Selvaraj, N. Kayalvizhi, 200, 231*n*26
Seven Samurai (movie), 115
17th Constitutional Amendment, 165
Shah, P. Daud, 45
Shanan (Nadar) protest (1858), 13–15
Shanmuga Rajeswara Sethupathi, 170
Shanmugasundaram, Anandhi, 113
Sharma, Pandit Krishan Chandra, 130–1
Shastri, Lal Bahadur, 155, 242*n*14
Sherring, M.A., 53
Sikhs, 192
Simon, Lourdammal, 181–2
Singapore, 140
Singh, V.P., 191
Sinhala (language), 124
Sivagnanam, Mylai Ponnuswamy, 117
Sivalingam, 140
Sixteenth Constitutional Amendment (1963), 24, 102, 125, 130–1, 133, 187, 189, 239*n*43
social pluralism, 6, 68, 87, 94
Soundarapandian, W.P.A., 15–16
South Indian Liberal Federation. *See* Justice Party
South Indian People Association (SIPA), 51
South Indian Teachers' Union, 112
SRC. *See* States Reorganisation Commission (SRC)
Sreeramulu, Potti, 116
Sri Lanka. *See* Ceylon
Sri Lankan Civil War, 204
Sri Lankan Tamils, 124
Srinivas, M.N., 44, 45
Srinivasan, Kasturi, 150
Stalin, M.K., 196, 201, 211–12
Stalin, Udhayanidhi, 200, 206
State Assembly elections (1967), 1, 3, 17, 20, 21, 25, 68, 86, 148, 167, 172

States Reorganisation Act (1956), 24, 102, 116–21, 123, 224*n*8
States Reorganisation Commission (SRC), 116, 117
Subbarayan, Paramasiva, 103, 135–6, 239*n*45
Subramaniam, C., 115, 124, 127
Subramanian, Narendra, 4, 5, 6, 7, 8, 16, 19, 28–9, 65, 68–9, 94, 95, 133–4, 146, 194
Supreme Court, 104, 191–2, 203, 228*n*39, 248*n*35
Suri, K.C., 12
Swamy, Arun, 4, 16, 19 on populism, 5–6, 7
Swatantra Party, 18, 119, 151, 160, 172
  DMK alliance with, 126–8

Taiwan, 143
Tamil Arasu Kazhagam (Federation for Tamil Autonomy), 117, 159
Tamil Desiya Katchi (Tamil Nationalist Party or TNP), 126–7
Tamil language, 1, 35, 37
  identity and, 9–11
  journalistic activity in, 22, 77–8
  political shift, 2
  reviving, 5
Tamil Nadu Congress Committee, 162, 183
Tamil Nadu Legislative Assembly, 192
Tamil Nadu Toiler's Party (TTP), 83, 107, 112, 151241*n*6
Tamil Oratory and the Dravidian Aesthetic (Bate), 10–11
Tamil Virtual Academy, 206
Tattuva Vecini (magazine), 39
TDP. *See* Telugu Desam Party (TDP)
Telangana, 116
Telugu Desam Party (TDP), 12, 212
Telugu identity, 11–12
Thailand, 143
Thambikku Annavin Kadithangal (Annadurai), 77
Thamizhan (magazine), 36
Thangappan, T., 170
Thani Arasu (newspaper), 82
Thani Tamil Iyakkam, 37
Thanjavur, 138, 140
Thendral (newspaper), 82
Theosophical Society, 36, 40
Thinker, The (magazine), 39
Thirumaran, 126, 157–8, 164–5, 169, 241*n*8
Thirumavalavan, 198
thirunangai (transwoman), 192
Thirunavakkarasu, K., 78, 81, 82
Thiruvilayadal Puranam, 38
Tholkappiyam, 32
Thoothukudi, 208
Three-Cornered Protests. *See Mummunai Porattam*
Tilak, Bal Gangadhar, 135
Tillin, Louise, 13, 133
Tirupathi, 140
Transgender Persons Welfare Board, 192
Travancore, 100, 232*n*31, 234*n*3
Trichy Conference (1956), 119–20, 139
Trichy, 105, 121, 139, 153, 237–8*n*32, 239*n*46
TTP. *See* Tamil Nadu Toiler's Party (TTP)

Udayars, 108
UDF. *See* United Democratic Front (UDF)
Udhaya Suriyan Mandram (Virudhunagar), 91–2
Union of South Indian States, 133–4

Union Public Service Commission, 140, 162
United Democratic Front (UDF), 107, 150–1
United Front, 159–62, 165, 168, 172, 182
United Kingdom, 213
United States, 213, 240*n*52
uravinmurai, 15
Uttar Pradesh, 12–13, 101, 178, 198–9, 202, 207, 247*n*25

"*Vadakku vaazhkirathu, therku thaeikirathu*", 132, 235*n*16
Vaiko, 196
Vaikom Satyagraha, 153, 241–2*n*11, 249*n*51
Vallalar sect, 39
Vanniakula Vilakkam (Nayakar), 36
Vanniyar Sangam (Vanniyar Caste Association), 196
Vanniyars, 14, 33, 36, 39, 108, 109, 121, 128, 172, 246*n*18
  cabinet berths, 175, 176*t*
Varanasi, 207
varna system, 4, 13, 32
Varuna Darpanam, 36
VCK. *See* Vidhuthalai Chiruthaigal Katchi (VCK)
Veerapandian, Suba, 78
Veerappan, R.M., 166
Velamas, 12
Vellalars, 33, 37–8
Venkatachalam, Jothi, 181–2
Venkatachalapathy, A.R., 38, 75
Vidhuthalai Chiruthaigal Katchi (VCK), 197–8, 199, 214
Vidivelli (newspaper), 82
Vijayabaskar, M, 193–4
Virudhunagar, 14, 15, 17, 18, 20, 24, 25, 140, 162–3, 165–6, 183
  reading rooms, 66, 68, 86–9
  self-respect marriages, 69–70
  See also reading rooms (*padippakams*)
Virumbi, Viduthalai, 80
Visalandhra Movement, 100, 116, 118
Visalandhra, 118
Visswanathan, E. Sa., 29, 30

Walch, James, 151
Wardha Scheme of Education (1937), 111
Washbrook, David, 3, 4
West Bengal, 140, 188
Women's Reservation Bill, 201–2
World War II, 130
WPA Soundara Pandian's Tenure in Tamil Nadu Legislative Assembly (Rajadurai), 15–16
Wyatt, Andrew, 66, 108

Yadav, Lalu Prasad, 212